THE YELLOW JOURNALISM

Medill School of Journalism
VISIONS *of the* AMERICAN PRESS

―――――◇―――――

General Editor
David Abrahamson

Other titles in this series

Herbert J. Gans
Deciding What's News: A Study of CBS Evening News, NBC Nightly
News, Newsweek, *and* Time

Maurine H. Beasley
First Ladies and the Press: The Unfinished Partnership of the Media Age

Patricia Bradley
Women and the Press: The Struggle for Equality

David A. Copeland
The Idea of a Free Press: The Enlightenment and Its Unruly Legacy

Michael Sweeney
The Military and the Press: An Uneasy Truce

Patrick S. Washburn
The African American Newspaper: Voice of Freedom

THE YELLOW JOURNALISM

THE PRESS AND
AMERICA'S EMERGENCE
AS A WORLD POWER

David R. Spencer

Foreword by Geneva Overholser

MEDILL SCHOOL OF JOURNALISM

Northwestern University Press
Evanston, Illinois

Northwestern University Press
www.nupress.northwestern.edu

Copyright © 2007 by David R. Spencer
Published 2007 by Northwestern University Press.
All rights reserved.

Printed in the United States of America

10 9 8 7 6 5 4 3 2 1

ISBN 978-0-8101-2331-1

Library of Congress Cataloging-in-Publication Data

Spencer, David Ralph, 1941–.
    The yellow journalism : the press and America's emergence as a
world power/ David R. Spencer ; foreword by Geneva Overholser.
        p. cm. — (Visions of the American press)
    Includes bibliographical references and index.
    ISBN 978-0-8101-2331-1 (pbk. : alk. paper)
    1. Press—United States—History. 2. Journalistic ethics—United
States—History. 3. Journalists—United States—History. 4.
Sensationalism in journalism—United States—History. 5. Press—
Influence. I. Title. II. Series.
    PN4864.S64 2007
    071'3—dc22

                                        2006025060

To Judi

CONTENTS

FOREWORD

Geneva Overholser

As vigorously and frequently as journalists are reviled today, they can always find refuge in this comforting thought: at least they don't live in the era of (shudder!) *Yellow Journalism*. Nothing so says "journalism evil" as this Victorian-era chapter of press history, when publishing titans like William Randolph Hearst and Joseph Pulitzer went head to head—with flamboyant and often irresponsible results. But is this relief-by-comparison really justified? As you read this insightful volume by David Spencer, do not be surprised if the charges about Yellow Journalism ring familiar, for they are the very charges favored by journalism's twenty-first-century critics: The blurring of fact and fiction. Hyperbole and sensationalism. An overemphasis on the negative. The undermining of society's essential institutions. And, perhaps most chilling of all, the notion of journalism as mere commodity.

If Yellow Journalism has provided our era with a quiver full of proven insults, it has given us much more besides. Indeed, it has substantially shaped today's press, for these Yellow journalists were nothing if not innovators. As Spencer so ably shows us, they gave us the modern newspaper—advertising-supported, rich with graphics and photographs and lively writing, catering to the people, competitive, aspiring to ever-greater success in the marketplace. To be sure, some of this inheritance feels lamentable. Take commodification: however much they led the way, even Hearst and Pulitzer would be amazed to see how crushingly commodified today's press has become, giving Wall Street more say about the future of a given newssheet than its readers could ever hope to have.

But the legacy is more complex still. While we never utter the words *Yellow Journalism* without distaste, it is worth considering that Pulitzer's own vow was to provide his readers with "Brilliant Humor, Splendid Illustrations and Stories by the Greatest Authors." There's a formula with merit. And those "great authors" the era's newspapers employed—writers like Stephen Crane, editors like Lincoln Steffens—did not save their best talents for the books we now know them for. Steffens, as this volume notes, once assigned a story about a man who hacked his wife to death, and here is what he told the reporter: "That man loved that woman well enough once to marry her, and now he has hated her enough to cut her all to pieces. If you can find out just what happened between that wedding and this murder, you will have a novel for yourself and a short story for me. Go on now, take your time and get this tragedy as a tragedy." Better advice than that I never gave as an editor. The Yellow journalists had other appealing traits. Think Nellie Bly's brave tales from the Women's Lunatic Asylum in New York. Think newspapers competing with one another to hand out bread to the needy. Think well-told tales, booming circulation, and crusades on behalf of social reform. Hmmmm . . . sounds pretty good, doesn't it?

Of course, we mustn't skim lightly over the egregious sins of Yellow Journalism: the warmongering, the screaming headlines, the blatant sensationalism and woeful unfairness. But it does not take subscribing to the worst of the many unfair charges hurled against journalism today to acknowledge that our own media are not all finely tuned instruments of noble betterment either, much as we like to comfort ourselves with the distance between our world and the Yellow one. I remember a session at a 1989 editors' gathering on the topic of sensationalism. Our panel included Phil Donahue, Morton Downey Jr., and Geraldo Rivera. I, by contrast, was one of the "respectable" journalists and all too proud of it. Then the inimitable moderator, Fred Friendly, held up a copy of my newspaper, the *Des Moines Register.* Across the front page ran this teaser: "WAS CARY GRANT REALLY BISEXUAL?" I've been a little less sure ever since about the dividing line between the virtuous and the not so virtuous, journalistically speaking.

To a degree (and it probably was true in the Yellow Journalism era, too), people find comfort in blaming the press for their own appetites. The press in turn reassures itself that it cannot be faulted for giving readers what they want, for it does, after all, want to be read. And of course, the line between good and bad journalism *is* unclear. Rich narrative to one reader is blurred fact to another, and the headline that compels me to enter the story may strike you as hopelessly hyped. But one thing is clear: the commitment to serve the broader public good is no good at all without the tools and talent to bring the individual along for the trip.

Now, here's a happy thought: Yellow Journalism's excesses were offensive enough to help spawn, in direct response, something truly fine—the best newspaper in America, a model of dignified and reliable journalism. The *New York Times* was born when Adolph S. Ochs arrived from Chattanooga in 1896 to inject a very different model into the tawdry New York City newspaper scene. As the late Edwin Diamond noted in his book, *Behind the Times,* Hearst was said to have wanted his *New York Journal* readers "to look at page one and say 'Gee Whiz,' to turn to page two and exclaim 'Holy Moses,' and then at page three, shout 'God

Almighty!'" In contrast, Ochs's sober credo was "All the News That's Fit to Print," and he pledged "to give the news impartially without fear or favor, regardless of party, sect, or interest involved."

So here we are in the twenty-first century, and Yellow Journalism's counterparts are easily spotted, from one cable channel's frenzy to top the others on the latest blonde-gone-missing story to the blogger-world's mountains of invective. Yet we can take heart. Out of Yellow Journalism's excesses came a fine new model of newspapering, and Pulitzer's name is now linked with the best work the craft can produce. And today, in what seems to some another nadir for the press, new forms of media are springing up everywhere. Who knows what models will prevail? We can hope for new heights of fairness and balance and commitment to the citizens' needs. Throw in a little humor, splendid illustrations, and killer writing talent and salvation could be right around the corner.

PREFACE

Every summer when I finished teaching journalism history to incoming graduate students, I used to take one morning to talk with the class about where we had been and what we had done during the semester. There was nothing really unusual about that approach, save the fact that most of my colleagues set aside a whole day to do exactly the same thing. So, I decided that press history should have a different sort of climax. I created a library of films that dealt with some aspect of journalism history and spent the final day eating popcorn and downing sodas with the students while showing them a feature film about the world, real or imaginary, that they were going to enter. The films covered the works of Ben Hecht, Orson Welles, Damon Runyon, and, of course, Robert Woodward and Carl Bernstein. Although I had long been convinced that my chosen field of research was one of the more interesting aspects of my existence, I also realized that it was not something I could take for granted with graduate students.

Through no fault of their own, the students had, at best, only a limited knowledge of the history of journalism. Often, the fault, as Edward R. Murrow so eloquently stated during his McCarthy broadcast, lies within ourselves. What have we been doing all these years to promote journalism history and make it one of the most exciting courses of study in the university calendar? In some cases, a lot; in others, not much. So, each of us, in our own way, can contribute our blood, sweat, and tears to the cause, which is why I took on this project when approached by senior editor David Abrahamson.

The Yellow Press was of particular interest to me, not because I am a great fan of sensationalism but because the emergence of the genre came at the tail end of one of the most exciting centuries in the history of the world. All those things that had happened since the invention of lithography came into force in the strange worlds of William Randolph Hearst and Joseph Pulitzer. We can certainly look at those developments one by one, from the telegraph of Samuel Morse in 1844, which fundamentally changed the way news was gathered, to the creation of the telephone correspondent by Charles Chapin on the eve of the twentieth century. What started out as a collection of dots and dashes was available in real language just over a half a century later.

During the Gilded Age, it seemed that every day would bring a new invention to the world. Thomas Edison had not only captured sound on a wax cylinder, he had also experimented with lighting city streets with something called electricity, and just for good measure, he used his competitor's invention of alternating current in the world's first electric chair. No one would make more of an impact on the collection of news than an eccentric inventor from Rochester, New York, named George Eastman, whose invention of celluloid film provided a base for visual journalism and led to the creation of the motion picture. It also made photography a critical player in the interpretation of important events. Then along came Hearst and Pulitzer, who introduced color in their Sunday supplements. The massive expansion of the railway system gave newspaper owners and editors the impetus to start seeing the country as one large media market, although it would be many years before true national media would be in place.

Of course, one of the most critical developments was the laying of a transatlantic cable, which brought America to the world and the world to America. The collapse of international obstacles would give America yet one more impetus to play a major role on the world stage. And the media would play host to the country's dreams and ambitions. They would indeed be the first witnesses to history. Hearst and Pulitzer would be at the forefront of the drive to make America a world power.

I have always been interested in storytelling. For the scholar, the study of the Yellow Press is a gift in this respect. A number of America's better-known writers were journalists, some of whom wrote in the late nineteenth-century scandal sheets. That community included Stephen Crane, author of *The Red Badge of Courage* and *Maggie, a Girl of the Streets,* Ambrose Bierce, a columnist for Hearst on the West Coast, and Mark Twain, who needs no introduction. They saw the Yellow Press as a tuition-free postsecondary school in which they could hone their skills in their pursuit of literary excellence. It is little wonder that truth often suffered in this kind of environment.

One must ask whether the world really needs another book on the Yellow Press. In my view, the response is emphatically *yes*. It is true that other scholars, such as Sidney Kobre, W. Joseph Campbell, and Ted Curtis Smythe, have studied this subject phenomenally well. The stories have been told as to how Hearst and Pulitzer ended up in New York and founded a newspaper culture that, in many respects, continues to function to this very day. My volume would have to be different. I was not going to compete with the basic premise that these authors used in their respective works. So, what is so different about this book?

First of all, it is not a narrative history, as are most other works on the Yellow Press. It deals with the evolving culture of Victorian journalism in America and how that culture was both adapted and shaped by the Yellow Press, as well as the impact that culture had on twentieth-century media. There will be no recounting of the specific events of the Spanish-American War, although the reasons expressed for the war by New York journalists and the impact of the press on this conflict will be told. Further, there will be a discussion on the role of visuals in the age of the Yellow Press because both Hearst and Pulitzer relied on illustrations in their journals as a key means to reach their target constituencies. This volume is intended to complement the fine work already under-taken on the Yellow Press.

As with any form of investigation, there is always a sense of ex-citement when one unearths material that could make a difference in the study in progress. One such discovery was a collection of speeches by Pulitzer and Hearst alumnus Morrill Goddard, deliv-ered in the mid-1930s in New York City. This man, reputed to be the founder of the Yellow Journalism genre, gave an impas-sioned defense of his role over a series of six evenings. His com-plicity, if you will, was no longer in doubt.

And then, there were the great artists. I had searched for works by Homer Davenport, Walt McDougall, the man who kept James Blaine out of the White House, and Bob Carter and other edito-rialists on the films containing both *The New York Journal* and *The World New York.* I found a memoir written by Davenport in 1910 in which he painfully described his firing from the *Portland Ore-gonian,* an event that led him to take a train to San Francisco, where he was eventually retained by the *San Francisco Examiner;* that position, in turn, would lead to a job in New York, where he would find fame and fortune with Hearst at *The New York Journal.* And finally, there was Richard Felton Outcault, creator of the first

comic strip, *The Yellow Kid,* which some believe gave Yellow Journalism its name. Outcault worked for both Hearst and Pulitzer before creating Buster Brown, a comic character who later became
synonymous with children's shoes of the same name.

In the year and a half that this study took, I felt I had personally
gotten to know all of these characters. At the same time, friends
became more like strangers during this period, though they were
very tolerant of my work. Without their support together with
that of my wife, Judi, my colleagues at the University of Western
Ontario, and David Abrahamson, this volume would have been
far more difficult to complete. Enjoy the read.

David R. Spencer

ONE

INTRODUCTION

When dismembered human remains floated to the surface of New York City's East River in June 1897, the publisher of *The New York Journal,* a young, devil-may-care college dropout named William Randolph Hearst, decided that his newspaper would beat the city's police department—the self-proclaimed "finest"—in discovering the culprit or culprits who had perpetrated this heinous crime. Pulling out all the stops, Hearst's Murder Squad, a group of investigative reporters, uncovered not only the identity of the murderer but also a sordid extramarital affair involving the guilty. The lurid descriptions of the untimely demise of a bathhouse masseur that appeared in *The New York Journal* pushed the limits of both credibility and social acceptability in those times. In a stroke of opportunism, the Yellow Press had been born.

For Hearst, Joseph Pulitzer, and scores of other editors and reporters across urban America who worked in the newspaper industry in the late nineteenth and early twentieth centuries, crime reporting was a godsend. It tugged at the emotional heartstrings of readers, and its violence and often graphic descriptions of the fate of the deceased touched sensitive nerves in those who advocated quick dispatch for individuals accused of such misdeeds. As historian Joy Wiltenburg recently observed, "Representations of crime influence people's conceptions of their lives and communities far out of proportion of the actual incidence of criminal activity." Little has changed over the past century and a half. Crime reporting was not the only avenue traveled by what would soon be called the sensationalist press, but it was undoubtedly the trendsetter for tales involving political corruption, sexual deviance, and other forms of thuggish behavior. But as we shall see in the story to come, Hearst and Pulitzer were only following a tradition that had begun to take shape some three centuries previously. It was not a tradition that was consequence free.

In most respects, the owners and editors who perfected the Yellow Press were creatures of their time and space. They lived in one of the most technologically productive centuries in human history, one that accelerated the new, soon to be literate world that had been born with the invention of movable type. Although not the only catalyst that propelled the evolution of the press into a significant player in a free-market society, the role of technology cannot be ignored. The first major invention that later became incorporated in the nineteenth-century press was lithography, the creation of one Alois Senefelder in Germany in 1798. Although visual images were rare in the daily newspapers until the rise of the Yellow Press, they were frequently used in specialized magazines during the first half of the nineteenth century. Of course, not all publications followed the techniques laid down by lithographers, who used polished limestones with ink based in oil to create a publishable picture. However, the invention of lithography gave rise to the concept that visuals could be part and parcel of storytelling, which in the hands of the Yellow Press left little to the imagina-

tion. By the time that Hearst and Pulitzer went to circulation warfare in the late years of the century, American journalism was a
battleground of both words and images.

By the 1870s, unlike the practice in the early years of the century, pictures were no longer produced by an engraver sitting at a
desk and working his tools into a slab of virgin wood. News was
being captured on celluloid film, the invention of a Rochester,
New York, eccentric named George Eastman. Coupled with the
invention of halftone reproduction, photography became a powerful addition to a Gilded Age journalist's arsenal. Hearst, Pulitzer,
and their imitators all exploited photojournalism shamelessly in the
late 1890s and early 1900s.

Like many other inventions that came to light in the same period, photography had no single inventor. It was as much the creation of the Frenchmen Joseph Nicéphore Niepce and Louis Da-
guerre as it was of the Englishman William Henry Fox Talbot.
When Talbot published a collection of twenty-four pictures in his
book *The Pencil of Nature* between 1844 and 1846, it would only
be a short fifteen years before photographers were capturing the
carnage of the War between the States almost as it happened.

Virtually every technological advance that American inventors
could create finally found its way into the collection and distribution of news. We need not account for each one in detail, but let
it be said that it is doubtful that Melville Stone of the Associated
Press (AP) could have exerted the same influence on American
publishers without having the telegraph in the AP's bag of good-
ies. It does not take a serious stretch of the imagination to realize
the impact of Richard Hoe's rotary press when it entered the
newspaper world in 1847. And to all these marvels of the century
can be added the motion picture, the Linotype, paper production

based on wood as opposed to rags, recorded sound, and the first static crackling of radio sound waves in precisely the same years as the Yellow Press rose in New York City.

But the rise of the Yellow Press must be seen as something well beyond the emergence of new technologies. As much as these inventions gave publishers and editors opportunities they could only dream of in the previous century, it was a set of ideas, philosophies, and concepts, deeply rooted in American life, that determined the behavior of the Yellow Press. In fact, the very role of the newspaper in the late nineteenth century came under a microscope both by those who were entertained and informed by the extravagances of the day and by those who were critically offended that such distaste could actually appear and flourish in one of the world's great democracies. It is a battle that continues to this very day.

The debates that would finally result in the First Amendment began, as did the use of sensationalism, long before the daily press became an economic linchpin in America's ever-growing urban environments. Frederick Siebert and his colleagues at the University of Illinois were convinced that the press in the Victorian age evolved from an essentially authoritarian model prevalent before the eighteenth century to one of virtually unlimited freedom to exercise what it saw fit, a condition that Siebert and his fellow authors called libertarianism. It was an age of great excess, one that eventually inspired new definitions of the press based on social responsibility that rose at the end of the Gilded Age in reaction to the Yellow Press.

Both the casual observer and the more clinically inclined scholar will recognize the influence of three major thinkers in Siebert's conceptions of the role of the press in late Victorian America. With no respect to order or influence, they are John Milton, Thomas Jefferson, and John Stuart Mill. In rethinking Siebert's philosophical approach, media scholar John Nerone noted that none of the three could be accused of holding any form of rabid libertarian beliefs, although he observed that Mill is more often than not placed in that kind of ideological straitjacket. Certainly, one might be tempted to add Alexis de Tocqueville to the mix.

It is undoubtedly safe to say that John Milton had no conception of anything like the Yellow Press when he rose in the Puritan Parliament in 1644 to make a passionate plea against press licensing. Milton was far more interested in promoting spiritual salvation than defending freedom of the press. However, he was concerned with the kind of moral issues that appeared in print in his day and continue to the present age. His argument was based on the belief that practicing Christians needed to be exposed to various forms of theological impurities in order to distinguish between good and evil. Although theological issues did not appear with any great frequency in the press world of the late nineteenth century, readers of the Yellow Press were bombarded on a daily basis with graphic and ghastly tales of murder, incest, poverty, infidelity, corporate fraud, and any number of imagined or real evils. In concert with the reader of Milton's age, these consumers of news were often faced with real and parallel dilemmas of a moral nature.

As much as Milton saw the press in the role of social purifier, Thomas Jefferson believed that a free press, along with accessible public education, was critical for the health of a democratic society. Writing to Charles Yancey on January 6, 1816, Jefferson argued:

> If a nation expects to be ignorant and free in a state of civilization, it expects what never was and never will be. The functionaries of every government have propensities to command at

will the liberty and property of their constituents. There is no safe deposit for these but with the people themselves, nor can they be safe with them without information. Where the press is free and every man able to read, all is safe.

Yet the press of Jefferson's day was still deeply entrenched in the process of paying homage to various political leaders and their organizations, if for no other reason than survival. Nonetheless, the groundwork was being laid for a press literally without borders.

In his most famous political treatise, *On Liberty,* John Stuart Mill argued that "the time it is to be hoped, is gone by, when any defense would be necessary for the liberty of the press as one of the securities against corrupt or tyrannical government." Mill pointed to the great press prosecutions of 1858 as a symbol of a continuing political maturity in the press in Great Britain. Although disappointed that the government had swooped down on a number of journals that opened a dialogue on tyrannicide, the author was relieved that the discussions regarding those political institutions seen to be a part of the debate were not involved in the prosecutions. In addition, he was pleased that the government eventually decided to drop the case and leave the press to its own wiles.

In many ways preceding Mill but following Jefferson, Alexis de Tocqueville made many of the same arguments, placing the press at the center of a democratic society. Yes, freedom of speech was to be a treasured part of any liberal concept of the state, but de Tocqueville was also interested in examining the role that newspapers took in the establishment of communities. As he stated, "There is a necessary connection between public associations and newspapers: newspapers make associations and associations make newspapers." It is within this concept that the Yellow Press will be situated in this study.

Nonetheless, one must not overstate the importance of the press in creating associations. As historian David Paul Nord observed, the press does not create associations by itself. What it does is deliver the information to constituencies capable of using that information to build their own communities or, in modern parlance, interest groups. Pulitzer's appeal to newly arrived immigrants with at most a scattering of English is, in one sense, a good example of the interplay between the press and one of its constituencies. In many respects, the Yellow Press, as we shall observe in upcoming chapters, provided glowing examples of community constructions before moving from an approach based on conversation and the exchange of facts and ideas to what media theorist James Carey referred to as "a model of information," which, for him, was a far from positive move.

In many if not most ways, the Yellow Press was a classic example of the newspaper genre Frederick Siebert described as libertarian. In his rethinking of the Siebert concept, John Nerone noted that "the notion of the marketplace of ideas is central to libertarianism's model of political communication." It is lodged in the belief that the press can be an agent of change in which interest groups, political parties, and religious organizations can vent their beliefs in the press in the hope that other persons who share those concepts can create what we have previously noted as communities. The concept is based in the idea that readers are rational and can make rational choices. In every respect, the marketplace of ideas that drove the Yellow Press was not that different from the economic marketplace that drove late Victorian industrial society.

The press world of the late Victorian age was characterized not only by the vicious circulation wars undertaken by Hearst and Pulitzer but also by a further division in practice between elite editors and those in the Yellow Press, whose approach to journalism was not considered to be objective. James Carey saw these two positions as a conflict between what he termed a model of information and a model of conversation. And, as noted earlier, by the outbreak of World War I, the model of information dominated the practice of the daily press in America.

Carey's assessment of the behavior of the press can be seen in its need to conquer space and exercise control over the flow of information in the constituency it purports to serve. Carey called this concept, which I have simplified to a significant degree, the transmission model. Of course, this model is far from exclusive in dealing with the press in general and is not specifically targeted in Carey's thought to the Victorian press of the late 1890s. But to a large degree, it can work with the newspaper scholar in the never-ending attempt to rationalize both how the news was delivered and what news managed to get delivered. As Carey noted:

> If one examined a newspaper under a transmission view of communication, one sees the medium as an instrument for disseminating news and knowledge, sometimes divertissement, in larger and larger packages over greater distances. Questions arise as to the effects of this on audiences: news as enlightening or obscuring reality, as changing or hardening attitudes, as breeding credibility or doubt. Questions are also raised concerning the functions of news and the newspaper; does it maintain the integration of society or its maladaption? Does it function or misfunction to maintain stability or promote the instabilities of personalities?

As we shall see, these issues manifested themselves in various forms and actions as the nineteenth century progressed. But for now, we need only look to Carey's second mode of interpretation—that which he named a ritual view of communication, an idea more closely related to the concept of the press as a vehicle for conversation:

> The ritual view of communication, though a minor thread in our national thought, is by far the older of these views—old enough in fact for dictionaries to list it under "archaic." In a ritual definition, communication is linked to terms such as "sharing," "participation," "association," "fellowship," and "the possession of a common faith," . . . a ritual view of communication is directed not toward the extension of messages in space but toward the maintenance of society in time; not the act of importing information but the representation of shared beliefs.

In the final analysis, Carey saw news as a form of culture that was created by the middle class beginning in the eighteenth century. The kind of news that emerged in the late nineteenth century was the inheritor of processes put in place by its predecessors. But in Carey's assessment, as the century passed, the ritual approach to news treated it not as pure information but as high drama. Unlike the transmission view of communication, news in the ritual sense does not relate events in the world as fact influenced by fact but as struggles between opposing forces and the actions that they take. Carey reminded us that this sits within a historical period in which participants were invited to become activists and take on social roles as an outgrowth of press agitation. As we will see, the Yellow Press came closer to a ritual interpretation than a transmission one, although its need to conquer the spaces in which it lived cannot and must not be dismissed as illegitimate.

One cannot separate the rise of the industrial urban complex from the growth of the newspaper industry as an industry in the closing years of the nineteenth century. The cylinder press, the web press, the Linotype, and the stereotype were all influential in bringing about massive increases in production of the daily newspaper. In 1887, American newspapers could produce forty-eight thousand copies of an eight-page newspaper per hour. A short five years later, this volume had increased to ninety-six thousand pages per hour.

Smaller communities living on the periphery of larger urban centers were often absorbed into the bigger metropolitan entity, with the consequence that their specific identities were either reduced to some form of historical curiosity or forgotten altogether. The more fortunate communities, while surrendering economic and often political independence, retained some aspects of self-governance. But in the final analysis, their newspapers and their openings to a larger world were determined not in their own backyards but by press denizens a short commuting distance away.

So it remains for us to discuss precisely what kind of reading material was being fed to a public that was increasingly literate and increasingly fascinated with virtually all forms of the printed word. Journalism became the mode through which authors on both sides of the Atlantic were able to sustain themselves by writing throughout the nineteenth century. In Great Britain, Charles Dickens made his mark as a contributing journalist, as did the radical wallpaper designer William Morris. They happened to have arrived on the literary scene when the business of patronage by royal and noble households was on its last legs. In the United States, union organizer Eugene Debs appeared regularly in print, as did Samuel Clemens (better known to his readers as Mark Twain), Henry James of *Turn of the Screw* fame, Nathaniel Hawthorne, and Henry Wadsworth Longfellow; America's poet, Walt Whitman, made regular appearances as well. It is easy to understand why storytelling, in contrast with pure fact reporting, was the predominant literary style in the American press until the Yellow Press turned the concept on its head, which in turn contributed to its ultimate decline.

As much as the nineteenth century was a period of intense technical innovation, it was also the backdrop to an elevated form of social turmoil that would radically transform Victorian society and the newspapers that depended on it for their continued existence. When Whitman, the poet of America, died in Camden, New Jersey, in March 1892, he was carried to his last resting place by the reformist Canadian psychiatrist Richard Maurice Bucke, on one side of the coffin, and American freethinker and self-proclaimed atheist Col. Robert Ingersoll, on the other. The funeral service was punctuated by readings from Whitman's classic *Leaves of Grass*, interspersed with passages from Confucius, Buddha, the Koran, and the Bible. Organized religion as it was known in the late Victorian age was coming to an end, as were other linchpins of the closed and smothering social system. The Yellow Press, always conscious of its need to tell the best of stories unimpeded by minor problems created by fact, would be there to do what it did best— excite the soul and sell newspapers. Both the content and the style that appeared in the journals run by Hearst and Pulitzer would open wounds within the profession, primarily dealing with the abstract notion of objectivity.

Two major issues emerged in the world of journalism as the penny press gradually became the daily and very commercial press. One was the debate over professionalism, the other the continuing argument regarding objectivity. Journalism, like most other forms of activity, had both its respectable and its not-so- respectable actors. And like those many other forms of activity, journalism tended to be identified with its less-than-savory elements. Proponents of disseminating all the news that was fit to print were more often than not forced to defend that approach when someone published all the news that was *not* fit to print. Needless to say, the excesses of the Yellow Press were embedded more in the public mind than in the fact-driven pages of the *New York Times*.

To the uninitiated, the Victorian reporter could only be found on the bottom rungs of the social ladder. News workers were hardly a glamorous lot. They were rough. They drank too much. They cheated on their wives if they were married. If they were single, most would have suffered through multiple divorces. They would never let any moral questions stand in the way of getting a good story. They were not to be trusted. They were usually overworked and badly compensated. But on the odd occasion, they rose to the surface to expose graft, corruption, and deception in the highest of places.

Representative of this group were the reporters who appeared in Ben Hecht's classic but frantic screenplay and Broadway play called *The Front Page,* which first appeared in 1928 and later emerged under a number of different names, including the 1940 film edition, *His Girl Friday,* with Cary Grant and Rosalind Russell. Hecht was well positioned to describe the life of the "typical" reporter, since he had covered crime and corruption in Chicago after dropping out of the University of Wisconsin. Like many others, he had humble beginnings. Before joining the *Chicago Journal* and later the *Chicago Daily News,* he had worked as a circus acrobat in Wisconsin. After being sent by the *Daily News* to cover events in Berlin in 1912, he became a fixture at the reporters' watering hole at the Adlon Hotel. Hecht was known to hold court until the wee hours of the morning, often playing the piano while his comrades emptied bottles of cognac, scotch, and numerous Rhine wines while puffing on exotic European cigarettes and Havana cigars. Not quite so romantic were the characters who appeared in Fred Fedler's historical analysis of the role of reporters. Their watering holes were a hop, skip, and a jump from their places of work and the dingy boardinghouses many called home. Drinking and working was a way of life to many a reporter who would never see Europe.

While laborers and skilled artisans formed trades unions to fight for their rightful place in the new industrial world of America, journalists, among others, were beginning to debate how they could improve their status both materially and spiritually. The word *profession* began to appear in the odd document as a prelude to wider debates on the politics of uplift. Other professionals, especially those in medicine, had formed self-governing societies in which there were strict rules for membership. Only the qualified could enter. And more important was the fact that these professionals could write the rules of their existence by themselves and for their peers without undue interference from the authorities. That very concept would prove to be the downfall of the notion of professionalism for journalists. Unlike physicians and teachers, who regarded themselves as members of a much larger entity in which values were shared, journalists have never been known to be communal.

It was Pulitzer, ironically, who made the first mainly public gesture to bring the concept of professionalism to journalism and journalists. The publisher of *The New York World* had attempted to donate a considerable sum of money to New York's Columbia College in 1892, with a view to establishing a journalism school on the campus. The administrators at the school had rebuffed his attempts even though he was a member of the city's social register. As one of the two most identifiable persons associated with the raucous Yellow Press, Pulitzer was an outcast and a social leper, not to be included with the more "respectable" gentry in New York—a group that included J. P. Morgan, William Rockefeller, and John Jacob Astor, among others.

Pulitzer, in spite of the editorial approach of his newspaper, always believed that an effective and efficient journalism was critical to a giant democracy such as the United States. With this in mind, he constantly wrestled intellectually with the problem of standards in the profession and the best ways to incorporate them in a journalistic culture. He was of the opinion that excellence could be encouraged if the right persons were hired to be journalists and properly trained in standards that governed the endeavor, which he believed were linked to the question of professionalism.

In the summer of 1902, he approached the president of Columbia, Nicholas Murray Butler, with an offer to fund the establishment of a journalism school that would recruit well-known journalists and ambitious and skilled students. To upgrade the existing practices in the field, Pulitzer offered to fund a series of prizes in his name for journalistic achievement. Butler was intrigued with the offer but was well aware that *The World* and its publisher were not held in overly high esteem by the academics at Columbia. He did not reject the offer outright but agreed to take the matter under consideration. Pulitzer was also facing contemptuous remarks from his colleagues in the field who believed that journalists were born and could not be created, a viewpoint that continues to infect some newsrooms to this day.

In the spring of 1903, Pulitzer upped the ante by increasing the gift to $2 million. The next stumbling block that faced *The World's* owner was the reluctance of Butler to have the president of Harvard University on the proposed school's advisory council. Pulitzer insisted that Charles W. Eliot be included. He finally lost patience with the affair and told Butler to accept or reject the offer as it stood. Butler surrendered, and journalism became a fixture at Columbia, with a mandate to improve and inspire the profession as it entered the twentieth century. Interestingly, Columbia was not the first postsecondary institution to offer education in journalism. Cornell had offered a certificate in journalism as early as 1874, and in 1893, the University of Pennsylvania offered a degree program in journalism. Following Columbia's lead, other postsecondary institutions founded journalism programs, which remain in significant number in the United States and around the world. But alas, Pulitzer's dream of a self-governing profession never took root in the same way it did in teaching, medicine, and the academy. And journalism continues to attract derision as a field populated by gossips, fearmongers, charlatans, and sensationalists.

Mark Twain once referred to the daily press as the "palladium of our liberties," a key player in the promotion and preservation of democracy. As well, he argued that the publication of newspapers was the first step in creating a national focus on advanced literature, which he also regarded as vital in developing a high culture. He winced and complained when some members of New York's robber baron upper class, such as Jay Gould, showed an interest in bringing newspapers into their kind of capitalist world. In an essay entitled "The License of the Press," Twain offered his reservations on what he termed the new journalism, which we may term Yellow Journalism. Specifically, he was upset that some journals in this genre had attacked religion and that these attacks "had made scoffing popular." Scoffing, indeed! What Twain was really complaining about was what we would now called a lack of objectivity.

Throughout the nineteenth century, the process by which news was delivered to a consuming public had strong parallels in the ancient art of storytelling. But in the mid-1860s, the seeds of destruction of the genre had been planted with the invention of the inverted pyramid. The adoption of the inverted pyramid, no matter whose version of its invention one may accept, was based on the concept that the most important aspect of news delivery was tied to facts and that somehow or other those facts were not tainted with personal agendas. Further, some facts were more important than other facts, and the facts with the greatest importance should be those first read by the newspaper consumer. There were those who believed that the increasing use of telegraph sources, which rose significantly in the 1860s, created a news culture that depended more on fact than on fiction.

As Mark Twain noted, the Yellow Press seemed to stand in perfect conflict with those who advocated the collection of facts and the diminution of storytelling. A sophisticated public deserved no less, according to the critics of the Yellow Press. Ted Smythe observed:

> The Yellow Journalism of the late 1890s was a product of hyper sensationalism and competition between Pulitzer and Hearst. It was New Journalism carried to an extreme. Headlines were larger and bolder and scare heads attracted readers. Illustrations no longer reflected reality. They were designed to supplement the scare heads, wow readers and get them to buy newspapers and to talk about the *World*.

Indeed, in the late nineteenth century, newspapers had joined the world of capitalism, for better or for worse depending on one's perspective. The journalism of the closing years of the century was becoming part and parcel of the world of marketing, in which business practices became essential for profit making and, in some cases, survival. Companies buying advertising space wanted to know to whom they were appealing, and as a consequence, circulation figures had to be published and verified. A whole new middle industry—advertising—rose in most major metropolitan centers in the country, with agencies where trained persons were paid commissions to place advertisements in prominent newspapers. It was at this period in history that the department store and the journalism industry forged a partnership that was to last well into the closing years of the twentieth century.

In its simplest form, objectivity was regarded as the reporting of news in which the facts that appeared on the printed page were totally separated in terms of human value from the person who collected those facts and assembled them for newspaper consumers. In this concept, then, the reader was given the task of analyzing and assembling facts gleaned from the daily press to form his or her own worldview, or, as we saw earlier, the potential creation of communities. Yet the difficult question remained: can anyone's value structure remain independent of the facts one collects? It is hard to imagine that a reporter brought up in a middle-class and relatively affluent environment would not allow the value systems accompanying his or her upbringing to at least filter some of the facts. And of course, the same could apply to persons from other backgrounds.

As media scholar Michael Schudson observed, the quest for objectivity in a business designed to bring in income and show a profit is "a peculiar demand to make of institutions which as business corporations, are dedicated first of all to economic survival." Certainly, any concept of objectivity took a back seat in the editorial rooms of Hearst's *New York Journal* and Pulitzer's *New York World* in the closing years of the nineteenth century. In fact, it was difficult to separate the news from the news makers. Both papers took up causes, beginning with Pulitzer's exploitation of Nellie

Bly's "Ten Days in a Madhouse," an exposé of conditions in a city asylum for women, and eventually involving Hearst's ambitions for high political office. Neither publisher even pretended that objectivity was a goal to be achieved. Intervention into the various aspects of New York life, by contrast, *was* a goal to be achieved and not denied, and it was not. As media theorist Marshall McLuhan concluded: "Real news is bad news—bad news about somebody; for months without a newspaper, the chief of police said, 'Sure, I miss the news but so far as my job goes, I hope the papers never come back. There is less crime around without a newspaper to pass around the ideas.'"

In the final analysis, it was the reporter who provided the filter through which much of the world arrived at the various kinds of social visions created in the age of the Yellow Press. It was never value free. As historian Hanno Hardt wrote: "Media work focuses on the construction of realities and helps maintain the institutional power of the media; it involves the labor of journalists, among others, who are hired to perform to the expectations of their bosses and in the name of freedom of the press."

TWO

THE INHERITANCE

As with all historical phenomena, the exact origins of the conditions that brought about in the Yellow Press are difficult to determine. However, one factor does stand out—namely, the integration of the concept of freedom of the press and the ability to survive in a newspaper marketplace that, throughout the nineteenth century, became more and more integrated with the market economy emerging before the Civil War. As a consequence, boundaries that had been defined by political power brokers and their fellow travelers underwent various severe tests. As editors sought to expand their influence and increase their respective circulations, stories that would not have appeared in a previous era took root in the contemporary one. Gradually, the press evolved from being a servant of the political structure to one of its harshest critics. Commentary that would have, at the very worst, landed a newspaper editor in jail or, at the very least, resulted in the loss of the business began to become commonplace, especially during the 1830s. As a result of one significant incident in eighteenth-century New York, the fear of retribution by persons maligned in the press was significantly reduced.

Getting into trouble with the authorities was a journalist's lot in life until John Peter Zenger appeared on the scene in 1733. One of his predecessors, a certain Benjamin Harris—founder, publisher, and editor of the seventeenth-century Massachusetts publication *Publick Occurrences Both Forreign and Domestick*—caught the attention of the colonial governor when he issued the first volume of his journal; in it, he gleefully related the shenanigans of certain royal personages in Europe. Harris, who had a dubious background at any rate (having spent time in a British debtors' prison), often made his living selling splendid elixirs at county fairs, liquids guaranteed to wipe out any number of maladies, both short-term and terminal. His work as America's first journalist hardly inspired confidence in the craft. Yet his so-called exposé of wrongdoing at the highest level would once again surface in New York City in the mid-eighteenth century, and the legal processes that resulted from it would impact journalistic practice to this very day.

Zenger entered the world of New York politics as an impoverished young European who had come to the United States searching for new beginnings. He served an apprenticeship in a print shop, saving enough money to buy his own press and set himself up as both a printer and a part-time journalist. While Zenger was seeking to make life easier for himself, one person who did not have to suffer, Governor William Cosby of the New York colony, found himself in a bitter battle with the colonial council over a number of matters, most notably his salary, which the council deemed excessive. Cosby ran headlong into a war with the chief justice of New York's Supreme Court of Judicature, Lewis Morris. When Morris resisted Cosby's pleas, the governor responded by firing the chief justice and replacing him with one of his cronies. The move did not sit well with many New Yorkers, particularly John Peter Zenger.

Zenger issued a pamphlet condemning the governor's actions
and supporting Chief Justice Morris. He immediately attracted
support from the antiroyalist factions in New York, with the consequence that he turned his pamphlet into a newspaper called the
New York Weekly Journal. His friend and legal adviser, James
Alexander, acted as editor and assisted Zenger, whose command
of English was anything but secure. The two decided to cover an
election in Westchester County in which Morris was running
against one of Cosby's appointees. In spite of some interference
by the local sheriff, Morris won the seat handily. However,
Zenger and Alexander decided to lampoon the sheriff, whom
they described as a monkey. The assault did not go unnoticed,
especially when the tirade against the governor continued on a
weekly basis.

Zenger appeared to be in the clear when a grand jury, though
pressured by Cosby and his friends, refused to issue an indictment
for seditious libel against the journalist. However, the governor
was not one to give up, and eventually, the colonial administration issued its own warrant. On August 4, 1735, Zenger went to
trial. Much to the shock of Cosby, as well as his appointee, Chief
Justice Delancey, and several other hangers-on, the jury refused to
convict. The argument that truth was a defense against charges of
libel and slander had entered the law books.

The colonial authorities were unwilling to overturn a jury ver-
dict, knowing as they might the kind of social unrest such an action could encourage. Although British law at the time and American law subsequently did not recognize jury verdicts as
precedent-setting, the case began to be used by defense attorneys
with some success. In 1742, *Boston Evening Post* journalist Thomas
Fleet used the truth-as-defense argument in a conflict with Sir
Robert Walpole. When William Parks of the *Williamsburg Gazette*

accused a politician of stealing sheep, he, too, was vindicated because he was able to prove the charges were true.

So, what does all this have to do with the emergence of the Yellow Press? Quite simply, when editors, publishers, and commentators no longer feared that a stint in prison could follow a damaging article, they began to explore the limits of public tolerance, all in a desire to accumulate readership that in turn would result in higher circulations and thus higher financial returns. And when the penny press began to appear on the streets of New York, one could easily determine that matters such as political corruption, lurid crime, and financial skulduggery would find their ways to the front page, and they did. The penny press would expand the borders of journalistic culture in early nineteenth-century America.

The birth of the penny press took place in Boston on July 24, 1830. The event would change the course of American journalism for all time to come. Its founder, Lynde M. Walter, a Harvard graduate with few worries about income, entered a world that had only begun to emerge from the relative instability of the eighteenth century. In 1830, there were only 65 daily papers in the country, supplemented by 650 weeklies. Population growth was hardly explosive during the 1830s, increasing from 12.9 million to only 17.1 million by the end of the decade.

The new penny press of the 1830s had little in common with the primarily political press that preceded it, with the possible exception of some factors of physical form. Prior to the 1830s, many newspapers were owned and operated by printers who also provided typographical services in order to make a living. These so-called printer's newspapers focused on events in Washington as a primary activity. Suffering in this respect were the events in the local communities around the nation, which sorely lacked local news coverage.

John Nerone and Kevin Barnhurst have referred to news gathering in the years prior to the 1830s as passive. Reporting had yet to emerge as an essential player in newspaper culture. Editors and owners seldom if ever wrote articles for their own journals. To a large degree, content consisted of material pirated from other newspapers, political news as noted previously, and correspondence both written and oral from readers and local gossipmongers. Needless to say, *fact checking* had also not yet entered the journalistic vocabulary.

Neither had the advantages of unique designs been explored. In terms of form and style, one newspaper looked very much like another. Publishers and owners were constantly struggling with cost obstacles, to the point that most newspapers were quite small, about the size of a standard sheet of modern typing paper. Even the most important stories were often reduced to a few clinical lines. As for the number of pages per issue, it was usually four. As Nerone and Barnhurst observed, "The printer's newspaper had been a gentleman's conversation about the colonial world and then a citizen's town meeting." The rise of the penny press would put this era to rest once and for all.

As a model for what would follow, Walter's paper made a number of significant innovations that would eventually find their way into the New York newspapers later in the decade. For one, he increased the size of each page from 8.5 inches by 11 inches to 10 by 15. The face page was devoted to advertising, a tradition that continued well through the nineteenth century and into the early years of the twentieth. As opposed to some of his successors, Walter saw to it that the content of his *Boston Transcript* was usually in very good taste, specializing in covering literature and theatrical events. Although the journal itself was fairly conservative in its outlook on life, Walter took it upon himself to defend Boston's largest minority, the boatloads of unkempt Irish immigrants who were changing the very character of the city itself.

The penny press arrived in New York on January 1, 1833, when Horatio David Shepard teamed up with Horace Greeley and Francis W. Story and issued the *Morning Post*. Although both Greeley and Story went on to fame and fortune in the New York press world, the concept of bringing out a penny paper belonged exclusively to Shepard. He made a habit of taking daily walks through the teeming streets of the Bowery, where he observed merchants selling small items for a penny a piece. He also took note of the fact that sales were brisk. Shepard correctly sensed the viability of the marketplace, a world the press would soon enter.

Of course, any item that sells for a mere penny or two is not likely to attract an elite purchaser. Prior to the rise of the penny press, only those with some sense of literacy and the financial means that usually went with it could afford to subscribe to newspapers in the Jacksonian era. Until the emergence of popular newspapers, most journals depended on subscription rates of anywhere from $8 to $10 a year. The penny press reached well down on the class ladder to a new constituency, one that would eventually be inherited by William Randolph Hearst and Joseph Pulitzer. At the risk of simplifying a relatively complex issue, it can be claimed that any form of anarchy that existed in the city's streets and neighborhoods supplied fodder for the press. The decorum that was achieved by the polite relating of political tales was replaced by a hurly-burly, headlong plunge into a nether world inhabited by crooks, murderers, petty thieves, and numerous persons whose names regularly appeared on police blotters. As historian James Melvin Lee noted, "The penny papers went on the principle of what the Lord let happen ought to be printed in their sheets." Needless to say, the approach did not sit well on upper Fifth Avenue.

Yet in many respects, the penny press became the laboratory in which journalistic experimentation took place. A sense of competition started to take hold, with editors and publishers fighting it out to see who could be first to report stories of significance. Rather than just be the voice of various political leaders, the penny press decided to take on the role of protector for those who could not fend for themselves—the huge population of working-class individuals who lived marginal existences in New York's overcrowded tenement slums. For the first time in the history of North America, newspapers became totally integrated into the culture of their respective communities. With the impact of the new industrial age about to be felt, new technologies such as steam presses increased the ability of publishers and editors to rapidly expand their activities and increase the size and content of their journals. More and more Americans were learning to read and write, creating an ever-increasing constituency for the press. There was no looking back.

The first penny press newspaper to make a quick impact was Benjamin H. Day's *New York Sun*. The opening issue was anything but impressive. Day relied on past practice to design the paper and determine its content. It was a four-page publication set upon 8.5-by-11-inch pages with three columns of type. There was no sense that something called original reporting should be done. This first issue was cribbed from a number of existing New York dailies and weeklies. Day mounted the first issue with one helper and two printers.

Yet though the layout and design followed some predictable patterns, the content did not. And when the New York marketplace got wind of what Day was publishing, the circulation of the paper jumped to four thousand copies a day. Readers could not easily turn away from a story with the tantalizing headline "MELANCHOLY SUICIDE," which appeared on page two. The center of reader attraction was the sad saga of one Fred Hall, who had moved to New York from Boston. Apparently, the young lovelorn man was rejected by his intended, with the consequence that he took his own life with an overdose of opium. What made him and his dilemma newsworthy was the simple fact that Fred Halls existed everywhere in daily life in large, urban areas. What made telling Hall's story significant was the simple fact that for the first time in its history, journalism turned its attention to the previously anonymous people who constituted the bulk of American society at the time.

What Day learned from the Hall affair was that the seamy side of life paid. In fact, so did crime. Preceding Damon Runyon by a century or so, Day turned his attention to the police courts, whose goings-on were directly related to his desire to hire more writers to make sure that no good story was missed. Taking his cue from a British newspaper called the *London Morning Herald,* Day treated his readers to a continual parade of petty thieves, hookers, confidence artists, homeless transients, and a host of others who had shadowy connections on the wrong side of the law. Although Day was probably not conscious of the fact at the time, his obsession with covering police stories likely marked the first instance in American journalism when the craft of reporting and storytelling actually began. As Nerone and Barnhurst pointed out, two forms of reporting culture began to take shape in the Victorian age. On the one hand, there was the scavenger, who was "not a persona but a completely anonymous news hound, combing first the exchange papers, then the police courts, the theatres and the taverns for bits of information that might be conveyed in a sentence or a paragraph or that might be turned into a story of a column or so." On the other hand, there was the correspondent, who was "a manly observer of events and personages in distant and usually powerful places; he (rarely she) was a persona, although pseudonymous, who conveyed subjective impressions with an air of authority and confidentiality, like the colonial letter writer."

However, Day did not depend solely on news about events that actually took place. In August 1835, the *Sun* carried a story about sensational astronomical discoveries on the moon made by a noted scientist, Sir John Herschel. Herschel was reportedly involved in significant advancements in telescope design and had an observatory in South Africa. His name gave immediate credibility to the story that was to follow. He was the son of Sir William Herschel, the man who had discovered the planet Uranus.

Day's first story contained few details but enough teasers to bring readers back for a second go. Eventually, the newspaper got down to printing so-called facts about life on the moon, which included several in-depth analysis paragraphs about vegetation and one tempting tale about a creature that supposedly existed on the planet's satellite. While Day was publishing this most sensational material, other New York newspapers figuratively bit their collective tongues until they bled. In the end, they could suffer the humiliation no longer. Day's articles began to appear one by one in the pages of his competitors' papers. But the final humiliation would come when Day revealed that not one of the tales of life on the moon was true.

Apart from new content, the rise of the penny press produced other significant changes in American journalism that would also find their ways to the Yellow journals of the late 1890s. The need to market the newspaper forced owners and editors to seek revenues beyond subscription fees. Following Walter's innovations, the concept of advertising became a permanent part of the journalistic culture. So did street sales, often the vocation of underpaid and overworked urchins called newsboys who lived in a world of their own. Above all, the penny press was still an urban phenomenon situated primarily on the upper East Coast.

When Day launched his *New York Sun* in 1833, New York City was the most productive urban area in which to found a penny paper. In 1830, the population reached two hundred thousand. In twenty-five short years, this number would increase to a million. The city was attracting immigrants internally from farming communities and smaller towns and villages across the country where employment opportunities were limited. It was also the main Atlantic port of entry for literally thousands of poverty-stricken Europeans desperate to land somewhere where the sanctity of life was not cruelly tied to politics and religion. These communities would prove to be the rock upon which Yellow Journalism would be constructed.

It was easily predictable that Day's success would breed a number of imitators. In 1834, the *New York Transcript* began its five-year run. It was founded by three printers who hired a professional editor and a professional court reporter. The *Transcript* appeared to be a very exaggerated version of Day's *New York Sun*. It looked like the *Sun,* it behaved like the *Sun* on both its editorial and its news pages, and it patterned its commercial agenda after that of the *Sun* as well. The owners exploited editor Asa Greene's previous profession as a humorist, encouraging him to apply his candor and wit to the many characters whose lives were unraveled in its pages. The newspaper built its success on what historian and professor Frank Luther Mott described as "illicit sex relations, prizefights, and criminal trials." But it also began the tradition of sports reporting in the daily press. The *Transcript* was a thorn in Day's side, but he had yet to encounter the man who would become his most fearsome rival.

It was the seamy side of life that eventually drew James Gordon Bennett to the press scene in New York City. Along with Horace Greeley, he was to emerge as one of the two most influential journalists in mid-nineteenth-century America. Greeley postured himself as a sartorial nightmare with a high IQ, but Bennett had no such pretensions even though he was the better educated of the two. Greeley had a passionate interest in the political life of the day. Bennett had long since divorced himself from any faith in the system. And while Greeley felt the role of the press was to present, discuss, and analyze contemporary issues, Bennett was only interested in what he determined was news and the people who read what he published on a daily basis. His writing style was often provocative, a literary fist to the face. He was obsessed with facts and often cast himself in the role of reporter, a vocation he thoroughly enjoyed.

When Bennett returned to New York from newspaper assignments in other places, he was immediately drawn to Benjamin Day's *New York Sun*. He had come with a solid tradition of in-your-face journalism, which he had learned during a brief tenure at the *Courier and Enquirer*. That journal was the handiwork of one Col. James Watson Webb, a retired veteran of the War of 1812 with a reputation as a successful Indian fighter. As Bennett would discover later in life, Webb was no pussycat. He was a physical and violent man who often fought his rivals in the street. He also had a criminal record, having spent two years in Sing Sing Prison for violating New York State's antidueling laws. Whatever competitive spirit may have lurked in Bennett's heart, his tenure with Webb did little to discourage it.

Bennett was nearly forty years old in 1835, and in a historical period when growing old usually meant lasting until one was sixty years of age, he had entered the second phase of his life with few prospects of wealth and influence. He had approached Day for a position but was turned down. So, with a small nest egg of $500, he decided to go into business for himself. He recruited several colleagues with whom he had associated as a member of Webb's newspaper staff. They set up shop on lower Wall Street, and on May 11, 1835, the first edition of the *New York Herald* hit the streets.

Bennett was convinced that truth was often stranger than fiction. He had no need to publish fake moon probes, since, as he argued on many an occasion, great tales in the human experience existed right beside him. All he as a journalist had to do was to find the facts of these great tales, deliver them in an attractive package, and enjoy the results. Bennett also believed that good stories never began and ended within a defined, twenty-four-hour period. The great adventures of his time, he thought, could carry over several days or, if need be, several weeks. It was the journalist's job to determine where a story began and where it ended or, in simpler terms, when the readers began to lose interest in the tale. Bennett's greatest journalistic success would follow this pattern flawlessly.

Bennett may have found acceptance with his ever-increasing readership, but he was not loved by his competitors in polite New York press society. In fact, he was not loved in impolite New York press society either, whose chief representative was the volatile Webb. While out walking on Wall Street on January 19, 1835, Webb confronted Bennett about a series of provocative articles that Webb felt maligned his reputation. Furious at Bennett's refusal to take his charges seriously, Webb pulled out his cane and beat the helpless Bennett to within an inch of his life. Following the attack, Bennett included a response in the *Herald*. He began by stating, "I have to apologize to my kind readers for the want of usual life today." Then, directly referring to Webb, he wrote:

> By going up behind me, [he] cut a slash in my head about one and a half inch in length, and through the integuments of the skull. The fellow, no doubt, wanted to let out the never failing supply of good humor and wit which has created such a reputation for the Herald, and appropriate the contents to supply the emptiness of his own thick skull. He did not succeed, however, in rifling me of my ideas. He has not injured the skull. My ideas in a few days, will flow as freshly as ever, and he will find it so, to his cost.

Bennett's encounters with Webb did not conclude with the events of January 19. On May 9, 1835, Webb once again confronted Bennett on Wall Street. This time, he pushed the owner of the *Herald* down a set of stone steps, after which he landed upon him and delivered several blows to his body on the doorstep of a local stockbroker. Bennett's response was one of clear defiance:

> As to intimidating me, or changing my course, the thing cannot be done. Neither Webb nor any other man shall or can intimidate me. I tell the honest truth in my paper and leave the consequences to God. Could I leave them in better hands? I may be attacked, I may be assailed, I may be killed, I may be murdered, and I never will succumb. I never will abandon the cause of truth, morals and virtue.

Although the reasons for Webb's anger were never recorded, it is known that Bennett took special delight in poking pointed remarks at the character of the *Courier and Enquirer*'s editor. His remarks included commentary about Webb's physical characteristics as well as his ability as a journalist. Bennett should not have been surprised by the results.

On April 11, 1836, James Gordon Bennett made newspaper history. He published the first installment of a series of articles about the grisly murder of a New York prostitute named Ellen Jewett, which had taken place the night before in a house of ill repute called the City Hotel, at 41 Thomas Street. Jewett was the perfect candidate for such treatment. She was the daughter of a poor shoemaker in Maine. She took employment in the home of a judge who was determined to give the girl a break in early nineteenth-century society. When he sent his daughters off to a private school for girls, he included Ellen. However, she was either unwilling or unable to accept the restrictions of an upper-middle-class existence, a life she abandoned for work as a prostitute. After wearing out her welcome in several other American towns and cities, she landed in New York.

For Bennett, the demise of the unfortunate Jewett was an opportunity he could not miss, especially because her accused slayer, Richard P. Robinson, was the son of a socially connected Connecticut family. The young Robinson was, by nineteenth-century terms, a handsome rake with an excess of charm and charisma. He was gainfully employed by a New York merchant firm owned by a man named Joseph Hoxie. He was hardly one's ideal candidate for the bludgeoning and attempted burning of a lady of the evening.

Bennett gleefully exploited the demise of the unfortunate streetwalker and noted in his memoirs that just a decade previously, Ellen Jewett had been a regular on Sunday mornings in a downtown church presided over by the Reverend Mr. Tappan. Bennett was determined to leave no secret unturned about the unfortunate life of Ellen Jewett. He became his own detective and his own reporter. He delved into her past, discovering her modest existence in the state of Maine and her fall from grace after leaving the employ of the judge. He read her letters and published intimate details of her life in a soap opera–like serial in the *Herald*. Jewett became the centerpiece of a series of tales that historian David Anthony described as "a mix of deadly erotics and aesthetic beauty." Bennett made the dead body of Ellen Jewett the central factor in the ongoing coverage of her passing. He even reported that a crew of local coroners had exhumed her remains under a full moon under the pretext of conducting a more detailed post-mortem examination. Then, he stated, the good doctors carried what was left of Ellen Jewett to a secluded place in the cemetery, where they proceeded to dissect her. There was only one problem with the story. It never happened.

And what happened to the young man accused of dispatching Ellen Jewett to her eternal rest? Bennett, for one, decided he was innocent of the crime. Robinson confessed to visiting her regularly but denied he had seen her the night of the murder. A hatchet found in the rear yard of the City Hotel that was identified as the murder weapon supposedly had been stolen from the store where Robinson was employed. A cloak that witnesses reported they had seen on Robinson was a critical piece of evidence, but the accused man denied owning it. As the trial progressed, more and more doubt was raised about Robinson's complicity in the crime. Bennett agreed, and the front page of the *Herald* eventually contained an article declaring that Robinson had nothing to do with Jewett's death. A jury concurred, and Robinson walked out of a New York court as a free man.

Bennett's reputation would be attacked by a number of his enemies. The editor of the *New York Evening Star,* Mordecai Noah, was reputed to have proof that Bennett had extracted a sum of

$13,000 from a well-known man who was in the house of ill re-pute the night that Jewett was murdered. Noah told his friends and colleagues that the man was terrified of being identified in such a place, especially considering the events of the night of April 10. Bennett recorded the accusation in his memoirs and dismissed the story as ridiculous. There was no proof to support the accusation.

Bennett had stirred readers' lust for more and more gore and vi-olence in the daily press. As one story reached its climax, editors sought out others to replace it, even if that meant testing the boundaries of credibility and good taste. When a cigar store em-ployee named Mary Cecilia Rogers was lured from the shop to her death, the local New York press missed no opportunity to relay even the most remote details of the case. The man who created the North American crime novel, Edgar Allan Poe, adapted the story, resetting it in France: the unfortunate and very late Mary Cecilia Rogers became immortalized as Marie Roget. Once these two cases passed into history, others, such as the murder of Har-vard researcher George Parkman by Professor John Webster in 1849, filled the pages of the country's penny press.

It appeared that the nation was awash with more crime than it could handle and that the press was merely revealing how bad the situation had become. In 1843, the *United States Gazette* reported that in the half year from January to July, there were no less than 215 murders by gun and knife. There were a further 56 fatalities due to the careless handling of guns. In addition, 45 persons died from having their clothing take fire, and 43 were killed by falling from horses or having carriages land on top of them during acci-dents. And to top it off, 83 persons took their own lives. What was proving to be a monstrous social headache for authorities was also prime fodder for the likes of James Gordon Bennett and several of his colleagues.

While Bennett was rampaging around the New York press scene, the journal that began it all, the *New York Sun,* had been passing through a number of hands. Benjamin Day had sold the newspaper to his brother-in-law and bookkeeper, Moses Y. Beach. Beach operated it until 1848, when his two sons assumed the mantle of responsibility. In terms of journalistic battles, the *New York Sun* was a minor player in comparison to the papers owned by Bennett and his rival Horace Greeley.

As the nation attempted to recover from the ravages of the Civil War, it was desperately in need of a respite from all the grief that set of events had caused. Charles Dana was more than willing and able to turn attention to more interesting and, of course, more sexually lurid matters. His journalistic sense would provide the perfect diversion.

Dana's approach to entering the New York market was quite different from that of the men who had preceded him. Instead of founding a new journal as had Day, Greeley, and Bennett, Dana opened his wallet and purchased the *New York Sun* from the descendants of Benjamin Day in 1868. It would prove to be a symbol of stability in a world of uncertainty. Dana's *New York Sun* published well into the twentieth century. It would also be better known as a newspaper that, like those of Day and Bennett, catered to the seamier side of life. His chief rivals in the newspaper battles of the late 1860s and early 1870s were soon to throw off their mortal coils, leaving the downside of New York life to Dana. James Gordon Bennett passed from the scene in 1872, the last of the great triumvirate of Day, Greeley, and Bennett to do so. There were few real obstacles on the road to success for Charles Dana.

Dana recognized the value of covering political news, theatrical performances, financial news, and popular lectures as well as copious amounts of crime. This kind of reporting had been long established in the New York area, and clearly, there was a market for it. But he also added something he referred to as human interest stories—tales of everyday folk doing everyday things. Over time, this coverage expanded into what could aptly be described as the curiosity market. Dana reported on matters such as the latest style in mustache grooming, the origins of slang expressions, strange ships with strange flags in the city's harbor, and the peculiarities of certain kinds of dress among visible minorities. A number of writers who would soon be famous worked for Dana, including Henry James, Robert Louis Stevenson, Walt Whitman, Rudyard Kipling, Bret Harte, Ella Wheeler Wilcox, and William Dean Howells. The groundwork for a new kind of journalism had been laid, which would be built upon, first and foremost, by Joseph Pulitzer. The adventures that reporter Elizabeth Cochrane, aka Nellie Bly, would soon embark on had a solid precedent in journalism's historical practice. As newspaper historian George Douglas noted:

> Much of the glitter of Pulitzer's *World* when it was founded in the 1880's could be traced to the influence of Dana and his staff of writers. So, too, much of the writing that was found in the *Herald,* the Hearst papers, and yes, even the more stolid *Times.* The *Sun*'s style seeped into the famous humor magazines of the late nineteenth and early twentieth centuries—*Judge, Puck,* the old *Life.*

Dana was hardly a shrinking violet when it came to singing the praises of his newspaper. To be sure, he was publishing much the same kind of content as the *New York Herald,* but there were differences in approach between the two rivals. Both newspapers had added the interview style of reporting. The front pages and glaring headlines pushed sensationalism to the limit in each. But as the

1870s dawned in New York City, Dana ran advertisements in his rivals' newspapers, declaring, with no sense of modesty, that the *Sun*'s "news is the freshest, most interesting and sprightliest current, and no expense is spared to make it just what the great mass of the people want." What the people want, indeed! These very words would be recycled over and over again by both Hearst and Pulitzer.

When James Gordon Bennett finally passed from this earth, his son, James Jr., took over the reins at the *New York Herald*. His journal would prove to be the first physical connection to what was to become the Yellow Press. Bennett Jr.'s world was also changing as the newspaper market began to rationalize itself. The old tried-and-true method of managing a newspaper with a person of strong journalistic sense in charge was giving away to hiring a professional chief operating officer who knew a lot about cost analysis and virtually nothing about journalism. Yet Bennett Jr. remained, to a significant degree, a chip off the old block.

He had been prepared for a newspaper career by his father. The senior Bennett moved his son from department to department so that he could learn the ropes of the industry. In fact, the younger Bennett had contributed directly and quite positively to the strength and popularity of his father's enterprise. But he fell out of favor in New York's tight social circles when, while quite intoxicated, he urinated into a fireplace at a social function attended by his fiancée's parents. He left the city to take up residence in France, where he spent the majority of the rest of his life. However, his interest in journalism did not wane. He continued to manage the newspaper on a long-distance basis and did so quite successfully.

Interestingly, one of the most important figures in nineteenth-century journalism was not a journalist but an artist and art teacher from New York City, Samuel Morse. His electric telegraph, introduced to the world in 1844, would also play a significant role in the emergence of Yellow Journalism. In fact, the telegraph was one of the main reasons why Yellow Journalism could spread its wings and become international in scope before the turn of the twentieth century. In the late 1850s, American and European entrepreneurs were actively working on connecting the world by telegraph by laying a cable under the waters of the Atlantic Ocean. By the time that James Gordon Bennett Sr. decided to take advantage of this technological feat to break one of the most sensational stories of his time, cable transmission from America to Europe and back, although suffering from frequent breakdowns, was generally reliable. Knowing that he could scoop his rivals by using the telegraph from Britain to America, Bennett sent Henry Morton Stanley to Africa to find the English missionary David Livingstone, who reportedly had been lost somewhere in the "dark continent" for three years. *Herald* readers were shocked when they opened the paper on July 2, 1872, to read that Stanley had been successful in his effort and that Livingstone had discovered the source of the Nile River.

Rather than be content in just reporting the news, Bennett Jr. wanted to *make* the news. One of his war correspondents was present at the opening of the Suez Canal and reported on the veteran explorer Samuel Baker's expedition up the Nile. *Herald* reporters told tales about the Russian invasion expedition to Khiva, and they covered events in such far-off places as Baghdad and Persepolis. Later, on the homefront, the *Herald* provided free ice to tenement dwellers in New York's working-class districts during an especially brutal summer heat wave. The newspaper's efforts and reporting success were commended by the Fleet Street press in Britain.

In Chicago, the *Daily News* decided to take a leaf out of the *Her-*

ald's playbook when a bank manager named Spencer disappeared with about $500,000 in cash from his employer. The journal's reporters followed the trail to Stuttgart, Germany, where the felon was captured. In Albany, New York, the local newspaper located a kidnapper and his victim after the police admitted they had no clues as to the whereabouts of either party.

The rise of the Yellow Press, although influenced primarily by the actors who preceded it, can also be attributed to some of the more unconventional journals that rose up during this period. Quite simply, if the illustrated press, the free love press, the socialist and labor presses, and the libertarian press could push the boundaries of journalistic judgment and manage to survive (although somewhat contentiously in many cases), so could the daily press. The nineteenth-century press was at one time the most effective communicator of a variety of social values, even as it was enmeshed in a grand experiment that would play out in the closing years of the century. From the vicious and mind-numbing newspaper wars that eventually took their tolls, the nation was given the gift of an effective pillar of republican democracy sometimes known as the daily press.

An event in Britain that would, in time, find its way to North America took place on July 17, 1841. On that day, the satiric journal *Punch* was born, selling some five thousand copies in two editions. Its first *Punch Almanack* appeared the following year and sold some sixty thousand copies, while its creator languished in debtors' prison. Although its first few issues did not contain any illustrations, founding editor Mark Lemon decided that, for effectiveness, *Punch* should become an illustrated journal. And so it did.

Illustrated journalism arrived in America in 1855, courtesy of an expatriate Englishman named Henry Carter. Carter, who adopted a professional name and emerged as the pictorial journalist Frank

Leslie, had extensive experience in the business of visual journalism. Prior to moving to New York City in 1848, he had worked as an engraver on the *Illustrated London News.* It did not take Carter long to come to the conclusion that the United States needed an illustrated press and that he was the person to run it. It took him far longer to convince the skeptics, especially the skeptics who had money to invest in the venture. Although normally confined to weekly publication, the illustrated journals introduced the concept that pictures, even those drawn by hand, were an integral part of reporting the news. Proponents of these journals believed, as did many others, that one picture was really the equivalent of a thousand words. After all, readers no longer had to rely on reporters who published their interpretations of daily events. Readers, so they thought, could now make their own value judgments. Pictures didn't lie, did they?

Although a concerted attack on the political ways and means of William Magear (sometimes known as Marcy) "Boss" Tweed began in the fairly staid *New York Times,* it took the illustrated press, in particular *Harper's Weekly,* to capture the hearts and souls of normally insulated New Yorkers and convince them of the extent of the crime perpetrated by Tweed and his pals at Tammany Hall. Rumors floated around New York that the ring had extorted literally millions of dollars from the city treasury. When the *Times* printed a special Tweed supplement, the journal reported that invoices paid for renovations at the city's courthouse "totaled $9,789,482.16, little of which, it appeared, actually got to the building's renovation fund."

It was Thomas Nast, more than most others, who refined the art of political commentary through the use of imagery. The campaign in *Harper's Weekly* to destroy Tweed began in the late 1860s and continued throughout the 1870s, when the infamous political

ward heeler finally paid the price for his crimes. In Nast's drawings, Tweed took on several different forms. At one point, he was
drawn as "fat and bloated, with a long nose and deep-set eyes." In
another drawing, he was transformed into a vulture. But no matter what the artist decided to do with him, Nast's Tweed always
wore a huge diamond stickpin to remind readers of the extent of
his plunder.

New Yorkers took to the illustrated press almost as readily as
they accepted the scandals of the penny press and its successors. Although always teetering on the edge of a financial nightmare, the
irrepressible Frank Leslie continued to add to his stable of publications throughout the 1870s. At one time, he employed three hundred to four hundred people, publishing fourteen magazines, all
aimed at different constituencies. If a publication became successful, he would eventually add "Frank Leslie's" to the masthead. No
part of New York life—including its Spanish-speaking population—was exempt from Leslie's desire to blanket the marketplace
with illustrated journalism.

In 1873, two Canadian publishers, Georges Edouard Desbarats
and William A. Leggo, launched the first illustrated daily in New
York City. Their publication was significantly different from the
other illustrated journals in the city. The *New York Daily Graphic*
actually published pictures along with other forms of illustrated
commentary. Although the subject is disputed in some circles, it is
widely accepted in Canada that Leggo was the inventor of the
halftone process in photography, which allowed reproduction of
viewable photographs in the daily press. For his part, Desbarats had
extensive experience in the illustrated press. He had come from a
long line of Canadian printers whose connections extended back
beyond the founding of the nation. In December 1869, he
launched the *Canadian Illustrated News,* and in the winter of 1870,

he founded a French-language version, *L'Opinion Publique.* His publications lasted well into the 1880s.

Initially, the illustrated press was saved by the fact that the reproduction of photographs in the daily press was still an expensive proposition. It was not until the late 1880s and early 1890s that photographs began to appear in the daily press. Yet with some exceptions, the general use of photography did not make an impact in journalism until well into the twentieth century. And as much as drawings fell out of favor when photography began to make its way into journalism, they did not disappear altogether. They just changed form. The old political cartoon type of illustration made a successful jump from the illustrated press, normally published weekly, to the daily press. Cartoonists who had been accustomed to relaxing over an idea or two through a five-day workweek now found themselves under the gun to produce daily. The use of the political cartoon is reported to have saved the early 1880s' *New York World* from extinction. On August 10, 1884, an artist drew a very unflattering cartoon of two presidential rivals, James Blaine and Grover Cleveland. Entitled "Belshazzar's Feast," the picture was an instant hit, and later that month, the newspaper began to publish political cartoons in its Sunday editions. Over time, political cartoons made their way to the daily press as well. The political cartoon and its coinhabitant on the printed pages, the comic strip, would become essential players in the rise of the Yellow Press.

In the spring of 1865, journalism and its approach to facts changed significantly. Under the tutelage of Edwin Stanton, President Lincoln's secretary of war, the inverted pyramid came into use. Replacing a style of reporting that had depended on citing tales chronologically, the inverted pyramid was primarily designed to relay facts rather than tell a good story. And by implication, reporters and editors would be forced to arrange facts in order of importance and emphasize only that which directly affected the information. In other words, the inverted pyramid and objectivity were seen to be closely related. Thus, when John Wilkes Booth shot Abraham Lincoln at Ford's Theater in Washington, Edwin Stanton assembled the facts of the case in order of importance and relayed them to a body of waiting reporters.

But not all journalists were interested in relaying just the facts. In the late 1820s, a dissident and strident press arose in the United States to support organized labor, abolition of slavery, and woman's rights. Well into the twentieth century, advocacy journalism kept rearing its head as one issue was replaced by another. Life in the dissident press was far from comfortable. Editors and owners struggled from issue to issue, wondering just when the cash flow would cease and the journal would be forced to quit publishing. Furthermore, their journals, which did not subscribe to the so-called journalistic ethics of the day, were often ridiculed by the mainstream press. Yet the editors and owners struggled on, convinced of the righteousness of their respective causes and knowing, above all, they could never get access to the large, urban dailies to spread the word about who they were and what they wanted.

One could easily count the number of journals that rose and fell during the nineteenth century that espoused some form of dissident thoughts—or any kind of advocacy that was not readily accepted by the ruling establishment. An early example was a journal published by Elizabeth Cady Stanton and Susan B. Anthony, with the very scary name *The Revolution*. Stanton and Anthony, both Republicans, had attempted to convince their party to accept the principle of one person one vote, irrespective of gender considerations. The party refused, opting instead to support suffrage for male African Americans. The two women left the party and hung their hats with the Democrats. When the same subject arose at a convention at Tammany Hall in 1868, Stanton was rudely laughed out of the meeting room.

The Revolution stayed alive simply because it had a male bene-factor, George Francis Train, who was willing to pick up the tab for its publication and distribution at least in the beginning when cost coverage was most critical. Needless to say, the journal was hardly objective. Considering the rationale for its existence, it could hardly be so. It argued for equal gender rights at the ballot box but took matters beyond that point. Both Stanton and An-thony wrote on the touchy subject of divorce. They published ar-ticles that argued that marriage was a civil contract, one that could be abolished if a marriage partner, especially the male, violated the sanctity of the union through bad behavior such as consuming too much alcohol, bedding down with other women, or inflicting physical damage on a spouse. They also argued that prostitution should be legalized.

Although its approach to gaining rights for women was often strident and militant, *The Revolution* was the creation and commu-nications vehicle for fundamentally middle-class, white women. As much as the quest for suffrage was the core around which the newspaper and its editors revolved, other controversial subjects regularly surfaced at meetings of professional women in New York City, most of whom supported the work of Stanton and An-thony. It was not uncommon to hear discussions on the legitimacy of abortion, the legalization of prostitution, and the role of female physiology in sexual practices. But there was not universal agree-ment in the ranks of disgruntled, Victorian women. Stanton and Anthony were regularly condemned in some circles for allying themselves with forces anxious to prevent African Americans from taking their rightful positions in society. The two women were flanked by relatively conservative women who were content with the way things were, on one side, and, on the other, by those who wanted to take a more visible and more flamboyant approach to securing woman's rights.

So often with reform movements, a radical fringe arises, in many cases drawing attention from the center to the periphery of the political spectrum. Gilded Age America would prove to be no exception in this regard. A sexual reform press began to emerge in the early 1870s and was accused of promoting free love. In the context of the times, free love actually meant matters such as sex education, common-law relationships, the use of sexually explicit language, the right to deny sexual favors to abusive spouses, and promiscuity. A twenty-first-century observer would hardly be shocked by the content of some of the free love journals, but nineteenth-century America clearly was. Riding to the rescue of pure America was one Anthony Comstock, a dry-goods salesman turned full-time antivice crusader who succeeded in getting the state of New York to pass a law prohibiting immoral publications in 1868. Five years later, he succeeded in convincing the U.S. Postal Service to place restrictions on the kinds of material that could enter the mail system. Later that year, he founded the New York Society for the Suppression of Vice, which went on a rampage that resulted in the destruction of some 160 tons of printed material deemed to be pornographic. But when two women journalists decided to publish the details of an allegedly illicit liaison between one of America's best-known clergymen, Henry Ward Beecher, and the wife of parishioner Theodore Tilton, the gloves were off in a battle between the puritanical and the permissive.

The conflict would pit Comstock and his allies against Victoria Woodhull and her sister Tennessee Claflin, publishers of *Woodhull and Claflin's Weekly* in New York City. The pair hardly fit the nineteenth-century ideal for women. Born in Homer, Ohio, Victoria spent part of her youth earning an income any way she could. She charged a fee for telling fortunes, sold liquor, and became a faith healer, among other enterprises. When the Civil War came to a conclusion, she teamed up with her sister in New York, where Tennessee was providing physical comfort to the newly widowed Cornelius Vanderbilt. Victoria also amused the elderly millionaire by conducting séances in which he reportedly spoke to his deceased wife. When he decided to remarry, he gave the sisters enough money to set up a brokerage firm in New York's financial district, and thus they entered a profession dominated by men. They made a substantial income from this venture, due in part to the notoriety they had gained through the publication of the free love journal that they launched in 1870.

Although hardly alone in the promotion of free love, the journal became the best-known advocate of the movement and was bound to attract the attention of Anthony Comstock. He was not the kind of person who would tolerate discussions of the kind found in the journal, a representative example of which appeared under the title "The Social Evil":

> The moral aspect of the whole question [of enforced monogamy] lies with society at large, especially with the women, the mothers, the female leaders. Legislation can do little in a matter which concerns the natural instincts of human nature. But it can do something. The stupid practice of making arrests and midnight descents is as great an immorality and public disgrace as the evil itself. It is too frequently a means of black mail. It is in a way a scandal. Such coarse brutal repression does not touch causes. . . . The only repressive agency admissible is a system of police license

and rigorous visitation. This is not authorizing sin by statute but simply recognizing social and physiological facts. In this way, and in this way alone, until a wholesome moral sentiment can be induced, can legislation deal with the subject.

Victoria knew of what she spoke. For a time, she was an active participant in the world's oldest profession.

Comstock was not about to be denied his revenge on the sisters. After reading Victoria's account of Beecher's alleged infidelity, he had her charged with publishing obscenities. The case dragged on for over a year and a half, until she finally got her day in court. Eventually, she made a deal with some of Beecher's parishioners, agreeing to turn over any evidence she had about his clandestine affairs (she had nothing but hearsay) in return for getting the charges dropped. She succeeded but remained in a legal mess and over $500,000 in debt. She lost everything—including her husband, who had tired of her numerous dalliances with other men. She finally had to resort to the lecture circuit to make a living. In June 1876, she closed *Woodhull and Claflin's Weekly.* It became part of Comstock's 160 tons.

When Victoria Woodhull exited the world of sexual journalism, there was no shortage of successors. In 1872, Ezra and Angela Heywood founded *The Word* from a base in rural Massachusetts. Considering the climate of the times, it is actually somewhat surprising that the journal lasted until 1893. The publication was both a labor reform and a free love enterprise. Ezra Heywood was not one to bow willingly or easily to the likes of Anthony Comstock and his crowd. Neither was his soul mate and equal partner, Angela. During the twenty-year life span of the newspaper, Ezra spent about as much time in jail as in his composing room.

If nothing else, the Heywoods were strong free speech advocates. *The Word* did not mince words, so to speak, preferring the graphic and the licentious to the often double-meaning dialogue that was typical of the period. They published a letter from a New York mother who related how her daughter received her first lesson in sex education. It went this way:

> The other day, the woman began, "My little girl, who is in her twelfth year, came to me and said, 'Mama what does fuck mean?'" When the woman asked where her daughter had heard the word, the girl answered "Today at school, Willie said to me, 'Mamie, won't you fuck me?'"

According to the Heywoods, this was enough of an incentive for the mother to enter the controversial field of sex education and explain the birds and the bees to her daughter. The mother confessed to the Heywoods that she had experienced sex for the first time at the same age as her child.

Of course, not everyone was impressed with the candid remarks that were seen on a constant basis in *The Word*. A reader named Laura C. Eldridge lost control of her temper upon reading yet one more sexually explicit commentary in the journal. Her response appeared in the September 1892 issue:

> You foul mouthed, disgusting thing! You ought to be tied to a whipping post until you promised to use decent language. Your demented old idiot of a husband isn't half so much to blame as you are. I think he would be half decent if it wasn't for you. . . . Of course Heywood will go to prison where he ought to go, only you ought to be there too—and put in close confinement— where you couldn't contaminate the rest of the felons with your dirty tongue. You nasty brute! You vilest thing in the country!

. . . Your children ought to be taken away from you and very likely will be.

The Heywoods also became cannon fodder for Anthony Comstock's crusade against vice as he defined it. Comstock arrested Ezra no less than five times, obtaining convictions on two occasions. Heywood spent four years in prison, leaving Angela to take care of their children and continue with *The Word*. It proved to be a daunting task. When Ezra emerged from prison in 1892, he greeted freedom as a broken man. His home was gone, and his journal had ceased publication. He attempted to revive the paper but without success. He was dead within the year.

While Ezra Heywood was struggling with Comstock and the law, a new journal made its presence known in the prairie towns of Kansas. Moses Harman's *Lucifer the Light Bearer,* named after the angel who led a heavenly revolt against God, was to prove just as controversial as anything published by Victoria Woodhull or Ezra and Angela Heywood. Harman had begun life as conventionally as most other Americans. At the age of twenty-one, he was teaching in a Missouri school when he met the love of his life. At that point, he decided to discard all the legal and moral trappings of marriage. His intended agreed, and they settled down to raise a family in rural Missouri. However, when Susan Harman died in 1877 in giving birth to their third child, the distraught Moses left the state and settled in the town of Valley Falls in eastern Kansas. It was there that *Lucifer the Light Bearer* saw the first light of day in 1883. Moses Harman began his journalistic career at the age of fifty. He soon gained a local reputation for being an abrasive ideologue.

No sexual or marital convention escaped Harman's wary eye. He even took on a discussion about the sexual habits of the Scots, in particular the poet Robbie Burns:

Sex was the rock on which Robert Burns split. He seemed to regard pleasure seeking as the prime end of life, and in this he was not so very far removed from the prevalent civilized notion of marriage. But it is a fantasmal [*sic*] idea and makes a mock of marriage, serving the satirist his excuse. To a great degree the race is yet barbaric and as a people we fail utterly to touch the hem of the garment of Divinity. We have been mired in the superstition that sex is unclean, and therefore honesty and expression in love matters have been tabooed. But the day will yet dawn when we will see that it takes two to generate thought; that there is the male man and the female man and only where these two walk together hand and hand is there a perfect sanity and a perfect physical, moral and spiritual health.

It was almost predictable that, sooner or later, Moses Harman would run afoul of the obscenity laws of Anthony Comstock, but their intrusion in his life was indeed a bit of a surprise. When his daughter Lillian entered into what she called a free marriage to a divorced man named Edwin Walker, the couple was accused of living together without the benefit of marriage, a crime at the time. They were arrested, convicted, and sent to jail, he for seventy-five days and she for forty-five. When they refused to pay court costs, their sentences were stretched to six months.

In 1887, Moses himself ran up against the law. He was arrested, charged, and convicted under the obscenity laws and sentenced to five years in prison. Lillian Harman kept producing the journal during the publisher's absence, and when he was released, he took up where he had left off, which inevitably brought about a second confrontation with the censors. Harman, at the age of seventy, spent another year in prison. A tired and broken man, he closed *Lucifer the Light Bearer* in 1907. He died three years later.

The contribution made by the free love newspapers of the late nineteenth century had a direct impact on the style of journalism that was about to emerge with the Yellow Press in New York in the mid-1890s. If nothing else, the constant harassment experienced by the likes of Victoria Woodhull, Tennessee Claflin, Ezra and Angela Heywood, and Moses Harman clearly defined the acceptable borders within which journalism had to operate. It was one thing to be loud and noisy about political corruption, squalid living conditions, and immigrant violence as long as the sex lives of those receiving the attention did not emerge. If nothing else, the sensationalism that hit the Yellow Press in the last decade of the nineteenth century was notable for its lack of discussion on sexual mores. But then again, everything else was up for grabs.

THREE

THE NEW YORK MARKETPLACE

As many other historians have recorded, New York City was not the only place in America or the world, for that matter, in which some variation of the Yellow Press existed and, in most cases, thrived. However, New York was the spiritual home of the genre of journalism that ruled the press environment in the hurly-burly days of the late nineteenth century. As a consequence, it is on that time and within that space that this study will now focus. With apologies to San Francisco, Chicago, Boston, Denver, and other important American communities reaching for greatness at that juncture of history, I have chosen to remain situated on the Hudson.

What was so special about New York in America's most creative century? For one thing, it paid homage to the rich and famous and denigrated the poor. Greed became the new secular religious experience, and as thousands sweated in slums, underfed and underpaid, colossal mansions rose on streets named Park Avenue and Fifth Avenue, built by the barons of a new industrial age who saw no shame in flashing the symbols of the wealth that afforded them that kind of lifestyle.

Like many other urban areas, New York had suffered greatly in the depression of 1837 to 1843. But from that time on, all indicators pointed upward. The U.S. population had increased by 50 percent, and the national wealth had doubled in value. Urbanization was on the march. The number of persons living in cities quadrupled in the four decades preceding 1900. All around, the telltale impact of new technologies was there to behold. Horses that pulled streetcars around the town were replaced by overhead electric wires. Americans were introduced to new treats such as the telephone, recorded sound, the typewriter, and, eventually, the radio and the internal combustion engine. Literacy increased, creating a demand for new media, of which the daily newspaper and the magazine were the largest beneficiaries in this brave new world, not to mention demands for new and better schools.

Blessed by a geographic location on the Atlantic Ocean, New York City strutted its advantages as an oceangoing port throughout the years prior to the Civil War. As happens in most times of economic growth and advantage, the benefits of possessing a lane to the sea inspired other industrial developments capable of taking advantage of the situation. The city remained a vibrant port during the middle years of the century, but entrepreneurs eager to expand their horizons eastward chose New York as the base for huge factory installations as well. And with prosperity came demands from the working class to share the wealth—demands that were not always met peacefully, as we shall soon see.

Writing under the pen name Edward Winslow Martin, James Dabney McCabe made this observation on life in New York's upper echelon in 1868:

Only wealthy marriages are tolerated in New York society. For men or women to marry "beneath" them is a crime society cannot forgive. There must be fortune on one side. Marriages for money are directly encouraged. It is not uncommon for a man who had made money to make the marriage of his daughter the means of getting the family into society. He will go to some young man within the pale of good society, and offer him the hand of his daughter and a fortune. The condition on the part of the person to whom the offer is made is, that he shall use his influence to get the bride's family within the "charmed circle." Such proposals are seldom refused.

One venue where this "trading of influence" took place was in the sanctuary of some of the city's better-known religious meeting places. Although many New York churches stood side by side, it was not hard to tell which were attended by the rich and which were frequented by the poor. They rubbed shoulders just above Fourth Street, where the very wealthy crowded out their equally pious but financially strapped Christian brethren by charging pew rents only the well-heeled could afford to pay. But in general, New York was not a hotbed for Christian spiritualism. The rich went to church to keep up appearances and to make inroads into New York's financial and industrial communities. The poor kept going in search of a better place to be.

It has been said that the railroad and the frenzy that evolved around it were responsible for two things—the health and the wealth of the New York financial community. Members of that community kept feeding money to railway barons anxious to expand their networks and to the infrastructure that fed the railroad, the many steel mills and iron foundries manufacturing the steam locomotives that pulled coaches full of settlers to the virgin lands of the West. Traders shouted out buy and sell commands on the New York Stock Exchange, while their poorer cousins set up shop on the streets outside to peddle stocks to the willing and the brave. New York brokers targeted anyone with a dollar to spend, taking down payments of 10 percent on purchase prices and hoping to cash in later when the inevitable climb upward neared its peak. It was not an economic climate for the faint of heart.

Ah, but as always, the bubble showed signs of some serious strain. The nation's railway capacity was severely overbuilt. Every rail baron wanted to dominate the country, controlling if not eliminating all possible rivals. At the top of the heap was the notorious robber baron Jay Gould, who controlled 15 percent of the nation's trackage. He was followed closely by William Vanderbilt, who was financing and laying track as fast as he could to keep up with Gould. Not deterred by this kind of risky venture was Edward H. Harriman, who held the controlling interest in the Illinois Central Railroad. Along with a group of New York speculators, these men applied so much pressure on the banking community that persistent failures became the mark of the day. The situation did little to inspire confidence in the workings of the American financial markets, and as a consequence, many European investors left the U.S. marketplace and vowed never to return.

Another spin-off from the relative prosperity of the 1880s in New York was the emergence of both advertising agencies and legal firms. The lawyers took their respective places in the industrial climate of the day as government became more and more involved in the workings of the economy, a factor that created a significant level of anxiety in the city's boardrooms. Meanwhile, advertising became a growth industry. In 1870, there were forty agencies operating in New York. Just two decades later, there were four hundred. The agencies were essential actors in the transformation of New York daily newspapers from political and subscription-supported journals to publications whose main income was to come from advertising. Circulation became the guideline by which advertising rates were set, which, in many cases, determined the behavior of the Yellow Press.

The newfound wealth was producing a new class of urban citizens in the country's largest and most important city. However, acceptance of these citizens by the city's established elite was not forthcoming. The nouveaux riches were regarded as uncivilized, uneducated, gross, and devoid of any social standing. As money poured out of Wall Street to this new class of businesspeople, a vicious confrontation between the established and the interloper began to take shape. Those seeking acceptance by the old guard kept upping the ante: "Dinner parties corkscrewed upward in lavishness—black pearls in oysters, cigars rolled in hundred dollar bills, lackeys in knee breeches and powered wigs." But as the ambitious nouveaux riches were to learn, getting into the inner circle involved more than an ability to spend at will. When William H. Vanderbilt offered an unheard-of sum of $30,000 for a private box at the Academy of Music, the old guard rejected his offer.

But the new guard was not about to accept this kind of humiliation. Gathering a ton of money from his friends and colleagues, Vanderbilt moved uptown to create his own opera house. If it had one consistent mandate, it was to be more opulent and elegant than the Academy of Music on Fourteenth Street. When completed, the new Metropolitan Opera House at Broadway and Thirty-ninth Street could seat thirty-six hundred opera lovers, with an additional seventy comfortably taken care of in seventy private boxes. The theater opened on October 22, 1883, with a performance of *Faust*. The combined wealth of those present was estimated to be $540 million. The guard had certainly changed. The old Knickerbockers no longer ran New York.

Yes, wealth was a wonderful thing, especially for those in the receiving line. But it brought with it another kind of downside, apart from the frequent bank collapses and almost predictable recessions. The new problem had two faces—political corruption and seemingly intractable poverty. It is hard to say whether New York was ready for the likes of Boss Tweed. Certainly, the city had been home to a rather interesting cast of characters during the nineteenth century, but Tweed was to be the first notable victim of what journalists refer to as the brown paper bag syndrome—in other words, the package delivered in the dead of night by a unknown source with the clear intent to damage the career and life opportunities of someone.

It is hard to feel sorry for Tweed. He was the architect of his own downfall, although the *New York Times* and Thomas Nast, the cartoonist at *Harper's Weekly,* were also critical players in the Tweed drama. Both journals set a tone that would emerge some thirty years later in New York's Yellow Press. Tweed was a rather large firefighter who had a thirst for politics. In 1860, he worked his way into the leadership of the Democratic Party's New York social club Tammany Hall; eventually, he became the chair of the city's Democratic Party machinery. Tweed understood a lot about accumulating power in an urban setting that was undergoing such rapid change as New York City was. He paid back loyalists with patronage appointments. He doled out money to the poor, especially newcomers to the United States, and he initiated huge public works projects; ironically, one was the construction of a new courthouse, which would become the conduit through which Tweed received hundreds of millions of dollars siphoned off from funds designed for the project.

In 1871, two disgruntled civic employees let the cat out of the bag. Tweed's ability to rob the city of a reputed $100 million was out in the open. Documents showed that Tweed had paid workers on the courthouse job thousands of dollars for a few days of work. Stone was purchased from quarries in which the Boss had a financial interest, and to top it all off, there was evidence that a thermometer had been purchased from a businessman with Tammany connections for $7,500. The Boss was about to go from being a celebrity in political circles to a pariah, a fall from grace that was effectively hastened by two New York journals. He was indicted and went to trial three times, ultimately dying in custody in 1878.

If immorality was rampant in the confines of Tammany Hall and the civic government, the behavior of New York's finest was something else to behold. Concerned about constant rumors of payoffs and corruption, the state senate launched an investigation of the police force at the midpoint of the final decade of the nineteenth century. The investigating committee issued a 10,576-page report detailing virtually every form of illegal activity one could imagine. The police were accused of rigging elections to keep police-friendly politicians in office, bribery, job peddling, and any number of lesser evils. Although many civil servants knew about the problems at police headquarters, fear of losing their jobs or lives kept them silent. The senate report would provide a launching pad for the career of a man who would later become president of the United States, Theodore Roosevelt.

Members of the new upper class of New York society reveled in luxury as they enjoyed the melodic airs in their freshly minted opera house and a host of activities in the cultural institutions they built in the city. But there was another New York as well, one that would be dutifully exploited by the newspaper barons of the late nineteenth century, in particular those who created what would become the Yellow Press. In 1884, radical journalist John Swinton, a former city editor of the *New York Times* and now a publisher of his own socialist-oriented journal, *John Swinton's Paper,* remarked that "the city is the headquarters of the new slave trade, although the barracoons have not yet been erected along the water front." What Swinton was observing was the presence of an emerging underclass populated by immigrants from central Europe, in particular from Hungary and Italy. And as Swinton so accurately noted, these people were not being imported into the New World to contribute to its intellectual and artistic endeavors. It mattered not if they could think and appreciate beauty: it was their physical strength and stamina the New World needed.

The corporate employers who lined up along the docks to meet the incoming ships cared only that these workers would place far less of a financial burden on their respective enterprises than American workers—most of whom were actively joining unions to seek a better life and to share the wealth that existed around them. The employers were not concerned that these workers would congregate with their own kind, filling up crowded slums that became the breeding grounds for illness, pestilence, and violence. On the Lower East Side, the former homes of the elegant Knickerbocker class were being "nearly obliterated by over crowded, sunless tenements built for two families but housing ten. People lived in filthy cellars, on fire escapes, door stoops, church corners and wherever they could fund a suggestion of shelter."

As in many an American city today, one could turn a corner in nineteenth-century New York and find oneself in a totally different world. It was only a few minutes' walk to cross two of the city's most traveled streets. One was the wealthy and fashionable Broadway, where the new affluent class paraded in the latest fashions past Stewart's Marble Palace; Delmonico's Restaurant, which provided take-out service to the assassin of New York's most celebrated architect, Stanford White; the Broadway theater district, which gave birth to the entertainment orientation that exists there today; and, of course, numerous shops appealing to the nouveaux riches or those close to that status.

In contrast, the folks who walked the other prominent street, the Bowery, came primarily from the Sixth Ward, which included the notorious Five Points sector of town. It was a neighborhood where three out of four residents had, since the mid-1850s, originated from places other than the United States. There was a smattering of African Americans seeking to avoid the slavery and, later, the segregation in the South; a colony of German-speaking immigrants; Polish Jews; Italians; Dutchmen; and, of course, the Irish, many of whom were descendants of those who had emigrated to New York earlier in the century. Into this mix came numerous small colonies of people of various other origins, from places such as China, India, and points farther east. In 1890, the Five Points area reported that 49 percent of the residents were of Italian extraction, 18 percent Jewish, 10 percent Irish, 5 percent Chinese, 1 percent German, and 17 percent of unknown origins.

When people began to set up housekeeping in the Five Points area in the 1820s, the district soon gained a reputation for being hospitable to the establishment of liquor stores, gambling houses, and, naturally, bawdy houses for prostitution. Anyone who had an entrepreneurial spirit, especially one not tempered by moral concerns, could do well in the Sixth Ward. And those who did had no hesitation taking their ill-gotten gains up to mid-Manhattan, where money of questionable background was soon turned to other forms of capitalist enterprise. Money was the god that New Yorkers sought. Some said that if Saint Peter himself were to show up in New York without sufficient funds, he would be kicked out

of the city until he could return in a more affluent state. For those
who failed, the Sixth Ward was to be home for life. As James Dabney McCabe observed in 1868:

> It is a horrible place, and you shudder as you look at it. The streets
> are dark and narrow, the dwellings are foul and gloomy, and
> seem filled with mystery and crime. It is the worst quarter of the
> city, and from here, over to the East River, you will scarcely find
> it any better. Yet, bad as it is, it is infinitely better than the Five
> Points of fifteen or even ten years ago. Then the place was noto-
> rious for its crimes. Murders, robberies, outrages of all kinds were
> of daily occurrence. The officers of the law dared not enter the
> district for the purpose of suppressing crime, and fugitives from
> justice found a safe refuge here. A man who entered the district
> carried his life in his hand, and unless he was either in secret or
> open league with the denizens of the quarter was tolerably sure
> of losing it.

By the time that William Randolph Hearst and Joseph Pulitzer
shot the first salvos in what was to become the newspaper war of
newspaper wars, little had changed on the Lower East Side. Jacob
Riis, who found fame but not fortune in his photographic essays
on the situation in that neglected part of town, wrote that the area

> was clogged with ash barrels and refuse, cheap lodging houses,
> forlorn-looking shops and tenements, two-cent restaurants,
> opium joints, and stale beer dives—four thousand saloons below
> 14th Street. It offered an endless expanse of brick walls and nar-
> row alleys criss-crossed with pulley lines strung with ragged
> clothes and patched linen. The cobbled streets were jammed
> with horse-drawn cabs, peddler's carts, and poor immigrants;
> Arabs, Italians, many wearing yellow kerchiefs or red bandannas,

pig tailed Chinese, Greeks, Russian and Polish Jews, the men bearded and wearing skullcaps.

For Riis and others such as the cartoonist Richard Outcault, the Sixth Ward and, in particular, the Five Points district would be career builders.

But alas, the Gilded Age proved hostile to the seemingly uncontrolled open society. Permissiveness was bound to produce retaliation, and it did so in two different directions. First of all, it became apparent to the Protestant clergy that the kind of immigrant now settling in New York was prone to the wisdom of the Catholic faith, which took a more lenient view of matters such as consumption of alcohol and tobacco and participation in Sunday activities. By 1880, nearly 40 percent of Manhattan's residents reported they practiced the Catholic faith. In this respect, Catholics had much more in common with Reform Jews than did the Protestant clergy. Protestantism was also being challenged from the left by socialists, anarchists, and secularists. The ministerial ranks were well aware of the fact that any mission to control vice and corruption in the city had to be accomplished with the support of religious and community groups outside their immediate circle.

The Protestant clergy was convinced that New York was Satan's capital, an opinion offered in more recent years by the Baptist evangelist Billy Graham. As the ministers looked around, they saw that

> saloons were everywhere—the city seemed awash in liquor—and one Methodist speaker at the 1888 Chickering Hall Conference noted that where there was but one Protestant church for every 4,464 inhabitants, the saloon to inhabitant ratio was one to 150.

What was particularly galling to genteel opponents was the de facto legalized status of commercialized vice. The National Police Gazette reported regularly on the fancy life of theaters, gambling dens, and bordellos, and a new generation of sunshine and shadow writers provided salacious details on dives and opium dens.

The clergy took halfhearted stabs at the numerous German beer gardens that emerged in the late 1800s, but most of the ministerial wrath was directed at the concert saloons and the dance houses. Although the Germans, at least in the eyes of strict Protestants, defiled the Sabbath by drinking alcohol and betting on the outcome of games on that day, nearly 800,000 citizens of that birthright lived in the combined boroughs of Manhattan, Brooklyn, the Bronx, Queens, and Staten Island, and, by and large, they presented the city with few if any major social problems. The rest of the citizenry was another matter.

The large-capacity nightclub that is often a feature of urban life today probably owes its existence to the rise of the concert saloon. The phenomenon began shortly after the Civil War and remained a fixture of New York nightlife until almost the 1890s. James Dabney McCabe wrote:

> The concert saloons are among the social evils. They flourish in certain parts of Broadway, Sixth Avenue and the Bowery, and are simply so many places where the devil's work is done. They provide a low order of music, and the service of the place is rendered by young women, many of whom are dressed in tights and all sorts of fanciful costumes, the chief object of which is to display the figure as much as possible.

The specter of a free or very low-cost show was the lure that was thrown out to potential customers walking by these establishments. The shows were simply staged, often without proper sets. Taking a page from the Wild West of the time, the tinkling piano music was sufficient incentive for certain tables to attract a man with a gambling urge. Many of these concert saloons offered pleasures of the carnal nature for those willing to spend some time in private rooms upstairs, where their needs could be looked after. Not all concert saloons were brothels as well, but many were.

Several rungs down the moral ladder from the concert saloon was the dance house. McCabe described the houses as "lower and viler" than the concert saloons. These establishments did not pretend to be moral outposts. Most were located in dilapidated buildings close to the waterfront, where they could attract their main clientele—sailors on shore leave. The sailor would be treated to taxi dancing, now known as lap dancing, by the primarily female waitstaff. Once sufficiently stimulated, the sea-weary navigator would be invited to a room where, as in some of the concert halls, pleasures of the flesh would be offered. Unlike the concert saloons, the dance houses, owned primarily by men, were usually fronts for prostitution, although it was rare that gambling took place in those establishments.

McCabe did give the nod of approval (limited as it was) to Harry Hill's establishment on Houston, near Mulberry Street. Hill claimed that he would not hire women to work his concert saloon and that he ran a respectable establishment. He had house rules, which few owners did. He hung them on the walls around the hall for all to see. In essence, he banned profane language, indecent conduct, and overall rowdiness. Hill claimed his patrons often traveled from afar to enjoy a night at his place. The owner washed his hands of any activities that occurred outside, once a patron had left the establishment. But as anyone with eyes could attest, a significant proportion of the crowd in the place on any given evening

consisted of highly muscled Bowery residents. Nonetheless, Hill
pointed to the fact that his saloon had also been visited by James
Gordon Bennett Jr., one of New York's leading newspaper publishers, and the inventor Thomas Alva Edison.

Perhaps some of New York's upper crust paid a visit to two to
the concert saloon, but by and large, it was a place where those on
the lower rungs of the social ladder could drown their sorrows in
a glass of warm beer. Nineteenth-century New York was a city divided between those who had and those who did not have. And
for those who had and wanted to keep what they had, the welfare
reforms of the 1870s made that a clear possibility. The city got out
of the welfare game and passed the distribution of a very limited
charity on to private organizations, organizations imbued with the
belief that the tendency to poverty was the consequence of "individual moral and character defects (probably hereditary) and the
task of scientific charity was to dispense assistance, cautiously and
grudgingly to the deserving while incarcerating or rehabilitating
the remainder."

In a movement only exceeded in vigor and determination by
eugenics, civic authorities were determined to stamp out laziness
and immorality before it became endemic in a family setting. This
position was articulated by Protestant female advocates in the
Charities Aid Association and by Charles Loring Brace, a child-
protection advocate. Brace had little sympathy for keeping dys-
functional families together, believing that the children of these
unfortunate unions would be better off elsewhere. By 1895, Brace,
through his Children's Aid Society, had sent nearly ninety thousand New York children from poverty-stricken families out of the
city to homes in the rural regions of the Midwest, where he believed the children, exposed to fresh air and hard work on the

farms, would turn into model citizens for the brave new world of twentieth-century America.

As convoluted as Brace's ideas may seem by modern standards, in the period in which he lived and worked, concerns about civic morality were on the minds of most social leaders in New York both within and beyond the Christian church, and they had been for some time. And it was difficult to profess the belief that Brace and like-minded people were acting out of some kind of malice toward the poor. Everywhere one looked, as noted earlier, there was solid evidence that the moral fiber of the community was being severely strained.

As far back as 1866, Bishop Matthew Simpson of the Methodist Church made a speech about civic immorality before an audience at the Cooper Institute. Simpson dragged out some numbers that he had previously presented to his congregation in St. Paul's Church. He declared that New York had 621 houses of prostitution, 99 houses of assignation, 75 concert saloons of bad reputation, 2,670 public prostitutes, and 747 waiter girls who worked in drinking establishments.

Even New York's better neighborhoods, according to James Dabney McCabe, were not immune to this kind of carnal curse. As those who strolled Broadway in the daytime retired to their homes, female streetwalkers took over the sidewalks, looking for customers. McCabe noted that most of them were quite young, somewhere between seventeen and twenty. But he also reported that a number were much younger, children of twelve and thirteen who were also plying the trade. In general, most could be found around the city's many hotels and amusement halls. He also noted, "Some of the girls are pretty and modest, but the majority are ugly and brazen." He added that a significant turnover in talent took place, with newer recruits replacing those who no longer, for whatever reason, worked the streets.

But prostitution was not the only endeavor undertaken by poor, desperate New Yorkers. The city was rife with thieves, who could normally be found hanging out either along the East River or in the Five Points district. They perfected the art of picking pockets, often relying on female companions (who theoretically had a soft touch) to remove the belongings of the unsuspecting. They prowled the "ferry boats, cars, stages, crowded halls and public places." They preyed not only on visitors to the city but also on residents.

The various campaigns to stamp out immoral behavior came on two fronts. First of all, there was the law, which took a turn for purity under the leadership of Theodore Roosevelt. This change in essence cleansed the hands of the professional criminal for future labors in legal establishments—or so the authorities hoped. Then there were the campaigns to prevent the mind from contamination in the first place. Led by Anthony Comstock's Society for the Suppression of Vice, the same organization that did in Victoria Woodhull, the city's bookshops and libraries were among the first victims of the crusading moralist. Supported by the likes of J. P. Morgan and the New York Chamber of Commerce, Comstock constantly rewrote his definition of what constituted vice, a definition that eventually extended to art and music and information on birth control. Any establishment reputed to be involved in immoral activity could be and often was raided by Comstock's troopers. They left very few stones unturned, but in the long run, as had been witnessed elsewhere, the campaign to eliminate vice was unsuccessful.

For those unwilling or unable to follow a career in crime, joining a labor union was the next best option for working-class New

Yorkers, but it was not an easy or simple choice. Inevitably, any thought of sharing the wealth with the city's elites was rejected emphatically and often violently. Organized labor was no stranger to the cultural environment in the city. Under the banner of an umbrella organization, the General Society of Mechanics and Tradesmen, skilled workers regularly turned out for boisterous Fourth of July parades down Manhattan's wide avenues. The parades would end at one of the city's larger churches, where a host of speakers would pledge allegiance to the Constitution of the Great Republic.

It was a radical machinist named Thomas Skidmore who was the impetus behind the creation of the New York Workingmen's Movement. In 1829, he had published a tract entitled *The Right of Man to Property,* in which he criticized the unequal distribution of property in this capitalist environment. He was also a vocal abolitionist and supporter of equality for women. However, Skidmore's fellow working folks were far more interested in alleviating their impoverished status on a faster basis. They proceeded to enter the political arena, with middling success. They managed to send one person to Albany, but six others felt the sting of defeat. Skidmore, who had been dumped by the movement's leadership, was roundly blamed for espousing ideas about property and prosperity that many felt turned potential voters away.

Realizing that political success or, in this case, failure would not alleviate working-class concerns, trades unionists took to the streets to press their demands for a greater share of the economic pie. In 1833, the city's carpenters walked off the job to support demands for higher wages. They were not alone. Soon, they were joined by printers, tailors, stonemasons, brush makers, and tobacco workers, along with members of ten other skilled craft unions. The employers had no choice but to give in, making New York's first major strike a victory for working people. In the following year, nine unions attended the founding convention of the General Trades Union, an umbrella organization whose main role was to organize support for the individual demands of its member societies. The next few years would prove to be anything but peaceful in the city's labor relations environment.

Both skilled and unskilled workers began to form unions, especially in the years after the Civil War. In 1867, the powerful shoemakers' union, the Knights of Saint Krispin, was founded. The union was strong and effective. It recruited women workers, whom it organized into chapters called the Daughters of Saint Krispin. It reached out to immigrant workers, especially those who had been recruited from Asian nations to work in the emerging factory society of the United States for wages below than those paid to native-born individuals. In 1868, the city's large German community established the New York Arbeiter-Union, which was, in effect, a German-language trades council. The leaders established a chapter of Karl Marx's International Workingmen's Association in the backyard of American gonzo capitalism. The old organizations that stretched back to the General Trades Union finally gave way to new organizations, in particular the National Labor Union, which was born in Baltimore in 1866. It did not take long for the union to realize the potential of organizing New York's large working class. The die had been cast for a major confrontation between capital and labor in the country's largest urban conglomeration.

Late nineteenth-century New York was a journalist's dream. When events of significance occurred in the United States, they more than likely took place in New York. And the ambitious reporter could always dig out the indiscretions of the new moneyed class. Cornelius Vanderbilt's odd relationship with Victoria Woodhull would provide the fodder for the front page of numerous scandal sheets that preceded the Yellow Press in the constant search for wider circulation. The precedents set by James Gordon Bennett Sr. were enjoying a vigorous life in some of the city's more dubious newsrooms. And when Nellie Bly exposed the evils of Blackwell's Island, the city-operated hospital for female patients with mental diseases, it became apparent that any subject was fair game for reporters. The era of the "star" reporter was about to be born.

Grudging admiration came when one of the underclass took on the system and won. Photographer Jacob Riis discovered several instances:

> The Boston "widow" whose husband turned up alive and well after she had buried him seventeen times with tears and lamentation, and made the public pay for the weekly funerals. . . . The "gentleman tramp" is a familiar type from our streets and the "once respectable Methodist" who patronized all the revivals in town with his profitable story of repentance, only to fall from grace into the saloon door nearest the church after the service was over, merely transferred the scene of his operations from the tenement to the church as the proper setting for his specialty.

The Tenderloin district, home to much of New York's entertainment and vice, supplied the cultural setting for the novels of Stephen Crane, who acquired renown for *The Red Badge of Courage*. Although Crane made his fame and fortune through his work as a reporter, in particular the Tenderloin sketches that he wrote for William Randolph Hearst, his major contributions were novels about the people and the lives they lived in that part of town. One night while walking back to his lodgings, he witnessed a police officer attempting to apprehend two very reluctant women. One of the women pointed to Crane and told the arresting officer she was his wife. Nonetheless, she was charged with streetwalking. Appearing in local court the following morning, the woman, Dora Clark, was surprised to see Crane in the chamber. When Clark appeared before the magistrate, Crane stood up and told the judge that she was indeed his wife and that he was anxious to take her home. All charges were dismissed, and Crane had another subject for one of his compositions.

His first attempt, in 1893, to capture the life of the Tenderloin in the form of a novel was unsuccessful. Unable to find a publisher who would take *Maggie, a Girl of the Streets: A Story of New York*, Crane paid to have it published himself. However, when *The Red Badge of Courage* became a national best-seller, the publishing interests began to look more seriously at Crane's work. *Maggie* was reissued, and soon, *George's Mother* appeared on the bookshelves. Then along came the essays of *The Men in the Storm* and *An Experiment in Misery*. Crane, like many other reporters in New York, was careful not to advocate the kind of change in social relationships proposed by political radicals of various stripes. Although wrapped in the cloak of fiction, his novels and essays were based in the tragedy of real life. In every respect, the stories spoke for themselves.

New York was a market hungry for information. In 1890, domestic production of newsprint for American newspapers stood at 196,000 tons, or 8 pounds per capita. By the end of the decade, this figure had risen to 569,000 tons, or 15 pounds per capita. The price of newsprint collapsed from $344 per ton in 1866 to $36 in 1900. The resulting drop in price gave incentives to newspaper owners to print bigger and better editions. All this was helped by improvements in press design and press efficiency. A Hoe press sold to the industry in 1835 could print 22,000 pages on both sides.

In 1893, this number increased to 96,000. Modern television station owners well know that it takes a lot of money and a lot of work to fill a schedule that often covers twenty-four hours a day, seven days per week. In the closing decades of the 1800s, newspaper owners were faced with many of the same challenges. It was one thing to be able to print a hundred-page edition. It was quite another to be able to fill it with anything worthwhile. As a consequence, reporters had to reach far and wide for content. Bennett proved that crime could sell, and it became a staple of the industry following the Civil War. So did vice. The goal was to reach a daily circulation of half a million in the mid-1890s. A few papers succeeded in doing so.

Lest one be misled, it should be noted that crime and vice were not the only subjects that attracted readers to the daily press. There was considerable interest in financial news, since New York was quickly establishing itself as the center of commerce for the country. Following the lead set by Standard Oil in the early 1890s, ten other major oil-processing firms established trusts, and eight of them moved into central Manhattan. By 1897, eighty-six new industrial enterprises had been established with funding by Wall Street financial houses. Each was capitalized at over $1 million, a considerable sum by anyone's standard but particularly large at that time. The new wealth attracted many offshore investors who, as a group, committed more than $3 billion to finance American enterprises. The ratings houses, such as Standard and Poor's, Moody's Investment Services, and Dun and Bradstreet, all emerged in this period.

The city was taking on a new complexion. Downtown was the place to be, the area where Manhattan's skyscrapers would one day rise. But given the problems still faced by large cities in that era, getting there, literally, was not half the fun. The government

responded by creating the Rapid Transit Act of 1875, and speculators and entrepreneurs responded by starting construction on a
network of elevated, steam-powered commuter railways. In the
early 1880s, the first coal-consuming and pollution-belching
locomotives began pulling overcrowded passenger cars from the
suburbs to the city center. By 1891, some 196.7 million passengers
had used the various lines. The commuter system succeeded in
making Manhattan and its bordering cities into one vast economic
zone, a factor that eventually led to the merging of the island community and its neighbors.

By the time that Hearst and Pulitzer descended onto the New
York scene, the city was rapidly becoming a marvel of moderni-
zation. In 1880, the road to electrification began. The conversion
proved to be a boon to the denizens of Wall Street who initially
financed it and then took it over. In 1878, the city's first telephone
exchange began operating. By the mid-1890s, there were twelve
exchanges in operation. In 1879, the old gas lamps that adorned
many of the city's streets began to come down, to be replaced by
modern and mostly reliable arc lighting. In the late 1880s, horses
were retired from the job of pulling trams on the city's numerous
streetcar lines. Gradually, electricity became the norm in all aspects
of the transit system except the elevated railways, which continued to use steam power well into the twentieth century. By 1900,
middle- and upper-class New Yorkers could claim with validity
that they were living in a period of unprecedented prosperity and
progress. It would take publishers such as Hearst and Pulitzer to reveal that this did not come without a price—and a fairly steep one
at that.

In 1880s' New York, the modern newspaper had been born. As
it grew and matured in the closing years of the century, some

would find it humorous, others ingratiating. Some would be grateful that it took on corrupt business and political leaders. Others wished it would just go away. Yet no matter what position one took, the modern newspaper was here to stay, and New Yorkers, rich and poor, good and bad, would just have to get accustomed to having it around.

FOUR

GRAPHIC INNOVATION

Many innovations can be attributed to the emergence of the Yellow Press in the late Victorian age, but two in particular stand out: the increased sophistication of layout and design and the emphasis on language, which, for lack of a better description, focused on color. Mind you, these were hardly exclusive, as an upcoming chapter on the use of illustration will point out. But in a day and age in which the mass media were beginning to emerge as major civic players, both Hearst and Pulitzer recognized that communication with people of limited literacy, such as the urban poor and new immigrant families, presented some significant challenges. In fact, the very survival of the industry that both owners and their editors had so viciously promoted became an issue.

In many ways, the modern newspaper was born in those final three decades of the nineteenth century that culminated in the rise of the Yellow Press. Media analysts Meredith and David Berg have argued that both Hearst's *Journal* and Pulitzer's *World* were instrumental in design innovation, much of which remains with us today. Advances in the production of chemical wood pulp significantly reduced the cost of newsprint, meaning that newspapers could print longer and more elaborate editions as well as work toward a seven-days-a-week schedule. It is no exaggeration to claim that the battle for press supremacy took place largely in the marketing of the Sunday editions of major metropolitan dailies, especially in New York City. As photography expert Michael Carlebach noted: "By the 1890's the camera and pen were partners in daily and weekly journalism. Whether based on photographic originals or drawn by an artist, pictures by the thousands were printed in the nation's newspapers and magazines."

Visual journalism and its various stepchildren, such as comic strips, entered the world of the press in late Victorian New York. Yet by the turn of the century, original photography was still rare on the pages of the Yellow journals. Original photojournalism was more likely to be found in a press dedicated to that specific genre, as with the investigative work of Jacob Riis. The New York daily press had yet to exploit visual journalism in a fashion equivalent to earlier journals, such as the *New York Daily Graphic.*

The most significant scholarship on the major changes in design and layout that affected the American press almost from its origins was undertaken by Kevin Barnhurst and John Nerone in *The Form of News,* published in 2001. Their findings will provide the necessary background information in our examination of these issues in both *The New York Journal* and *The World New York,* the newspapers of Hearst and Pulitzer. It has been argued here and elsewhere that the birth of the modern newspaper can be directly connected to the innovations in the Yellow Press, and there is much truth in that declaration. But it was the modest changes that took place some thirty years before Hearst and Pulitzer came to dominate the press scene that provided the foundation upon which these two editors built their empires and redesigned a little more than the front page.

"The Arbiters of Taste": New York Journalism Figures, Early 1870s,
Punchinello, May 28, 1870

"Captain General Weyler and the War in Cuba," *The World New York,*
Sunday, January 4, 1897

What may be Expected.

ALL THE TERRITORY ON THIS SIDE OF JORDAN, JONATHAN CASTS A LONGING EYE UPON THE OTHER "ABSORPTION" OF SOME OF THE OTHER PLANETS. VENUS WILL BE THE FIRST ONE TAKEN IN, PROBABLY

"Brother Jonathan's Great Ambition," *Yankee Notions,* Vol. 2, No. 3, March 1857

"Returning from a Fenian Raid on British Colonies in Canada,"
Frank Leslie's Budget of Fun, July 1866

To Uncle Sam's Bird.—*A Map of North America to take home and Remodel.*

"Uncle Sam's Bird: Fixing North America," *Frank Leslie's Budget of Fun*, February 1866

WANTED—A WHALER.

OLD SAM.—Now, THEN, YOUNG 'UN, PUT IT IN, OR THEM DARNED ENGLISH FELLERS WILL HAVE HER.

"Who Will Get It First, Uncle Sam or John Bull?" *Vanity Fair,* June 2, 1860

stocks?"

"Why, y-e-z, zur, I stood in 'em once about four 'ours!"

"Vat mit be the reason dat Shosheph wouldn't shleep mit Botifar's wife?" inquired an honest Dutchman of his boy.

"Shpose he wasn't sleepy," replied the youngster.

"There's a woman at the bottom of every mischief," said Joe.

"Yes," replied Charley, "when I used to get into mischief, my mother was at the bottom of me."

Jonathan's talk with the King of the Sandwich Islands ; or Young American Diplomacy.

"Yer see, Gineral—yer Majesty, I meant to say—I'm sent as a depitation, I am, from Young America. We want to buy you eout, we do, stock, lock, and barril. Say, now, what'll yer take, old feller, for them ere melon patches of Islands, with all the improvements? Yer know yer can't hold 'em long—must give up. Now, we'll give yer a nice annuity, and send yer the Notions free, and take the hull consarn off yer hands. Come, now, what will yer take?"

"Brother Jonathan's Expansion Agenda, Like It or Not,"
Yankee Notions, Vol. 2, No. 2, February 1854

"Just Taking What I Think Is Mine," *Vanity Fair*, May 19, 1860

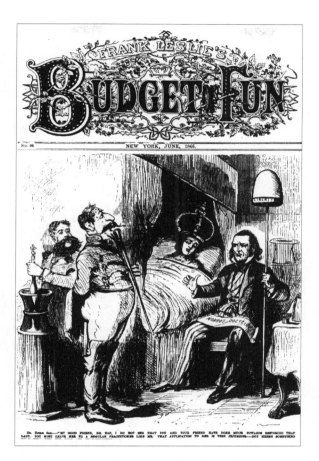

"The Monroe Doctrine and American Desires," *Frank Leslie's Budget of Fun,* June 1866

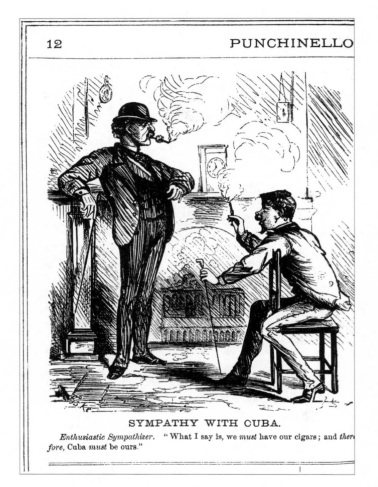

SYMPATHY WITH CUBA.

Enthusiastic Sympathizer. "What I say is, we *must* have our cigars; and ther*fore,* Cuba *must* be ours."

"Free Cuba from Spanish Rule. Good Cigars Demand No Less,"
Punchinello, April 2, 1870

ALAS! POOR CUBA!

Messrs. Fish and Sumner. "LET HER STAY OUT IN THE COLD."

"Hamilton Fish and Charles Sumner Get Cold Feet over Cuba Liberation," *Punchinello,* April 16, 1870

"Ulysses S. Grant and the New American Agenda of Imperialism," *Frank Leslie's Budget of Fun,* 1870

BEN AND BIZZY.

The Newspapers advise President Harrison to send Ben Butler with the Samoan Mission, as Bismarck could neither bully nor browbeat him.

"Ben and Bizzy: Thwarting the American Dream," *Judge,* Vol. 15, No. 385, 1889

King Edward.— " Build the canal ?   Why, certainly, you may do anything you please."
—*Cartoon from the North American, Philadelphia, Dec. 14, 1901.*

Apropos of the Isthmian Canal, Mr. Nelan attributes to sheer necessity the courteous attitude of England towards America. Shackled as he is by internal depression and external warfare, King Edward, it is suggested, can do nothing else than look on as pleasantly as he can.

"Giving Away to America on the Canal Building Agenda," *The North American,* Philadelphia, December 14, 1901

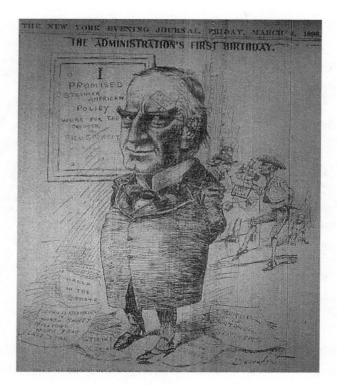

"The Great Fixer Mark Hanna," *The New York Evening Journal,*
March 4, 1898

"Anybody Wanna Fight Me?" *The New York Evening Journal,*
May 16, 1898

The multiplying effect can be seen in the figures collected by Barnhurst and Nerone regarding page limits and column design. Until the early 1870s, most newspapers, the illustrated press excepted, looked fairly much the same. Citizens with weak eyes or those who did not own a magnifying glass were unlikely to become regular readers. Small type was the order of the day, since editors wanted to cram as much information as possible into a limited amount of space. In general, readers were faced with row upon row of long columns with brief but different-sized headlines indicating the content that was to follow. The number of lines one could cram onto a page began to increase as early as the 1870s, when page length expanded. Longer pages could hold up to 225 lines. By 1872, this had increased to 275 lines, and by 1876, it had reached 300 lines. With improved typesetting techniques and longer columns, the newspaper of the mid-1870s was exceptionally dense.

As the accompanying front pages of the New York Yellow journals clearly show, the concept of rows of rigid columns was becoming a thing of the past by 1897. New designs, although based on an eight-column format, were more flexible, with pictures or charts allowed to overlap more than one or even two columns.

The Wednesday, November 3, 1897, edition of *The World New York (The New York World)* was far more disciplined than the Sunday, August 15, 1897, edition of *The New York Journal*. Of the two front pages, *The World*'s at least showed some sort of respect for the concept of columns. There were the equivalent of eight columns, four of which were consolidated into two larger columns, one dealing with the recent state and municipal elections. The state vote was presented by counties, and a full-length column detailed the city's results.

The Journal's front page paralleled the anarchistic approach to journalism that often was reflected on the pages of this newspaper. As one can clearly see, the two major stories were split between illustrations and written content. The type size was significantly different from that of *The World*. In the column on the Spanish Liberal leader Sagasta, two of the front-page paragraphs were highlighted in bold. The Tammany Hall story about Richard Croker did not contain a similar emphasis, but the whole article was summarized in eleven significant quotes taken from it, two of which were highlighted. This so-called fact box technique was revived in the late 1980s, when it became part of the redesign craze following the introduction of *USA Today*.

American newspapers were also beginning to break out of the page-limitation trap. By the time Pulitzer canceled a planned European vacation in 1883 and chose to stay in New York to buy *The World* from financier Jay Gould, many newspapers were expanding from the previously accepted four-page limit to double that size. As the age of the Yellow Press arrived, New York Sunday editions were printing anywhere from fifty to sixty pages. *The New York Journal* on Sunday, August 15, 1897, published no less than fifty-eight pages, and *The World New York* remained competitive with approximately the same number.

Shortly after arriving in New York and taking possession of the then virtually moribund *World,* Joseph Pulitzer revealed his first sensational marketing technique—the use of the banner headline. In every respect, it was a tease, much like the hanging plots of contemporary soap operas on television. The banner headline resembled those old-time posters that drew customers to theaters before the television age. It was designed to draw the reader in, playing on the natural human instinct of curiosity. In most cases, the technique worked.

In the two samples we have been using, we see two different

kinds of headlines designed to achieve different results. When R. A. Van Wyck became mayor of the soon to be amalgamated New York City on the Tammany Hall ticket, his victory banner ran from side to side in Pulitzer's Wednesday, November 3, 1897, edition, in bold type three-quarters of an inch in height. Van Wyck's victory story contained a further seven headlines, one of which—the lead announcing his plurality—was set in emphasized bold. The remaining headlines dealing with the election were rather spartan. Most of the stories were announced by two short headlines; the story about Van Wyck's mysterious absence from his campaign headquarters rated only one.

To put it mildly, Hearst was somewhat more emphatic than his rival in terms of the use of headlines. He had abandoned the older front-page style of stacking headlines in order of importance to tell the tale contained below. His piece on the Spanish Liberal leader had only one major headline above the illustration, but breaking with the convention of the time, he added another below the drawing. His story on John Sheehan and Richard Croker showed the same approach to the use of headlines. And there was a headline both above and below the Tammany story. Pulitzer used headlines in a significantly different manner. He seemed content with one blazing front-page headline complemented by several short and more informative ones as his story expanded. By contrast, Hearst clearly showed that he had no use for brevity. The stacked group of headlines was replaced by multiple-line headlines that teased but revealed little of the major part of the story being told. What was also noticeable was the increasing variety of fonts in varying sizes and textures on the pages of the daily newspapers. The fundamental purpose of these techniques was to draw the reader to the story.

As noted earlier, photography as an instrument of journalistic process was a latecomer to the press, but illustration was not. The role of illustration will be dealt with in terms of its style and content in a later chapter, but it deserves to be noted here as one more example of the advances in technology that impacted the Yellow Press in the late Victorian age. As early as the 1830s, illustrations began to appear in journals in both North America and Europe. The invention of the daguerreotype in 1839 suggested that photography could also be a tool used by journalists. But it was not to be until the creation of halftone photographic technology in the early 1870s. So, while photography took a back seat in journalism, various other formats, such as woodcuts and wood engravings, metal engravings, and lithographic reproductions, often found their way into the press technology.

Illustrated journals began to pop up everywhere at the midpoint of the century. In the United States, the expatriate Englishman Henry Carter was about to become famous as Frank Leslie, the pseudonym under which his first illustrated newspaper was sold on the streets in 1854. In 1873, the *New York Daily Graphic* was introduced to New Yorkers by the Canadian publishing company of Georges Edouard Desbarats, who had launched two very successful illustrated papers in Montreal. Journalism would be profoundly affected by this trend: the evidence is clear in both of New York's major Yellow journals.

One of the more noticeable changes was the shift of advertising from the front page of most pre–Civil War newspapers to the inside and back pages of the major metropolitan dailies. Also noticeable was the increased reliance on advertising. The only advertisements on our two model front pages were those that promoted the papers themselves. *The New York Journal* boldly claimed, "IF YOU DON'T GET THE *JOURNAL,* YOU DON'T GET THE NEWS." And just in case a reader's wandering eye missed one insert, the newspaper carried the claim on both sides of the masthead. *The World New York* was no less modest and, in fact, made several other claims. Noting that his newspaper had "ALL THE NEWS ALL THE TIME," Pulitzer took the next step and declared that his journal carried "BRILLIANT HUMOR, SPLENDID ILLUSTRATIONS AND STORIES BY THE GREATEST AUTHORS." He may have had some genuine claim to the last declaration, as one of his contributors was Arthur Conan Doyle, creator of the British detective Sherlock Holmes: Doyle's tale *Burger's Secret,* complete with a centered sketch of two of the combatants, Kennedy and Burger, appeared in the Friday, October 15, 1897, edition of *The World*. Pulitzer also laid bare his political allegiances in the advertisement that appeared on the right side of the masthead. He argued that the thrice weekly version of *The World New York* was an unapologetic mouthpiece for the local Democratic Party. It would not be long before Hearst challenged what Pulitzer believed was the exclusive right to champion that party.

As the Monday, August 2, 1897, edition of *The New York Journal* showed, Hearst's designers fell back on some traditional forms of layout while adopting new techniques. Page five of this issue demonstrated clearly the combination of the old and the new. The column designs resembled those in newspapers of a bygone era, some three decades previously. The typefaces were small, and each column was headed by a multiplicity of headlines summarizing the accompanying tale in order of declining importance. The story of the resignation of the Reverend Dr. R. Marshall Harrison, pastor of the Bedford Heights Baptist Church in Brooklyn, provides an excellent example. It would appear that the good reverend's departure was connected to the fact that a trolley transfer station was located just one block away from his church. He found himself continually frustrated when trying to inspire his parishioners with the Holy Word of God, for he had to compete not only with trolley bells but also with the songs of revelers on their way to and from the Coney Island amusement park.

The story contained a drawing of the good pastor as well as an insert featuring his church. The headline above the story pointed to his frustrations, indicating that the primary complaint was with the constant singing and ribald sounds coming from the passengers. "GAY SONGS DROWN ALL HIS SERMONS" was the word from on high. The second headline read, "REV. DR. HARRISON CAN'T VIE WITH MERRYMAKERS SO RESIGNS." The third headline was related to the second one in noting that the problems took place "ON THE CONEY ISLAND ROUTE." The concluding headline, "HE KNOWS ALL THE POPULAR AIRS, SUCH AS MY GIRL'S A HIGH BORN LADY," strongly suggested that these lyrics were learned in spite of a determined effort by the minister to ignore the passing crowds outside.

There were two major advertisements on the same page, both of which featured limited illustrations. The larger of the two announced a furniture sale at Wanamaker's Store. The name of the establishment was illustrated. The advertisement, in spite of the drawing, was basically information-driven. Among other things, it listed the prices charged for a variety of beds on sale. It also noted that Rodman bicycles made for men were on sale for only $24.50. Yet in keeping with a so-called sales approach that took on more prominence in the early years of the twentieth century, there was language in the advertisement that made direct appeals to buy. Under the headline "THE SITUATION THIS MORNING WITH ROD-MAN BICYCLES," the advertiser noted that several boxes containing Rodman bicycles were opened on the prior Saturday morning, and all the women's machines were sold out by noon. It also noted that there were a limited number of male versions still available and that time was of the essence. Although the language of advertising had yet to reach the frenzied pitch that was to come, the point that the sole intent was to create sales was not lost on those who designed and paid for these print commercials. The Yellow Press could not deny its role as a critical player in an emerging market society.

The design and layout of the rest of the newspaper replicated that seen on page five. News stories had multiple headlines, and there was ample use of illustration for any number of reasons. Page nine was filled with sporting news in a format familiar to modern readers. The page contained a drawing of past and present tennis champions, positioned in the middle of the page above the fold. The feature story concerned the races at Saratoga, New York. There was news of an unfocused discus thrower who nearly decapitated a number of spectators who came to witness his prowess. News of a racing competition on water was among other stories. The page was completed by the addition of baseball box scores and the standings in both major and local minor leagues. Not surprisingly, there was a small advertisement for Mastiff Smoking Tobacco, with a brand name that could only appeal to males. The remaining pages were devoted primarily to classified advertisements, news of the performing arts, and financial news.

In comparison, Pulitzer's *The World New York* was tame; in terms of layout and design in 1897, it was close to being pedestrian. The second page of the Monday, February 15, 1897, edition contained eight columns laid out in a very traditional fashion. Most were headed with multiple headlines, which, as in the Hearst newspaper, told the story in brief sentences in order of importance. The one notable exception was the lead story, which targeted one John Searles, whom *The World* claimed was the secretary treasurer of a major sugar trust. The headline above the story was somewhat inflammatory, reading "SUGAR TRUST DEMANDED AND RECEIVED

ABNORMAL PROFIT FROM ITS HELPLESS VICTIMS." Certainly, the notion of just the facts and nothing but the facts had not come into play with the composing of this headline, given the language used.

At the core of the story was an investigation being conducted into the sugar industry by the legislature of the state of New York. *The World* accused the aforementioned Searles of showing nothing but contempt for the state because he took a journey out of town and refused to divulge why or where instead of showing up to explain his industry's conduct in front of the investigating committee. Of course, the newspaper found this action to be contemptible and noted that had a businessperson of something less than Searles's stature done the same, that unfortunate would be serving time for contempt.

In a separate window at the top of the page next to the main story on the left-hand side, the newspaper listed the financial implications of the sugar trust's impact on the citizens of New York State. Without offering any supporting corroboration, Pulitzer's editors claimed that Searles and his bunch had ripped off the public for $37,680,000 in excess profits over a ten-year period. The window contained information that showed the price of sugar and how it had changed from a five-year period before the trust had been founded to the present price. The gap was significant.

The next page was devoted primarily to the activities of President-elect William McKinley. It does not take long to realize that *The World* was not exactly fond of this high-profile Republican. The reporting focused on dissension in Republican ranks over his choice of cabinet members. But on a lighter note, it also had a short article on what Mrs. McKinley would wear to the inauguration of her husband in January. The page was rounded out by a political cartoon that lampooned the politician for selecting the wool of a Merino sheep for his inauguration clothing. In the drawing, the face of the sheep was replaced by a visage resembling McKinley's. The page also had a small advertisement on the right-hand side for Carter's Little Liver Pills.

In terms of layout and design, the rest of the newspaper, unlike *The Journal,* was quite dense. There was a noticeable lack of illustration as compared to the Hearst output. In fact, Pulitzer's newspaper looked more like some of the staid New York papers of the day—until, that is, one began to look beyond the layout and design and explore the content. The brief bits of sporting news and financial concerns that merited a page in the Hearst papers were included on the last page of each issue, along with a series of small advertisements featuring wines and liquors, teas, sewing machines, bicycles, gold rings, clothing dyes, stock market tips, seeds, wheels, and carriages. Some included small drawings, but most did not.

A significant amount of the competitive bloodletting at the height of the New York press wars was related to who could do the better Sunday edition. Joseph Pulitzer had long since realized that human interest stories dealing with crime and sex were bound to be big sellers. Under his tutelage, *The World New York* began to market some of the successful ideas that he had once included in his first major newspaper, the *St. Louis Post-Dispatch.* Pulitzer was also a believer in the communicative power of illustrated graphics. To that end, he had hired an obscure Russian artist named Valerian Gribayedoff to draw publishable sketches from photographs. Many of Gribayedoff's drawings of a shady statesman, a fugitive from justice, or an accused murderer appeared in the top right-hand corner of the front page of the daily edition. Soon, the fault lines between news and gossip became hard to detect.

Pulitzer's success in the New York market was not lost on William Randolph Hearst when he took over *The New York Journal* in 1895. In many ways, Hearst copied Pulitzer's concepts shamelessly, often succeeding in exaggerating an already exaggerated approach to contemporary journalism in the late Victorian period. Like *The World,* Hearst's *Journal* soon became the repository for lurid tales of demented criminal activity, stories of environmental revenge and natural disasters, an almost obscene fascination with the wonders of science, and hints of scandal involving those in high places, all of which were combined with literally thousands upon thousands of illustrations that were beginning to turn journalism into a visual as opposed to a written expression.

Of the two major competitors, Hearst's *Journal* had the most diversified content. Each Sunday, in addition to the regular news section, Hearst published the *Sunday American Magazine,* which the masthead described as "THE POPULAR PERIODICAL OF THE *NEW YORK JOURNAL.*" This pull-out section was supplemented by two other permanent inserts, the *American Woman's Home Journal* and the *American Humorist.* In the summer, the company also published the *Summer Resorts and Summer Sports* section.

All of these sections were highly illustrated. There were very few stories that did not include some kind of drawing, large or small, with the possible exception of those in the summer supplement, which seemed to be more interested in passing along vital information as opposed to titillating the curiosity of a reader or two. This is not to suggest that Hearst abandoned his goal of communicating the news through pictures. The front page of the Sunday, August 8, 1897, edition contained actual photographs of two men, one bowling a cricket ball, the other teeing off on a golf ball. But the headlines conveyed the supplement's more noble intentions. Slightly over half of the front page was devoted to a photograph of two very well-dressed young women who, according to author Edgar Saltus, would dearly have loved to find mates. He noted that in the spring, a young man's fancy turned to love; by the summer, the cycle was complete. Then, the inevitable line announced that the remainder of the article could be found on page thirty-two.

As the reader leafed through this section, a variety of stories emerged, the most important of which were complemented by accompanying pictures, both sketch drawings and photographs. In terms of layout and design, the inside pages showed a return to the traditional column style, with one notable exception. The stories that the editors clearly wished to have seen by all were dominated by multifaceted headlines. Four stories fit into this category, all of which had four headlines. The top headline had the largest font, about one-half inch in height. The second headline was somewhat smaller, but it was intended to connect the reader to other aspects of the story below. The third and fourth lines' fonts were approximately the same size as the second font. Although the concept of multiple headlines took root in the journalism of a much earlier period, the actual word count in the use of stacked headlines in the Yellow Press was noticeably limited. Most of the rest of the stories in the summer supplement contained two headlines, the first larger than the second. The remaining pages contained information on how to go deer hunting successfully, organized sports, and those matters deemed important to single women.

In many ways, the face page of *American Magazine* revealed much of the approach that designers took when working with newspapers of the period, in particular the Yellow Press. The lead item in the Sunday, August 8, 1897, edition of the insert was the story on the tragedy of Garrett E. Anderson and his wife. Details on the actual content will be discussed in the next chapter. The purpose here is simply to show how the story was presented within the boundaries of layout and design. The Andersons had ventured out into the summer heat of the Arizona desert to make contact with their son, who was supposed to meet them at a way station. The first thing a reader would notice was a large sketch stretching from side to side on the front page, taking up about 40 percent of all available space. The picture showed a couple in a carriage drawn by a horse that was obviously suffering from a lack of water. Several predatory birds were hovering over the couple, waiting, it would appear, before descending to pick apart the soon to be dead bodies. On the left-hand side of the page, there were two sketches portraying both of the Andersons. And in the bottom left-hand corner of the page, as if to set the appropriate mood, was a sketch of two desert coyotes howling at a full moon.

The main story, "Death in an American Desert," was laid out in the middle of the page, stretching from the bottom of the major sketch to the end of the page. The story was submitted to the journal by John Moore, who ran a freight business that crossed the desert. It was he who came upon the distraught couple while he was making a delivery. He was unable to get the dying Mr. Anderson to take water. In typical Hearst fashion, he was described as a "Journal Correspondent," although his actual role in feeding this tale of grief to the New York press is unknown. Difficult to miss were two windows on the pages. One was located just below the lead sketch on the left-hand side of the first page. It had a neat border and contained an appropriate teasing headline, "HOW I PASSED THROUGH THE VALLEY OF THE SHADOW OF DEATH BY MRS. GARRETT E. ANDERSON." The biblical metaphor was hard to ignore. However, that insert was designed to be a stand-alone, relating not to Moore's tale or that on the other side of the page, which was the story in Mrs. Anderson's own words. The most important point to note here is that the Anderson story took up the entire first page. This treatment became a common occurrence with the Sunday supplement. When the *American Magazine* revealed the tale of Chicago resident David Bates the following Sunday, it followed the same format. Bates, by the way, had collected no less than seven wives, which earned him the name "the Modern Bluebeard."

If any one descriptor could be applied to the second page of the section, it would be *gigantic*. The top of the page contained a sketch of a war machine being developed by the German kaiser. Apparently as large as a passenger car on the railways of the day, it was made of solid steel and ran on wheels, and it had the capability of hurling bullets and explosives at an enemy who would find it difficult to penetrate its armor. The sketch dominated the top third of the page. On the middle of the page was a drawing of a thirty-foot basking shark that had the misfortune to encounter a very skilled fisherman, although the report did contain the not so surprising news that it took a dozen men to lift the fish out of the water. Like the Anderson sketch, the picture of the unfortunate shark stretched from side to side on the page but only occupied a small percentage of the total page. These two drawings were complemented by three images depicting the "gigantic" wheat crop of the state of Nebraska. To make the point, the illustration, essentially a graph, depicted three stacks of wheat beside the 555-foot-tall Washington Monument; the assembled wheat packages would reach a height of no less than 1,223 feet.

The *American Journal* became the forum in which all of Hearst's journalistic fetishes could be displayed. Thus far in this limited discussion, we have seen a story about a terrible family tragedy and an obsession with size; now, we can move on to Hearst's interest with matters scientific. The supplement paid homage to the inventor Nikola Tesla, who claimed that he had invented a device that could shoot electrical energy around the world by taking advantage of nature's own capacity to store energy, or so he thought.

Tesla, of course, became famous by convincing George Westing-house to manufacture devices to produce alternating current (AC) electricity to compete with and eventually replace the more dominant direct current (DC) electric energy being promoted by Thomas Edison.

Obviously, Hearst was captivated by such an idea. Even though the story was published on the inside pages, Tesla's invention was given the full-page treatment. For fear that someone might miss the importance of the discovery, two lengthy headlines, out of character at that time in a Hearst paper, introduced the reader to the complexity of the find. Approximately the top right-hand third of the page was taken up with a large drawing of Tesla and probably one of his cohorts holding a device shooting large, lightning-like bolts out to a drawing of what was obviously the earth. Just below the primary drawing was another showing a circle that was reputed to be the core element of the device that theoretically could perform this miracle. Of all of Tesla's more important contributions, such as his early work in radio, this invention did not see the light of day beyond this coverage in Hearst's pages.

The *American Woman's Home Journal* was, in many ways, a hybrid of different concepts of the role of women in society and their interplay with the performing arts. Unlike the *American Journal,* the front page of this publication was not dominated by one large story with a predominant set of sketches. The lead story was about a performer named Gertrude Zella, who had been featured in what was called the latest theatrical novelty, the statue dance. The top of the page contained six photographs of Zella in the various movements that took place in the dance. Her costume and her motion were intended to replicate a dancing statue in ancient Rome, hence the name of the dance. Farther down the page, the paper announced that a woman, no less, actually ran a zoo in the

Western Rockies. Just in case there was a disbeliever among the readers, the one-paragraph story was supplemented by no less than four photographs of the zookeeper playing with some of her charges, including a kangaroo, an ostrich, what appeared to be two small tiger cubs, and one full-grown lion.

The following page was full of photographs, the first third of which were boldly titled "A Bunch of Famous Southern Beauties— Lovely Women Who Live Where the Sweet Magnolia Blooms." The center photographs showed a group of young women taking singing lessons, and the page concluded with a series of photos of recent attendees at a society ball, the majority of whom were female. Even though Hearst did not use the camera to any great extent in news coverage before the turn of the century, it played a significant role in the creation and maintenance of the Sunday supplements.

It could be argued with some credibility that most of Hearst's Sunday papers, if not all of his publications, were sources of pure entertainment, as opposed to fact-driven news reporting. There is little doubt that the *American Humorist,* the colored comic weekly of *The New York Journal,* clearly fit that bill. It was here that the world was introduced to both one-panel and multipanel illustrations of characters such as the Yellow Kid, a fitting name for the cartoon figure who appeared in the Yellow Press. The humor in the *American Humorist* was not restricted to the comics, although they dominated the section. A significant collection of light tales and anecdotes were woven in among the numerous drawings that covered most of the pages.

The front page of the Sunday, August 8, 1897, edition of the newspaper was a glowing example of how Hearst used comic drawings as part of his publishing agenda. In all, there were fourteen sketches portraying different aspects of the human experience, all intended to produce some form of humor. In one, a dapper businessman was depicted hanging about a pool hall and bookie establishment. Another showed an unsuccessful fisherman buying a catch at a local market. Of these drawings, two small ones appeared on either side of the masthead. The remaining twelve were distributed almost evenly throughout the main page. Nearly all of the captions were single sentences, of varying lengths.

Playing on some of the new technology of the age, page two contained a filmstrip of a rather dumb farmer who picked up a loose wire on the local interurban railway line. Needless to say, it was alive. The strip was called *The Journal Kinetoscope,* the banner of which was engraved. It had six frames, and as one might have guessed, the farmer survived his lesson in electricity, although he was somewhat battered by the experience. Some of the stories on the page, all of which were quite short (most not exceeding three paragraphs), dealt with a preacher whose sermon was mistyped in the local newspaper, a wife who complained to her husband about his chauvinism, a woman with a shopping list her father could not afford, and a few two- or three-line jokes. The page also contained a multiframe comic sketch of young people dreaming about their fantasies and a series of single-frame, joke-oriented comics. The majority of the sketches that appeared in the Sunday edition of *The New York Journal* were to be found in the *American Humorist* section. In comparison to the every burgeoning Hearst publication, Pulitzer's Sunday contributions were far more tame and less complex.

FIVE

FACT AND FICTION

In quiet and sometimes polite circles of mainly local and amateur historians, it has often been said that facts should never interfere with the telling of a good tale. Both Joseph Pulitzer and William Randolph Hearst must have been listening at the keyhole when such pronouncements were solemnly declared. After all, both were in the business of commercial newspapers, and their ability to continue to feed any form of public frenzy over scandal, crime, and sensational scientific discoveries depended on money. Pulitzer did not have access to a family fortune as did Hearst, and therefore, the immigrant publisher was obliged to depend on newspaper sales and advertising. These men had some experience in tapping the constituent imagination, so what took place in regard to both their papers and Yellow Journalism in New York in the closing years of the nineteenth century should have been no surprise to anyone with any observational skills regarding the state of American media.

Of the two men, Hearst proved to be the most accurate harbinger of things to come when, as chief arbitrator of bad taste in the big-city press in 1892, he took on Charlotte Perkins Gilman, a leading American feminist and notorious husband collector. Gilman was known as one of the leading icons for instability in family relationships at a time when divorce was still considered a moral scandal. In the *San Francisco Examiner* in 1891, a full-page and exceptionally inflammatory discussion was presented on the latest peccadilloes of the flamboyant Gilman, much to her distress. So, when a Hearst reporter appeared on her doorstep a year later to gather some comments about the whole business of getting divorced, Gilman would not cooperate. After she refused to consent to a formal interview, the reporter attempted to extract commentary by reverting to a casual conversation. When this did not achieve the desired results, he offered to pay Gilman; then, having had no success, he threatened to smear her name in the newspaper. But Gilman did not bend, and the reporter left her doorstep empty-handed.

Gilman's encounter with Hearst over her divorce scenarios led to her lifetime boycott against any Hearst publications, even though many an editor assured her she would not have to face the owner himself if only she would agree to publish in one of his journals. Speaking of the Hearst brand of journalism, Gilman wrote:

> [It] frankly plays on the lowest, commonest of its traits: tickling it with salacious detail, harping on those themes which unlettered peasants find attractive, and for which most people retain an unadmitted weakness. This is the secret of our "Yellow Press" and of the strange prominence given to unimportant stories of vice even in the mildly cream colored variety.

In Gilman's analysis of the Yellow Press, merely being associated with the likes of Hearst was grounds for condemnation. She took on the venerable Ambrose Bierce when he refused to stop writing rude remarks about the Pacific Coast Women's Press Association; she was particularly grieved when Bierce directed his attacks against the individual female members of the organization. She responded to his verbiage by noting, "That man ought not to go unwhipped." Gilman's distaste for Hearst continued to be expressed even after she took her own life in 1935. Her agent, Willis Kingsley Wing, attempted to abscond with her autobiography, which he wanted serialized in the Hearst-owned publication *Cosmopolitan*. Wing received a curt letter and direction from Gilman's daughter, Katherine Stetson Chamberlin, that even though her mother was now deceased, the boycott against Hearst would continue.

So, just what type of journalistic culture encouraged the kind of misbehavior that troubled Charlotte Perkins Gilman and those who agreed with her assessment of the late Victorian press? As historian Fred Fedler and others have noted, the demographic class occupied by working journalists was not far from the bottom of the social ladder. Most journalists were underpaid, drank too much, and were rude and ruthless and fundamentally dishonest. They could not hold a job and drifted from city to city, constantly looking for work. They struggled through long and exhausting hours of labor and lived in hovels on the wrong side of the tracks, often having only the local saloon as a place of comfort. As journalism history professors Steven Vaughan and Bruce Evenson discovered in their study of journalism on film, such images of journalists persisted well into the 1930s, as seen in Ben Hecht's play *The Front Page*. It was only when the American Newspaper Publishers Association began to complain that revisionist histories, such as *His Girl Friday* and the 1940 remake of *The Front Page,* began to soften the image of the hardened journalist.

One of the key problems affecting the journalistic era of

Pulitzer and Hearst was dishonesty. When pursuing a story, many reporters refused to identify their profession to potential sources. Prominent individuals frequently woke up to their morning coffee and papers and found themselves quoted, often in a very unflattering light. Journalists typically defended the use of this kind of deception as the only way a reporter could gain access to the facts of a particular case. One editor even boasted that no reporter who was *not* dishonest could succeed in the profession. Needless to say, the journalists' enthusiastic defense of the practice did not cut any ice with Gilman and those who thought like her. And not only did journalists routinely lie to get a good story, they also accepted bribes, eavesdropped on potential sources, and stole pictures and documents from reporters who worked on competitive papers. Hearst newspapers in both New York and Chicago were known for grabbing suspects off the street and grilling them in order to obtain good copy before turning them over to the police.

The problem of dishonesty existed not only in collecting information but also in publishing it. It was well known that many journals that followed Hearst's example printed material that was factually untrue. One of Hearst's most vocal opponents, E. L. Godkin, editor of the New York newspaper *The Nation,* pointed to the coverage of a theatrical event as handled by three different newspapers. The first account noted that the lower floor of the theater was almost completely filled and that the first balcony had three to four rows of chairs. The second reviewer proclaimed that the theater was only about a third filled. And the final account had the place packed, with no room left for anyone wishing to sit. Of course, deceptive and dishonest reporting reached its peak during coverage of the Spanish-American War, which will be dealt with in a later chapter.

The deceptive practices of the journalistic community were

well known among those whose circles included individuals with little respect for the law. On July 17, 1890, the *New York Times* printed an article cautioning local merchants about an elaborate swindle being perpetrated by a person using the newspaper's name. Apparently, this man would approach a business and identify himself as a *Times* reporter. In one case, he interviewed an eyeglass manufacturer and wrote a very flattering article on the man's business. He then told the businessman that the *Times* would publish the article if it was paid $10. The businessman felt that he had accomplished his goals when he bartered the swindler down to an $8 sum. The phony reporter left the premises with the money and the article, which, of course, never saw the light of day.

Why was there no wholesale rebelling against this kind of dishonesty? One factor was that people believed the press was simply in the business of being in business and that truth had to be sacrificed if the journalistic community wanted to continue to sell newspapers. In other words, scandal was profitable, and as long as money remained the root of the evil, the evil would continue to exist. The other factor was entertainment. Not only did the Yellow Press consolidate its readership in the lower segments of American society, it also appealed to the middle and upper classes. It seems that everyone in the new industrial America needed a diversion from the tensions of everyday life, and folks such as Pulitzer and Hearst were more than willing to provide the product. Their approach was not without controversy.

In spite of the popularity of the genre, the Yellow Press had its critics in the community at large. It was one thing for a member of the journalistic establishment such as Godkin to spout invective against Pulitzer and Hearst, but it was quite another to have criticism arise among other prominent community members, especially those who were generally regarded as leaders in Victorian society. The Yellow Press was not the first institution to draw attention from one of its own. In 1859, Lambert A. Wilmer's book *Our Press Gang, or, A Complete Exposition of the Corruptions and Crimes of American Newspapers* appeared in American bookshops. The volume did little to halt the march of sensationalism that most people at the time would argue had begun with Benjamin Day and his *New York Sun* of the 1830s.

A number of critics contended that in its extravagant detailing of the most heinous of crimes, the Yellow Press was actually providing a how-to handbook for young criminals. Some of the critics declared that the press did more than provide detailed methods by which successful criminal activities could take place: it actually, they said, encouraged those with no respect for the law to take up a career in crime. As one Baptist minister put it: "Do you suppose that your sons and daughters can grow up pure-minded and clean if their minds are fed on such filth in the formative period of their existence?"

Prominent academics regularly explored what they saw as the irrefutable link between sensationalist reporting and urban crime. In one article, the authors argued that the lower classes, by the very nature of their respective existences, were naturally prone to criminal behavior. These citizens were deemed far less advanced intellectually than those who held the levers of power, and they were considered more impressionable as well. In the age of eugenics, this was not an uncommon position. And where, according to the experts, did these underlings get their views on society? The Yellow Press, naturally.

The Yellow Press found itself in the moral crosshairs of Anthony Comstock, the notorious self-appointed guardian of the moral community in the nineteenth century. Comstock trotted out statistics that proved, in his mind at least, a definite connection between the kinds of stories that appeared in the Yellow Press and proven crimes. As journalism historian John Ferré discovered, the list of crimes was (as one might suspect) comprehensive, including arson, burglary, counterfeiting, assault, forgery, grand larceny, highway robbery, housebreaking, attempted murder, murder, perjury, petit larceny, drunkenness, and attempted suicide.

Any number of crusades were directed at the Yellow Press in the closing years of the nineteenth century. There were campaigns to limit the profits pouring into the coffers of Pulitzer and Hearst. None worked. Some opponents argued that establishing endowments similar to those enjoyed by universities, hospitals, and charitable organizations could lead to a cleaner and more responsible journalism. The concept was quite simple: if one freed the press from the basic need to attract advertisers, the quest for constant circulation increases could be dealt with. Steel magnate Andrew Carnegie called upon his friends to undertake such a course, but alas, the thought of placing their millions into a potential sinkhole was unappealing. So, too, was the campaign to buy out both Pulitzer and Hearst. In the final analysis, there were no takers. The line in the sand over which no responsible journalist could cross was only drawn after Hearst made the outrageous claim that corruption and bad behavior on the part of public officials could lead to legitimate assassinations of the perpetrators. Shortly after the editorial expressing this opinion appeared, President McKinley was shot down in Buffalo, New York. The Yellow Press had, in many ways, finally reached the zenith of its role as gossipmonger, social critic, and disturbing influence.

In spite of the fact that they were lumped together by those who condemned the Yellow Press, Joseph Pulitzer and William Randolph Hearst were very different people. As an eastern European Jewish immigrant, Pulitzer probably realized that he would never become part of the power-brokering establishment in New York City, regardless of his success and his great wealth. When he finally approached Columbia College about the possibility of establishing a journalism school on its campus, his dream was put on hold for well over a decade before he finally forced the issue. But Pulitzer did rely on New York society in a way Hearst did not.

In the influential circles in the city, Hearst was considered to be an appalling character. Most considered his newspaper a reflection of his character. The young student who had sent a chamber pot to the president of Harvard now regularly sent literary chamber pots to the citizenry of New York and often in the most provocative of ways. While Pulitzer worked with the newcomers to his city, Hearst rashly exploited them and their city. And when Pulitzer retreated to his yacht to deal with his strained nerves and increasing problems with blindness, Hearst was burning yet one more midnight candle in the cause of personal ambition.

It can be argued with some conviction that Pulitzer was the creator and Hearst was the follower. In spite of continuing debates over the influence of the two on late nineteenth- and early twentieth-century journalism, it is a fact of life that while Hearst was busily spending a good chunk of his mother's money long before he arrived in New York, Pulitzer was turning the journalistic community on its head with an approach to fact gathering and storytelling that would later be dubbed New Journalism.

For the reporter involved in the execution of the New Journalism, the city was theater. Stories had color and life, and if they did not, those attributes could be created. The reporter roamed the streets and back alleys of the metropolis, seeking out what Pulitzer anointed as the human interest tale. Peoples' trials and triumphs became the meat of the material that appeared under gaudy and often suggestive headlines. It was no longer good enough to report that a man bit a dog after the dog bit him. What happened during the attack, from the first crunch to the last bloodletting, in many ways defined the New Journalism.

In that world, it was also fair to create the news or at least the factors leading up to the news of the day. Pulitzer's paper was filled with endless crusades to stamp out corruption and poverty. The publisher's victims were numerous, and among the leading villains of the day were the Standard Oil Company, the New York Central Railway, the telephone monopoly, slum landlords, crooked contractors, sexual exploiters, and the railway lobbyists of 1887. And if a reader was in danger of being turned away by stories of the ill health of the nation, there was the amusement of the stunt to provide the proper distraction. In the fall of 1888, *World* reporter Elizabeth Cochrane (Nellie Bly) boarded a steamship in Jersey City to begin what would be a seventy-two-day journey around the world, beating that of the fictional Phineas Fogg of Jules Verne's exceptionally popular novel *Around the World in Eighty Days.* Needless to say, Pulitzer ensured that his journal covered every vital moment of the adventure, which captured the hearts and souls of many a resident of New York City and beyond.

For Pulitzer, the use of sensationalism was a means to an end. Hearst treated it as an end in itself. Pulitzer regarded himself as a champion for those with little or no voice in the community. Although the gory tales that appeared on page one sold his newspapers, they were actually designed to lead his readers to the more thoughtful commentary contained in the editorials inside. For Pulitzer, the editorial page was the heart of the Victorian newspaper and the page that mattered most.

But try as he might to excuse the rabble that appeared on page one, Pulitzer had unleashed a journalism that would eventually engulf the city and the country and place in the hands of William

Randolph Hearst a weapon that ultimately brought discredit to the institution of journalism in the United States. Until Hearst arrived on the scene in 1890s' New York, virtually every journalist working in the city was controlled by what appeared in Pulitzer's journal. Reporters lived in fear that they would miss an important story in *The World.* It was well known along the newspaper alley of Park Row that early editions of *The World* were snapped up by competitive journals and that *World* stories were often rewritten for consumption in those newspapers. The fearsome Charles Chapin, who would later become the subject of scandal himself, ran Pulitzer's empire in a bloodless and unfeeling manner. He eventually died in Sing Sing Prison, serving a life term for the murder of his wife.

Pulitzer had created the model and Charles Chapin set the tone for what appeared on page one. In 1884, James L. Wilson and his wife were brutally murdered in Winnetka, Illinois. At the time, Chapin was cutting his teeth on sensationalist stories for the *Chicago Tribune.* He learned his lessons well and eventually took his knowledge to New York and Pulitzer before his downfall. Chapin had noted that a similar murder had taken place in Lincoln, Illinois, some four months previously. Melville Stone, publisher of the *Chicago Morning News,* charged his reporters with not only covering a crime but also investigating it. The lessons of this so-called detective journalism were not lost on the young Chapin. He, too, conducted his own investigation into the Wilson murders and came to the conclusion that they were linked to the Lincoln case. Chapin also abandoned the inverted pyramid style of reporting for a series of articles on the case in which the readers were led along by a series of tantalizing facts that moved, step by step, in a logical order. In the end, in spite of his colorful rhetoric calling for justice in these cases, Chapin was unable to identify the murderer.

But his experiences would soon hold him in good stead in the hurly-burly world of New York journalism.

Until Hearst's significant faux pas in the McKinley case, journalism in New York had been resilient, existing for over a half century. When Lincoln Steffens returned to New York after a stint in Europe, where he attended university, the culture was alive and well. He noted in his biography that reporters were never allowed to get too comfortable in their role. In order to fight complacency, they were regularly shifted from department to department. Yesterday's police reporter could become tomorrow's art and music critic. As Steffens noted, "When a reporter no longer saw red at a fire, when he was so used to police news that a murder was not a human tragedy but only a crime, he could not write police news for us." When he finally became an editor with the *New York Commercial Advertiser,* Steffens gave this charge to a young reporter about to go out and cover a murder:

> Here, Cahan, is a report that a man has murdered his wife, a rather bloody, hacked up crime. We don't care about that. But there's a story in it. That man loved that woman well enough once to marry her, and now he has hated her enough to cut her all to pieces. If you can find out just what happened between that wedding and this murder, you will have a novel for yourself and a short story for me. Go on now, take your time and get this tragedy as a tragedy.

There was little doubt that the reporting of tragedy did much for a newspaper's circulation at that time in history. Previously, both Ellen (Helen) Jewitt and Mary Rogers had captured the fancy of New York readers in a way that neither would have preferred. Now, it was up to another woman, Nellie Bly, to put a female name on the masthead of one of the city's major newspapers, *The*

World New York. Bly had started a modest newspaper career in Pittsburgh, reporting primarily on what was known in those days as
women's issues. She had also convinced her editor to send her on
a trip to Mexico, where, in return for the newspaper's generosity,
she would report on life in that country. But when she returned
to Pittsburgh, she was once again forced to return to the women's
section of the journal. Fed up with these restrictions, she resigned
and made her way to New York in search of a career in which her
abilities as a reporter, regardless of gender, would be respected.
Her quest took her to Pulitzer's offices on Park Row and a meeting with his editor, Col. John Cockerill.

Since *The World* dealt in controversy for most its existence, access to the home office was difficult if not impossible for anyone
who had not been invited or who was not expected to be there.
Bly was such a person, yet she doggedly worked her way through
the strict security apparatus in the building to end up in Cockerill's presence. He was impressed with her determination but was
more reserved about her story possibilities. She proposed taking a
steamer to Europe and then posing as an immigrant to the United
States on the return voyage in order to explore the hazards experienced by the unfortunates housed in the steerage section of the
ship. Cockerill was not about to make any commitment, but he
paid Nellie $25 to keep her from approaching other newspapers.
He asked her to return on September 22, 1887, and she did.

Cockerill's reaction to the immigrant story was lukewarm at
best. He had other ideas for making a journalistic splash and testing Nellie Bly's courage and stamina at the same time. He pointed
her to a 120-acre site located in the East River. Its official name
was Blackwell's Island, and it housed several city institutions, including the Women's Lunatic Asylum. Cockerill suggested that
the young investigative reporter pose as a person with a mental

problem in order to get herself committed to the hospital. Her mission was to investigate the continuing rumors that all was not well in the behavior of certain individuals, including physicians, who were employed at the hospital. Bly regarded the challenge as a way to get into the newspaper, and whatever concerns she may have had about her own health and welfare were superseded by the knowledge that she was about to embark on a journalism career in the heart of American journalism, New York City.

Blackwell's Island and whatever went on there had come to the attention of most of the newspapers in New York at one time or another. In August of that year, 1887, two nurses went to the *New York Times* with tales of abuse at the hospital. The Blackwell's Island facility was not the only institution that had been accused of mistreating patients. *The World* itself had penned two editorials, one on July 3 and the other on July 9, calling for an investigation into tales that inmates on Ward's Island, just north of Blackwell's, were also the victims of abuse. The story began to take on a life of its own when two guards were charged with manslaughter in the death of an inmate whom they described as a lunatic.

If a story was dramatic, it made page one in Pulitzer's *World*. And if such New York events as the Festival of Connection, marking the opening of the Brooklyn Bridge, were considered to be worthy of front-page treatment, one can only guess the reaction in the editorial chambers of Pulitzer's fiefdom when Nellie Bly began to bang out her story of horror at Blackwell's Island. The story had it all and proved, if anyone doubted, that truth can be stranger than fiction.

Bly began her odyssey by booking herself into Matron Irene Stenard's Temporary Home for Women on Second Avenue. She used the name Nellie Brown at Cockerill's suggestion, just in case a forgotten monogram should appear on an article of clothing.

After having dined, she began a confusing and rambling conversation with some of the others in the working-class boardinghouse. She then feigned becoming more and more delusional, at which point some of the other guests began to fear for their lives. The proper authorities were called the following morning, and Nellie Brown was on her way to Bellevue Hospital for observation after a short stop in the courtroom of Judge Patrick Duffy.

Duffy was intrigued by the lost soul and suggested that New York's journalistic community might be of some assistance in attempting to define who this person really was and from whence she came. Nellie told the judge and the congregated reporters that she came from Cuba and that her real name was Nellie Moreno. The *New York Sun* took up the challenge by treating her tale as an unresolved mystery. Other newspapers followed suit, but *The World* remained silent on the issue. Nellie was finally on her way to a stay on Blackwell's Island that she would never forget.

When "Ten Days in a Madhouse" hit the front pages of Pulitzer's the *World New York,* it was an instant sensation. But was it sensational? The opening insert, which later became the first chapter in the book version of the story, was simply entitled "A Delicate Mission," hardly the kind of graphic design that would later appear in Hearst's *New York Journal.* The title of the second chapter was no more provocative: Bly modestly entitled it "Preparing for the Ordeal." In fact, Bly's reporting had almost a matter-of-fact approach. Describing how the story came to be told, Bly carefully pieced together her experiences:

> I succeeded in getting committed to the insane ward at Blackwell's Island, where I spent ten days and nights and had an experience which I shall never forget. I took upon myself to enact the part of a poor, unfortunate crazy girl, and felt it my duty not to

shirk any of the disagreeable results that should follow. I became one of the city's insane wards for that length of time, experienced much, and saw and heard more of the treatment accorded to this helpless class of our population, and when I had seen and heard enough, my release was promptly secured. I left the insane ward with pleasure and regret—pleasure that I was once more able to enjoy the free breath of heaven; regret that I could not have brought with me some of the unfortunate women who lived and suffered with me, and who, I am convinced, are just as sane as I was and am now myself.

Even when she told of torture and relentless abuse of the inmates, the text of her columns had almost a distant feeling:

Miss Tillie Mayard suffered more than any of us from the cold, and yet she tried to follow my advice to be cheerful and try to keep up for a short time. Superintendent Dent brought in a man to see me. He felt my pulse and my head and examined my tongue. I told them how cold it was, and assured them that I did not need medical aid, but that Miss Mayard did, and they should transfer their attentions to her. They did not answer me, and I was pleased to see Miss Mayard leave her place and come forward to them. She spoke to the doctors and told them she was ill, but they paid no attention to her. The nurses came and dragged her back to the bench, and after the doctors left they said, "After awhile, when you see that the doctors will not notice you, you will quit running up to them." Before the doctors left me I heard one say—I cannot give it in his exact words—that my pulse and eyes were not that of an insane girl, but Superintendent Dent assured him that in cases such as mine such tests failed. After watching me for awhile he said my face was the brightest he had ever seen for a lunatic. The nurses had on heavy undergarments and coats, but they refused to give us shawls. Nearly all night long I listened to a woman cry about the cold and beg for God to let her die. Another one yelled "Murder!" at frequent intervals and "Police!" at others until my flesh felt creepy.

Bly's caper was a Pulitzer classic. The publisher told friends and colleagues that he admired her courage and the down-to-earth, populist approach she took to reporting. However, not all persons in the journalistic community were turned on by Pulitzer's social agenda. Upton Sinclair, who was to have a little experience in exposé journalism himself, thought that Pulitzer and eventually Hearst were only taking up popular causes to increase circulation, which in turn was reflected in higher advertising rates, in order to become richer and richer. For Sinclair and like-minded individuals, the newspaper game was little more than an extension of the marketing mentality that gripped New York at the time. But it was not to be turned back just yet. Nellie Bly had opened the floodgates, and more startling revelations were to follow.

If Sinclair was concerned that Pulitzer was doing little more than reviving the legacies of Benjamin Day and James Gordon Bennett, he must have been horrified by what he saw when William Randolph Hearst took over the minor league *New York Journal*. The paper, with an average pre-Hearst circulation of some seventy-seven thousand, once thrived on reporting tales of the seamier side of big-city living. It was known in New York circles as the chambermaid's delight. Retreating from the tabloid approach, the newspaper's management decided to reform the journal, but it began a serious slide in circulation. It apparently could not compete with Pulitzer's journal, with its nearly half a million daily readers.

Pulitzer left most of the less savory side of the world to front-page reporting. Hearst has no such restrictions. He took on Pulitzer in Pulitzer's own backyard. When his rival began crusades to help the poor and homeless, Hearst not only copied his initiatives but also usually expanded on them. When Pulitzer's employees were passing out bread to starving New Yorkers, Hearst was giving away full meals and warm clothing.

There was always a school of thought in New York journalism circles that Hearst, as opposed to Pulitzer, was nothing more than a big kid at heart and that his newspaper world was his kindergarten. Certainly, much of the evidence in his behavior, which was later used in Orson Welles's *Citizen Kane,* tends to bear this out. One of Hearst's fetishes was to play fast and loose with New York's police force. As his biographer Ben Procter wrote, "Crime and passion, no matter how bizarre and grotesque, were the most pervasive themes in every *Journal* paper. Hearst seemed to be especially fascinated with police work, with sleuthing and the vagaries of the criminal mind." And as with all of his passions, Hearst pushed his obsession to the limit. He gathered his reporters around him one day in 1897 and announced that they were the founding members of his special "Murder Squad." Their mandate was to investigate and solve heinous crimes before New York's finest came up with the answers.

One can only imagine the horror experienced by three young New Yorkers as they attempted to beat the city's summer heat with a dip in the East River on the last weekend in June 1897. They were accustomed to sharing their swimming hole with fish, garbage, and marine traffic, but a headless body was one find too many. To William Randolph Hearst and the Murder Squad, however, it was a gift from heaven, so to speak. The Sunday news edition of *The New York Journal* laid out four screaming headlines on page one.

In large, bold type, the leading headline barked out, "BE-HEADED, CAST INTO THE RIVER." The second announced, "DIS-MEMBERED TRUNK OF A MAN FOUND BY THREE BOYS WHO WERE SWIMMING." Set in a descending size, the third read, "HE HAD BEEN MURDERED AND HIS CUNNING SLAYER SOUGHT TO FOREVER HIDE HIS CRIME." And finally, yet one more of Hearst's obsessions appeared via a headline that revealed, "SCIENCE HAS RECON-STRUCTED THE LIVING MAN FROM WHAT REMAINS OF THE DEAD ONE—PROBABLY DECAPITATED WHILE STILL ALIVE." Of course, two very obvious liberties in terms of accurate reporting were taken in these announcements. First, since the murderer had yet to be captured, how could one possibly know how cunning the criminal really was, and second, there was no way of knowing whether the unfortunate victim had his head removed while still living. The headlines were little more than Hearst hyperbole.

The body, which was wrapped in a decorated oilcloth, was that of a Turkish bath masseur named William Guldensuppe. His iden-tity would not be revealed for another four days. For the Hearst Murder Squad, the monetary value of the oilcloth was important. As one short headline noted, "THIS MAY BE A CLEW [*sic*]," and it would prove to be so. It would eventually connect the victim with Augusta Nack, a married woman who had ended their romance to take up with a barber named Martin Thorn. He should have known better.

The Monday edition of the newspaper was no less relentless in the coverage of the crime. Page one carried a graphic drawing of the victim's remains, showing in detail where the knife used to dismember the unfortunate Guldensuppe entered his body. The story revealed for the first time that along with his head, the victim was also missing his legs and arms, which were later discovered at separate locations along the river. When it came time to inter the bath masseur, it would be a challenge to reassemble him in death.

Along with the sketch of the body, Hearst's artists also drew pictures of the ropes used to tie the oilcloth together around the corpse. At the center of the visual treatment of the tale was a detailed sketch of the location where part of the discovery took place, at Cliff Avenue and 176th Street. For those readers captured by the lure of such a mystery, the saga continued on into the second page of the Monday edition. Again, the oilcloth with its unique diagrams was reproduced, as was a picture of the location on the river at Eleventh Street where the three young boys made the original discovery. And for those unaffected by squeamishness, a realistic drawing of Guldensuppe's slashed hand, with three deep knife wounds, accompanied the other drawings. Nothing was left to the imagination, unless it was Hearst's imagination.

By Tuesday, Hearst and his gang were in full coverage hysteria. The entire first two pages of their paper were devoted to the affair, with considerably large volumes of text supplemented by drawings related to the crime. The front-page headlines announced that the clothes belonging to the victim had been discovered, as was a valise that the newspaper claimed belonged to Guldensuppe, although no concrete evidence to link the findings and the victim was published. Hearst even hired a palmist to read the dead man's fingerprints for clues to his personality.

Day by day, coverage of the event took up more and more space in the first section of *The Journal*. Hearst even extended the story by inviting readers with missing relatives to contact him and his investigative team of journalists, delivering a faint hope of finding those who had gone astray. And then, Hearst dangled the temptation of a reward in front of his readers. In a can't-miss location on page one, he offered a $1,000 reward to anyone who could offer evidence that would result in solving the mystery.

When Wednesday arrived, the screaming headline on page one read simply, "DISCOVERED BY THE JOURNAL." So, what was discovered? First, Hearst's private police force had confirmed that the body found in the river was that of William Guldensuppe. Second and more important, they revealed that Augusta Nack had at one time left her husband to take up an illicit affair with the masseur. It also appeared that Nack had acquired yet one more devoted paramour, the barber Martin Thorn. Could she be involved, asked the newspaper? When the front-page story noted that she was under police surveillance, the least *The Journal* could do was to turn its attention away from the deceased to concentrate on the living. It was Nack's turn to lose any sense of privacy in the world governed by William Randolph Hearst. To ensure that no one could beat his *Journal* in revealing more of this lurid crime, Hearst rented out the entire building where the major suspect lived and placed guards around all the entrances to prevent rival reporters from gaining access to the soon to be accused or her living accommodations. It would only be a matter of time, one would suspect, before Nack and the unfortunate Thorn were paraded in front of a judge.

Throughout the summer, *The Journal* kept the drumbeats sounding. Day by day, the case grew more and more bizarre. Recognizing that it was very likely that the state of New York was reserving a place for her in the electric chair, Augusta Nack ultimately confessed her role in the crime but pointed to Thorn as the perpetrator. She told lawyers that she really loved William Guldensuppe but that Thorn had a better income, one that would help her enjoy a life of comfort. The prosecution bought her story. Nack, who was actually the person who dismembered the unfortunate Guldensuppe in a bathtub in New Jersey after Thorn had dispatched him with a barber's razor, finally entered Auburn Prison for a fifteen-year term early in 1898.

Thorn was not as fortunate. He was charged with first-degree murder and sentenced to meet his maker in the electric chair at Sing Sing Prison. Virtually every major New York newspaper followed Thorn's trial, conviction, and sentencing. Even the august *New York Times* devoted a column to the barber's demise on August 1, 1898. Apparently, Thorn walked coolly to the electric chair, followed by his spiritual master, one Father Hanselman. The *Times* reported that Thorn held his head erect while carrying a crucifix in one hand. At 11:17 that morning, the first jolt of 1,750 volts passed through his body, to be followed by a second charge of 400 volts at 4 amperes. He was dead in less than a minute. Following the customary autopsy, his remains were claimed by men named Hippe and Hinchliffe. They were his employers.

In comparison, Pulitzer's coverage of the Guldensuppe-Nack-Thorn affair was quite placid. In fact, the first mention of the case did not appear until page five of the June 30 edition of the newspaper. The story was less than a column long and featured six headlines, none of which indicated the scandal that was about to unfold. The lead, bold headline simply read, "DEEP MURDER MYSTERY," and the article recounted the discovery of the body in the East River and noted that the mysterious oilcloth was the only clue to the perpetrators. The second paragraph, quoted here, lacked any sense of emotion and was quite routine:

The facts are briefly these: the upper part of the headless body of a man was found in the East River on Saturday. It bore unmistakable marks of assassination. On Sunday the lower part of the same body, but legless, was found in the woods eight miles away. Both fragments were wrapped in oil cloth of a peculiar pattern. The head has not yet been found but a diligent search is in progress. There is only one mark on the body by which it may be identified. It bears a scar on one finger.

Unlike the Hearst publication, Pulitzer's paper contained no drawings in the initial story. That would change in subsequent coverage. Finally, on Friday, July 2, *The World* made the Guldensuppe murder a front-page story, supplemented by a medium-sized drawing of Nack appearing in Jefferson Market Court. Pulitzer's coverage of this spectacular case did not have the sideshow impact that Hearst had created. Hearst also pursued certain other aspects of the case, such as the rare experience of being able to report on a devious female murderer. In typical Hearst fashion, he gave her a day in court before the justice system was able to do so. The Sunday, August 1, 1897, edition of *The Journal* supplement *American Magazine* carried a full-length interview with the accused Nack in her cell in the New York jail, the Tombs, complete with extensive illustrations.

In subsequent editions, Hearst seemed to lose interest in the story, preferring to deal with political and social issues that were just as caustic as a good murder tale. As the tempo of rebellion increased in Cuba and as the legal profession in New York retreated behind closed doors to work on the Guldensuppe murder, the focus of sensationalism began to shift. And slowly but surely, Pulitzer would be dragged into Hearst's orbit, the prospect of which he detested. But with survival on his mind, when the opportunity to go head to head with Hearst presented itself in the form of the Spanish-American War, Pulitzer was about to show his mettle.

There is plenty of evidence that suggests Hearst's approach to selling newspapers was not significantly different from P. T. Barnum's approach to entertainment. The great circus and museum man had been dead some six years when Martin Thorn took his razor blade to the Murray Hill masseur, but there is little doubt that the worship of extravagance that he preached for many a year had an impact on the overall social structure of the city of New York. Both Benjamin Day and James Gordon Bennett were no strangers to the kind of hoaxes that Barnum sold as legitimate entertainment. Let us not forget that New York willingly bought into Day's fictional series about life on the moon. It remained for Hearst, as we will see in the next few pages and the following chapter, to prove just how profitable planned exaggeration could be.

As noted in the previous chapter on the use of graphics, Hearst's Sunday supplement of August 8, 1897, had carried the tragic tale of Garrett E. Anderson and his wife. Anderson was a well-known Wall Street broker who had ventured to the deserts of Arizona. The Andersons had started out on a journey of a mere twenty miles across the sands to meet their son at a place called Caverock Station. It took some time before the couple, not to mention their horse, realized that they had gone too far and were undoubtedly lost. The rest of the real-life script could have easily been turned into a movie had such a technology existed at the time.

Anderson fell ill from the scorching heat, and the horse refused to move. Mrs. Anderson realized that unless the party was found and found quickly, death would be imminent. Eventually, a Phoenix-based freighter named John Moore came upon the couple and their wagon. By this time, the day was ebbing into evening. Moore agreed to help the Andersons return to the point from which they had started. Moving slowly to prevent any more heat-driven fatigue and illness, the party took from sunset until eleven o'clock in the evening to make the trip. But alas, the stock-broker was no match for what Hearst's reporters called the Arizona Hell Patch, and he died on the way to rescue.

The coverage of this story rated a full first page, and beyond that, the Hearst reporters convinced Mrs. Anderson, in spite of the untimely death of her husband, to write her own tale of grief. Not only did the widow compose one fairly long remembrance under the provocative headline "HOW I PASSED THROUGH THE VALLEY OF THE SHADOW OF DEATH," she also telegraphed a supplement expanding on the role of John Moore in the tragedy. Moore as well was convinced to relate his view of the incident. Under the title "Death in an American Desert," he noted, "The desert kills, and no man knows why or how. The traveler faints from thirst with his canteen at his lips, his horse drops dead with his muzzle in the trough at the station." Certainly, if this view of the life-threatening qualities of the desert was accepted, few would venture into such an environment.

Along with tragedy, crime became a constant staple in *The New York Journal* of 1897, and it didn't even have to take place in New York. A small railroad in the center of America—the Missouri, Kansas and Texas, known affectionately as "the Katy"—had the dubious distinction of having more holdups per mile of track than any other railway in the country in the closing years of the century. The owners of the line, tiring of the constant interruptions to their service and the threat to their passengers, decided to fight fire with fire. As proof of their success, they mounted photographs of the highwaymen that the company had helped dispatch into the other world, men with colorful handles such as Chicken Elmer Lewis, Skeeter Baldwin, and Cherokee Bill, as well as the only female member of the gang of bandits, Jennie Metcalf, also known as "the Queen of the Rustlers."

Although most of the bandits had left this earth by acquiring a bullet to the brain, there were exceptions, the most notable of which was Cherokee Bill, the youngest member of the gang at age twenty-one. He had the misfortune to get caught alive. Cherokee Bill was reputed to be a person of mixed heritage whose various bloodlines came from African Americans, Creek Indians, and downright mean white folks. He had allegedly bolted from a Sunday school class when he was only fifteen, which launched him on a career of robbing, killing, and pillaging. When his luck finally ran out, he was sentenced to meet his maker at the end of a rope. Asked if he had any last words before the trap was sprung, Cherokee Bill replied, "I came here to die, not to talk."

If murder and robbery were not enough to capture the imagination of his readers, Hearst knew that infidelity on the largest scale possible was a guaranteed winner. His reporters uncovered the marital shenanigans of a man they dubbed "the Modern Bluebeard." The paramour, whose real name was David A. Bates, of Chicago, juggled no less than seven different households with seven different brides, putting to shame those globe-trotting sailors who claimed they had a girl in every port. This generous lover had apparently supported his seven women on a mere $60 a month, which led *The Journal* to refer to him as "A VERITABLE GENIUS ON THE ART OF LOVE MAKING AND MATRIMONY." However, when Bates was negligent in paying a doctor's fee, he set into motion a chain of events that eventually led to the discovery of his unusual lifestyle. No one could accuse him of cowardice: wives four and five lived next door to each other, completely unaware of anything being amiss.

Finally, one cannot leave any discussion of Hearst's extravagances without a mention of his almost demonic worship of things scientific. He devoted a full page, art included, to worshiping at the feet of the inventor Nikola Tesla. Electrical items were beginning to appear with some regularity in the industrial world, and it was only a matter of time before the world could take advantage of this new and inexpensive source of energy. Both Thomas Edison and George Westinghouse were expanding their manufacturing empires through electrical development. At that point, no one really knew whether AC or DC current would come to dominate the electrical industries.

Tesla had come up with the proposition that electricity could be transmitted through the air to all parts of the world. To this end, he had invented a large, eight-foot disc with brass electrodes that he claimed could transmit electrical energy. Tesla told *The Journal* he was confident that one day his device would be able to project electricity as far away as Mars. However, at the moment, the inventor was content to work out the details of sending electrical bursts to ships in the middle of the ocean. *Journal* reporter Julius Chambers called Tesla "the Wizard of Science," a man who had, by his own admission, "ENSLAVED EARTH'S MIGHTIEST FORCE FOR THE USE OF MAN." In spite of *The Journal's* obviously very biased worship of Tesla, he did prove to be a central figure in many of the electrically based inventions that first saw the light of day in the late nineteenth and early twentieth centuries.

If stories of unfortunate death, especially of elite persons, along with gross infidelity, train robbing, and an unquestioning worship of things scientific proved insufficient to keep Hearst busy, then something quite spectacular, such as a war, might help him stay in front of the circulation battles that were plaguing the New York newspaper market. Perhaps Hearst was not the catalyst who sparked the Spanish–American War, but he certainly exploited it to the fullest. Sensationalism and the Yellow Press were about to step out into the world at large.

SIX

THE SPANISH-AMERICAN WAR
AND THE HEARST MYTH

A famous comic once stood before an audience in a northeastern American city and told a story about a soft drink. What happened to the beverage is inconsequential. What happened to the story is enlightening. As it traveled from one person to another, the tale began to take on characteristics that were not included in the version that the performer divulged to his audience. And when the tale finally circled back to the creator, it bore little resemblance to the story as originally told. Anyone who has listened to tales of the "good old days" or corporate war stories related by any organization's senior citizens will certainly recognize the phenomenon. The fine line between fantasy and fact has more than once been blurred in the pursuit of material gain. Nowhere was this more evident than in the New York press wars that broke out in the closing years of the nineteenth century and, in particular, the shifting paradigm of what came to constitute journalistic practice in the coverage of the Spanish-American War.

The New York press and especially those journalists who fancied themselves as gifted storytellers have often been blamed for creating the fervor that surrounded the decision by President

McKinley to intervene in yet one more uprising on the island of Cuba against colonial masters based in Spain. There is considerable merit in blaming both Hearst's *New York Journal* and Pulitzer's the *World New York* for playing fast and loose with the truth in their respective attempts to garner larger and larger circulations. But to assert that these two journalistic enterprises were capable of dragging a reluctant nation into battle is both misleading and erroneous.

The early 1890s were, in all respects, lean years for Americans and their government. But by the midpoint of the decade, things were looking up, the economy was gathering steam, and industrial America was about to take on the world. Those whose opinions mattered most, namely, bankers on Wall Street, were less than enthusiastic about the prospect of a conflict that they felt could undermine the country's new financial growth as well as impact negatively on increasing foreign trade. The business community favored President McKinley's approach of exploring a negotiated settlement of the dispute between the locals and the Spaniards. Initially, the Emporia, Kansas, editor William Allen White denounced American intervention in Cuba. However, like many others, he eventually adopted the basic tenets of Manifest Destiny and, along with financiers such as John Jacob Astor, J. P. Morgan, and Thomas Ryan, became quite vocal in supporting an invasion of Cuba.

Other than the initial opposition to the war expressed by White, there was no real concensus as to what America should do about the festering conflict just off its most southern borders. As Professor W. Joseph Campbell observed in his study of journalism in New York in 1897:

It was [the time] when a choice would crystallize between rival and incompatible visions or paradigms for the future of American journalism—a choice between the self-activated, participatory ethos of Hearst's Journalism and the detached, sober antithesis of that genre, as represented by the *New York Times* and its lofty commitment to "All the News That's Fit to Print." Resolution of this clash of paradigms would take years and result ultimately in rejection of Hearst-style activism.

Although Hearst was a major player in the Chicago newspaper market as well, the same journalistic creed that brought him notoriety in New York brought him criticism throughout the country. In his home base, the *New York Evening Post* had joined the *New York Times* as one of the most vocal critics of Hearst's journalistic vision, calling it a national disgrace and a public evil and denouncing its journalists as sinners. In the Midwest, Victor Lawson, owner of both the *Chicago Record* and the *Chicago Daily News,* was bitterly opposed to the concept of sensationalism. Although war fever was starting to spread as early as 1896, the Lawson newspapers devoted much of their foreign coverage to rewrites of Associated Press copy, a good deal of which was submitted by the likes of Hearst and Pulitzer. The blazing rhetoric was seriously toned down, but when it came to factual reporting, editors and owners such as Lawson were at the mercy of the Yellow journals and their war coverage.

Lawson showed little interest in covering the uprising in Cuba until he attended an Associated Press meeting in New York in December 1896. On his way back to Chicago, he decided to open an office in Key West to cover events on the Caribbean island.

The journalist in charge of the bureau was to hire two more reporters, who would be based in Havana close to the action. Writing to his Florida bureau boss, Lawson issued these instructions:

> While the *Record* is anxious to get "all the news" possible from Cuba, I wish you to understand that the basic principle of its news service is truth. We do not want to fool our readers with sensational stories that have little or no foundation in fact. . . . We deem it of far greater consequence to retain the confidence of our readers than to startle them with sensational stories that must eventually be known as untrue.

Lawson then turned his attention to his major competitor, the *Chicago Tribune.* He accused that journal of transforming suspicion into fact, which in turn fed the hunger for the United States to enter the rebellion in Cuba on behalf of the insurgents. In the face of the bluster coming from Joseph Medill's *Chicago Tribune,* Lawson maintained that his own *Chicago Daily News* also approached reporting on this topic in a "cool, steady, peaceful and conservative" manner.

The farther one moved away from the northeastern seaboard, the less journalists were interested in the goings-on in Cuba. Eventually, William Allen White himself fell victim to the culture of the day in the Midwest that was rooted in various forms of ethnic prejudices, racism, and the almost theological treatment of Manifest Destiny. In neighboring Missouri, the issues were no less cloudy. The process of reformation, prevalent in the minds of most Americans since 1890, became the raison d'être for nationhood. America was going to take its place in the world, and God help any nation that stood in the way.

The new America was to be based on three pillars of nationhood as described by its advocates. The first was the silver crusade, or the campaign for a stable currency based on the free distribution of silver and elimination of the gold standard. The second pillar was nativism, or the desire to rid the country of foreign elements that, in the popular imagination, should not be there. Sentiment existed for sending African Americans back to Africa, and the humiliation of Chinese residents has been well documented. And as official attitudes would soon become apparent to all who could see, America, the only powerful nation without an empire, was about to embark on a military policy that was based on pure jingoism. For journalists in this part of the world, the campaign against the Spanish in Cuba had little to do with freeing that troubled land from Spanish domination.

The Missouri press had a substantial number of members who supported the concept of free silver. In essence, the press saw adoption of the silver standard, if it could be called that, as a direct challenge to the gold standard. They felt that support for gold was just one more way that Wall Street controlled American economic development at the expense of the Midwest and the western regions of the country. In the final analysis, the pro-silver press in Missouri saw the Cuban campaign as a "holy war in the name of freedom, humanity, patriotism and silver against Wall Street, Great Britain, Jewish bankers—the whole 'international gold conspiracy.'" In other words, the tub-thumping going on in the New York press was considered a juvenile, distracting concerto being mounted for all the wrong reasons.

During the time leading up to and including the brief few months of the Spanish-American conflict, there were thirteen daily newspapers published in South Dakota. These journals had lined up behind the two major political parties, the Democrats and the Republicans, and had no hesitation showing their respective biases. Debate over the legitimacy, or lack thereof, of entering the Cuban conflict usually reflected party positions. In most cases, the coverage lacked the blood-and-guts approach of the New York Yellow Press and, with some exceptions, revolved around editorial commentary on the behavior of President McKinley. Democrats and their allies regularly pummeled the president in the press for what they thought was his lack of initiative in seeking a settlement with Spain. Republican newspapers, of course, defended the president's noninterventionist approach, until public opinion began to swing away from it. Eventually, the president lost the support of nearly all of South Dakota's daily journals.

In many ways, some of the journalistic approach seen in the South Dakota newspapers reflected that of the wild and woolly New York press. Three newspapers—the *Deadwood Daily,* the *Pioneer Times,* and the *Aberdeen Daily News*—hopped onto the sensationalist bandwagon, joining the eastern press in an all-out attack on the Spanish-appointed Cuban governor, Valeriano Weyler. Where the eastern and midwestern newspapers divided can be seen in the reasons for publishing such inflammatory materials as they did. The eastern press was involved in a war to increase circulation and profits. The midwestern press was just trying to keep its head above water; feeds from the more rabid eastern wire services were seen as a godsend and little else.

It would seem that if any state were to have stepped beyond normal convention, it would have been Minnesota. It had long been home to viable third-party movements and had elected legislators who were neither Republican nor Democrat. But some would claim that the North Star State's considerable northern heritage, forged by immigrants from Scandinavian countries, could go a long way in explaining the commitment to different forms of political expression. The long and fruitful trek down the liberal middle of the road in municipal, state, and national politics was a state tradition and one that benefited the Land of Ten Thousand Lakes.

In every respect, the press's behavior differed little from that of its citizenry. When confronted with the razzle-dazzle of the eastern Yellow Press, members of the Minnesota press, with few exceptions, refused to become Yellow. It was not that Minnesotans did not take an interest in the events in Cuba, but the issue of free silver, which impacted Missouri and South Dakota, as we have seen, was far more important to local editors than a country occupied by a European power that was a considerable distance away. The dividing line between the Yellow Press of the East and the middle-of-the-road press in the Midwest was quite noticeable in the coverage of the sinking of the U.S. battleship *Maine* in Havana harbor. While the New York press howled for war, the Minnesota press urged caution and contemplation. As observer Mark Welter remarked,

> The Western press not only failed to mimic Eastern tactics but was openly and sharply critical of the lack of professionalism. After 10 days of viewing the journalistic pyrotechnics from the coast, the *Minneapolis Journal* declared that "sensational newspapers play on 'rumors' by manufacturing canards and scare news. . . . There is no story too improbable for these men to invent and circulate."

Our brief look at the attitudes of the American press beyond the borders of the northeastern industrial states will stop in Nevada. Although there was a general feeling that war could be supported by Nevada newspapers, there was little evidence that the press in the desert state followed the sensationalist leads of the New York press. Nevada had larger concerns on its mind, namely, the impact of the decline of the Comstock lode that began in the 1870s and brought a sudden and rough halt to an otherwise prosperous mining economy. To those living on the margins in the state, there was an obvious solution—free coinage of silver.

By the time that the 1890s rolled around, the state political structure was dominated by three major parties: the Democrats, the Populists, and the Silver group. They all supported the issuance of free silver, in contrast to their Republican foes. The tone of the newspapers was generally quite bitter, driven by a paranoia that kept reinforcing the supposition that Wall Street bankers, especially Jewish ones, were behind the campaign to keep the Nevadans down.

In general, the most jingoistic of the Nevada newspapers were also those who supported free silver minting. However,

> the Nevada press did not evidence the sensationalism that characterized many of the nation's metropolitan journals. There were no scare headlines, no pictures, no cartoons, no Sunday supplements, virtually no front page coverage and no evidence that the Cuban situation was being exploited for increased circulation. Nevada papers devoted little space other than editorials to the Cuban crisis.

So, if the Yellow Press was not solely responsible for driving Americans to war, what was? There is little doubt that the Yellow Press made an impact, an impact that will be reviewed in the remainder of this chapter. America was changing. It had suffered through a number of wars, including a vicious internal one, but at the same time, it had become one of the world's industrial and technological leaders. As historian William E. Leuchtenburg noted:

The United States in the 1890's became aggressive, expansionist, and jingoistic as it had not been since the 1850's. In less than five years, we came to the brink of war with Italy, Chile and Great Britain over three minor incidents in which no American national interest of major importance was involved. In each of these incidents, our secretary of state was highly aggressive and the American people applauded. During these years we completely overhauled our decrepit Navy, building fine new warships like the Maine. The martial virtues of Napoleon, the imperial doctrines of Rudyard Kipling and the naval theories of Captain Alfred T. Mahan all enjoyed considerable vogue.

And if one needed to hear it from the horse's mouth, the immortal words uttered by Senator Shelby M. Cullom of Illinois in 1895 offered further proof of a predator on the loose:

> It is time that someone woke up and realized the necessity of annexing some property. We want all this northern hemisphere and when we begin to reach out to secure these advantages we will begin to have a nation and our lawmakers will rise above the grade of politicians and become true statesmen.

In the final analysis, the Yellow Press played a significant role in mustering national feelings against Spain, but it would be a mistake to assume that it enjoyed little or no competition in that quest. In all, Yellow journals were in the minority. As we have seen with the press in the South and the Midwest, there was a significant amount of anti-Spanish feeling in the journals of these areas, but their approach was far more conservative than that of their eastern counterparts. But if the Yellow Press did contribute to the four months of slaughter in 1898, it was because of its ability to reach into the highest offices of the land. There, the Yellow journals were in the majority.

The troubles in Cuba had a long history, one that was constantly being observed and analyzed in the halls of power in the United States. However, at the midpoint of the century while rebels who were holed up in Cuba's hill country took on the legions of Spain, Americans were fighting each other. There was to be no intervention from a country with its own set of difficulties. But American money had gravitated to Cuba, in particular to the sugar trade; Cuban-processed sugar was allowed to enter the United States duty free until the enactment of the Wilson-Gorman Tariff of 1894. It was at this point that the insurgency against Spain was rekindled. It was not the first time that the colonist and the colonizer had come to blows. A decade-long guerrilla war had petered out in 1878 when limited concessions were granted to the islanders, principally the abolition of slavery. However, the main objective of the rebel army was to gain independence for Cuba. And in the rebels' minds, the imposition of the sugar tariff made the crusade even more important.

One of the key questions that continues to be posed focuses on why Hearst was so adamant that the United States remove Spain from Cuban soil and a couple of other places in the world, Puerto Rico and the Philippines. There is little doubt that the publisher regarded a good war story as a fundamental asset in a circulation confrontation in New York. But as his biographer Ben Procter argued:

> Hearst was ever sensitive to the American metabolism of the 1890s that craved recognition by the world community, that exuded pride both in individual and collective achievement, that reveled in the greatness of the United States and its people. He

therefore identified the *Journal* with national purpose and chauvinistic impulses. . . . But without question, Hearst believed that the culmination of all such expectations rested in American intervention in Cuba and the freeing of its people from a "tyrannous Spain," actions that would establish the United States as a formidable power in world politics.

The story of journalistic interaction with the events in Cuba began as early as 1895, when the uprising started. Spain, tiring of having to deal with the rebels, sent General Weyler, captain general of the Spanish armies, to Cuba with orders to crush the rebellion as quickly as possible. The general was no pussycat. He had acquired a reputation for significant brutality, accompanied with little regard for the value of human life. Upon his arrival in Cuba, he ordered the relocation of mainly rural peasants to areas close to military bases. He might as well have waved a red flag in the eyes of American journalists when he clamped a tight censorship regime on what news could and could not be reported from Havana. In many ways, Weyler's actions aggravated an already tense situation. American reporters had to rely more and more on unsubstantiated gossip, much of which ended up being treated as fact.

The Spanish authorities were not without blame when it came to the increasing specter of further hostilities. On March 13, 1895, Pulitzer's the *World New York* reported that an American steamer, the *Allianca,* carrying U.S. mail and flying the American flag, had been fired upon by a Spanish man-of-war, the *Venadito.* The journal declared that the attack, which took place in international waters off Cuba, had been unprovoked. Wishing to avoid any escalation in the unfortunate event, the Spanish admitted the error and apologized to the United States, an apology that was readily and willingly accepted. This story was, in every respect, Pulitzer's story. William Randolph Hearst would not arrive on the New York journalistic scene until September 25, 1895, when his purchase of the *New York Morning Journal* was finalized.

When Hearst did make his presence felt, he did so with a bang. Unfortunately, it was not the kind of bang in which the new owner of *The New York Journal* could take great pride. The *Olivette* incident almost led him into a disaster from which he would have had some difficulty recovering. When *Journal* reporter Richard Harding Davis boarded the American steamship *Olivette* in Havana harbor for a trip home to the United States in February 1897, he was about to become part of a story that nearly destroyed his credibility and did destroy his relationship with William Randolph Hearst. While awaiting the time when the ship would sail, customs officials boarded the vessel and searched Clemencia Arango and two of her traveling companions. The women were suspected of delivering illegal correspondence to rebel leaders in New York City. The officials demanded that a room be made available so that the women could be unclothed and searched in private.

Davis was not amused and immediately issued a report about the strip search to his editors in New York. When the story arrived, Hearst commissioned artist Frederic Remington to draw a sketch outlining the basics of the tale, or at least the basics as Hearst saw them. Remington agreed, and not surprisingly, his final product had little to do with the actual events. His drawing showed a young woman in only the "clothes" that nature had provided her in the midst of a group of leering government officials. An American senator named William Cameron announced he would introduce legislation that would prevent future incidents of this nature. Davis was so furious about the sketch that he sent a letter to Pulitzer's *World* denouncing *The Journal*'s article and Remington's portrayal of the incident. Pulitzer then sent a reporter to Tampa to ask the so-called victim Arango to explain exactly what had taken place on the ship. She confirmed that she had been undressed and searched but added that the investigation had been conducted in private by a police matron. For a time, Hearst retreated from his activist quests, but it would not be long before opportunities to make his presence felt would knock one more time. The haughty *New York Times* referred to the incident as the "rivalry of our esteemed freak contemporaries."

Ironically, Hearst's savior was none other than a Cuban American dentist named Ricardo Ruiz. Late in February 1897, Ruiz had been arrested and imprisoned by the Spanish authorities on suspicion that he was in league with the rebels. Like many other Cubans, he had participated in the ill-fated ten-year war and saved himself by escaping to the United States, where he acquired citizenship. When things settled down, he chose to return to the island, and there he set up a dentistry practice and eventually married and fathered children. When a train thought to be carrying government officials was set upon and robbed by rebels, the Spanish police went looking for Ruiz, among others. On February 20, 1897, the whole world knew about Ruiz and the fate he met in a Spanish prison. That day's *New York Journal's* front-page headline screamed out, "AMERICAN SLAIN IN SPANISH JAIL." There was no mention of the fact that Ruiz had spent the majority of his life outside the United States and had voluntarily returned to his homeland.

The headline was only the opening salvo in a series of articles that would appear in *The New York Journal* in the subsequent days and weeks. Hearst published an article in which he claimed that Secretary of State John Sherman was so incensed by the killing that he advocated war with Spain. Sherman responded to the charge by stating that all he knew about the Ruiz murder was what he read in Hearst's newspaper. Other notables in the high offices of government were also "quoted" in *The Journal*. As a final stretch of the imagination, *The Journal* claimed that Ruiz spoke to its reporters from the grave, telling them that he had scratched vital information about his treatment on the back of a chair while he was being murdered.

The story created a national journalistic firestorm. The *Chicago Tribune* came to the conclusion that Ruiz's death in a Spanish prison had to have been murder. Medill's newspaper offered no evidence to support such a claim. A few days later, the *New Orleans Times-Democrat* repeated the claims. Not to be left out of the increasing hostility toward Spain, the *New York Sun* added its voice to those who yelled "Murder." And the *Boston Herald* accused the Spanish of committing an outrage and insulting American citizenship in its treatment of Ruiz.

It is in this case that we can first see the slippery slope of sensationalism in Pulitzer's newsroom. Hearst was capitalizing on the affair, and others were only too anxious to join his parade. As *The New York Journal* continued to increase its circulation based on its emotional and hypersensitive coverage of events in Cuba, Pulitzer came to the conclusion—a conclusion he would regret later in life—that he had to challenge Hearst head-on by doing what he was doing, only doing it better. As a result, on February 22, 1897, *The World New York* devoted part of its front page to the Ruiz story. The tale included all the gory details, but it did not match Hearst's version when it came to colorful rhetoric.

On the bottom left-hand corner of the front page, a headline that stated "AMERICAN TORTURED AND SLAIN IN CUBA" opened a rather dense and, in spots, quite descriptive reporting on the legacy of the unfortunate dentist. The story forwarded the claim that Ruiz's body showed unmistakable evidence of severe beatings. However, the jail's governor told the press that Ruiz had committed suicide while incarcerated. The American consul general in Havana, Gen. Fitzhugh Lee, disputed the claim and demanded to see the body, which was being held in the Guanabacoa Jail just outside of the capital city. At first, the Spanish refused to respond to Lee's request, but in time, General Weyler's right-hand man, the Marquis de Ahumada, issued the necessary consent forms.

Lee barely made it to the prison before the Friday afternoon funeral service and subsequent burial was to take place. When he finally was admitted to the viewing room, he encountered a squad of guards protecting the plain pine coffin containing Ruiz's remains. Then Lee ordered that his investigation begin. In the words of *The World New York*:

> When the coffin was opened it was found that Dr. Ruiz's face had been so battered with blows and so cut with wounds as to be almost unrecognizable. The other prisoners said that piercing cries were heard from his cell on the night of his death. Gen. Lee could reach no other conclusion than that Dr. Ruiz had been murdered. He immediately ordered an autopsy to be made the result of which will not be known until late today. He cabled the results of his investigation to the State Department but again no response came.

The results of the autopsy were immaterial. The journalists had decided that Ruiz had suffered at the hands of his Spanish jailers and that he had been killed by them. Hearst constantly referred to Ruiz as "the murdered American."

However, the United States did not let the matter drop. The Wednesday, February 24, edition of *The World New York,* under the byline of correspondent Arthur E. Houghton, reported that Spain had agreed to conduct an impartial investigation into the death of Ruiz. The official Spanish investigation concluded that Ruiz had died from something called brain congestion. The press thought otherwise. Although it was too late for the unfortunate dentist, the American ambassador to Spain wanted to get concessions regarding the treatment of other Americans held in Spanish prisons in Cuba. Critical to that demand was the insistence that General Weyler be removed from his command. The Ruiz case became more important to the United States—and Pulitzer in particular—when it was discovered that the newspaper's chief correspondent in Cuba, Sylvester Scovel, was also being held by the authorities.

On August 17, 1897, *The New York Journal* published the sad tale of Evangelina Cosio y Cisneros, a strikingly beautiful eighteen-year-old who had been imprisoned in the Casa de Recojidas, Havana's most notorious prison for women; she was awaiting trial as an accused rebel. The young woman had the misfortune of being the daughter of a prominent but revolution-minded Cuban family. Her rebellious pedigree was not in doubt. Both she and her sister were considered to be dangerous persons by the Spanish rulers. Her father played a significant leadership role in the ten-year war that took place between 1868 and 1878. In 1895, he once again came to the attention of the Spanish authorities, who sent him to a prison facility on the Isle of Pines. He had been there for two years and possibly faced the firing squad when Evangelina conspired to free him. Hearst was determined to use his power as an editor and journalist to spring the young woman from Spanish custody.

Reporter Marion Kendrick's tale of the case appeared under a bold headline on page one, "THE CUBAN GIRL MARTYR." It was difficult not to feel some attachment to Evangelina; a seven-by-nine-inch sketch of her revealed a person who could just as easily have been an American Sunday school teacher. Kendrick noted that in keeping with Spanish judicial custom, Evangelina's conviction as a rebel, when it came, could not be announced until approved by General Weyler. Words from the tribunal were few and far between. Kendrick concluded this was almost certain proof that Evangelina had been convicted and faced a twenty-year term in the prison settlement at Ceuta.

Then Kendrick pumped up the rhetoric. She reported that Evangelina faced the wrath of a military tribunal after "a hideous imprisonment of nine months in a jail filled with the vilest women of Havana." Continuing, she wrote that "there is nothing against the black eyed, sweet faced young girl except that she was in the Isle of Pines when an outbreak of Cuban prisoners occurred and that she is the niece of President Cleneros y Betancourt who heads the civil government of the rebels in the jungles of Camaguey." But what exactly was Evangelina doing on the Isle of Pines? As the evidence clearly suggested, she was hardly a disinterested observer.

As the tale continued to be revealed, the tug on the heartstrings of *The Journal*'s readers increased. Kendrick carefully painted a picture of what life would be like for the unfortunate Evangelina should she be sent to the prison colony of Ceuta, which Spain operated for those whom it considered a threat to its peace. The compound was located on a small island not far off the coast of Gibraltar. Kendrick noted that because of the severity of the place and the type of prisoner usually sent there, Ceuta had never accepted a woman convict. Its population consisted, on one side, of "murderers, ravishers and robbers" and, on the other, rebellious Cubans who were "doctors, lawyers and literary men." And just to add the final coup de grâce, Kendrick wrote:

They work in chains, keeping entire silence. A single word brings the lash of the guard down on the offender and when his day's work on the stone pile is done, he is triced [*sic*] up to the prison yard and flogged until he faints. They are fed on food that has become foul under the fearful heat of the African sun, and they are tortured with all the ingenuity and ferocity of the Inquisition at the pleasure of their guards and governors whenever anything goes wrong at the prison of which they may have knowledge.

For the next three months, New York's grand manipulator was at his best. The *New York Journal* began a campaign in which it clearly placed the subject of the young woman's fate within the context of a gender issue. Let us not forget that at this period in history, women were taking control of their lives and expressing their independence in campaigns to acquire the vote and abolish the consumption of liquor. Hearst was the master of the daily installment; by modern standards, he probably could have been a scriptwriter for television soap operas. He kept his readers on the edge of their seats with lurid details of Evangelina's life behind bars while being subjected to a trial by an obviously prejudiced tribunal.

By soliciting women's groups and campaigning for a petition in the pages of his newspaper, Hearst collected fifteen thousand signatures regarding Evangelina, which he promptly sent to the queen of Spain. Among the signatories were Clara Barton, Julia Ward Howe, Jefferson Davis's wife, and President McKinley's mother. The suspenseful story finally reached an ending when an agent paid by Hearst, Karl Decker, succeeded in freeing Evangelina by bribing her guards and having her scale a ladder to gain entrance to a building with doors to the street. When Evangelina arrived in New York, Hearst arranged a grand rally at Madison

Square Garden for his new icon of freedom. She was eventually dispatched to Washington, where she was greeted by President McKinley. At Hearst's insistence, she embarked on a speaking tour of American women's clubs to thank them in person for their generosity in gaining her freedom from the Spanish. Hearst had enjoyed his first major success. It would not be his last.

There are those who would argue that some of the best scoops come in the aforementioned brown paper bags from people who apparently don't have names or have names that can be quickly forgotten. More often than not, the victims in these cases are persons universally despised by their colleagues or those who are just plain careless; in extreme cases, they have both qualities. Such a person was the Spanish ambassador to Washington during these years of crisis, one Dupuy de Lome. He was certainly no favorite of the American press corps in Havana, who firmly believed that he had hired Pinkerton agents to shadow the reporters to make sure that what they published was favorable to Spain. De Lome was also said to have a slush fund of some $15,000 per month that he used to thwart rebel activities within the United States. De Lome further infuriated American public opinion when, in response to the *Olivette* incident, he boldly declared that Spain had a right to search any American vessel that he felt was not operating in the best interests of his country.

De Lome's downfall began on February 9, 1898, when Hearst's *New York Journal* published a letter written by the ambassador but intended only for the eyes of Jose Canalejas y Mendez, a Spanish journalist and the editor of the newspaper *El Heraldo de Madrid*. In the next day's edition, the Hearst headline read, "JOURNAL'S LETTER GETS DE LOME HIS WALKING PAPERS." Lest any reader be allowed to forget the gory details of the scandal, *The Journal* carried on relentlessly in its campaign against the Spanish. On February 11, Hearst had the gall to declared in a headline, "JOURNAL'S LETTER FREES COUNTRY FROM DE LOME." Hearst's journey down the slippery slope leading to war was further hastened one day later when the headline read, "THREATENING MOVE BY BOTH SPAIN AND THE U.S." And finally, just before de Lome left his office, Hearst released one final salvo against the unfortunate ambassador. On February 12, he cranked up the campaign significantly and wrote, without any sense of the impact his words could create, "SPAIN REFUSES TO APOLOGIZE, ARMS 6 MERCHANT VESSELS."

How de Lome's letter got into Hearst's possession is only partially known. Apparently, the source was the Cuban rebel organization in New York known as the Junta. How the Junta received the correspondence is anyone's guess, but the war-driven folklore around the tale described a dangerous mission in which a rebel soldier broke into Canalejas's office in Havana and made off with the material at the risk of his life. The manner in which the letter got to Hearst is far less important than what it contained, namely, de Lome's candid and very undiplomatic view of no less prominent a figure than President McKinley:

> Besides the natural and inevitable coarseness with which he [McKinley] repeats all that the press and public opinion of Spain has said of [Captain General] Weyler, it shows once more that McKinley is weak and catering to the rabble, and, besides, a low politician, who desires to leave a door open to me and to stand well with the jingoes of his party.

But there were doubts that the letter was authentic. And in this regard, Hearst had the last word. He had managed to collect a series of letters that contained de Lome's handwriting. A comparison between those samples and the script on the letter was conclusive: de Lome was clearly the author. Hearst also reached back into de Lome's past, bringing up the ambassador's caustic comments on the state of American womanhood that he had published in a book called *From Madrid to Madrid*. Not to be undone, *The World* joined *The Journal* and dozens of other American newspapers in demanding that de Lome be recalled to Spain. Once Hearst released the letter to the Associated Press, de Lome's career in Washington was at an end, and the baying sounds of victory cries from *The Journal's* editorial rooms seemed endless.

In spite of the aggravations between the United States and Spain over the Cuban uprising, the two countries had thus far restricted their war primarily to one of words. When the battleship *Maine* sailed into Havana harbor on January 25, 1898, with the consent of the Spanish authorities, the world was about to change. President McKinley had long sought a negotiated solution to the Cuban uprising, but as time went by, it was becoming more and more apparent that the Spanish could not contain the rebellion; it was also apparent that the best that could be hoped for other than a negotiated end to the conflict was a stalemate. This situation did not bode well for American interests in Cuba. In spite of its dislike for the colonial government, the United States had invested quite extensively in the Cuban economy, most notably in the sugar-processing industry, as discussed earlier. The health of this and other adventures could only be negatively impacted by a bloody and drawn-out conflict. As a result, the United States sent the newly commissioned battleship to Cuba to remind the Spanish that patience was becoming less and less of a virtue and that the possibility existed that Americans might enter the conflict if their interests became threatened.

The story of the *Maine* has been well documented by historians who have focused on the Spanish-American War. Nonetheless, to come to grips with the behavior of both of the world's most renowned Yellow journalists, Hearst and Pulitzer, a brief summary of the incident is in order. Sitting just offshore in Havana harbor, there was little for the sailors on the *Maine* to do but watch and wait for the events on land to unfold. For nearly three weeks, the work undertaken by the officers and crew members was of a routine nature. Then, at 9:40 in the evening on February 15, the *Maine* blew up and sank, taking the lives of 2 officers and 264 sailors. The nation was horrified, and war became inevitable. Americans were exhorted to "Remember the *Maine*." And should they have a lapse of consciousness, the New York press corps would do what it had to do to refresh their memories.

Both Hearst and Pulitzer hit the streets in the early morning of February 16 with the *Maine* story. The *Journal*'s exaggerated and grotesque headline read, "WARSHIP *MAINE* WAS SPLIT IN TWO BY AN ENEMY'S SECRET INFERNAL MACHINE." Exactly what this infernal machine was supposed to be was never revealed. Pulitzer, who had ended up second in most of the major scoops that were published during the previous year, was not to be outdone by Hearst when it came to claims about the *Maine*. On that morning, *The World New York* devoted its entire front page to the story, complete with a sketch of the undamaged battleship at dock and a portrait-like drawing of the face of the *Maine*'s captain, Charles Sigsbee, who somehow or other escaped the carnage. The gripping but not overly exaggerated headlines took up the entire top third of the page.

What exactly did these words of wisdom tell readers? The lead and largest headline read, "THE U-S BATTLESHIP *MAINE* BLOWN UP IN HAVANA HARBOR." The second headline started to reveal more details about the situation, stating, "MORE THAN ONE HUNDRED OF THE CREW KILLED BY THE EXPLOSION WHICH OCCURRED WHILE THEY WERE ASLEEP." The specter of innocent bystanders began to make its way into the reporting. The third headline reported that Captain Sigsbee and two officers had survived the disaster but noted that there was, as yet, no certain cause for the explosion, a gray area that would be exploited by both Hearst and Pulitzer as war fever gripped the nation. What the headlines did report on that fateful day was the known fact that the explosion took place near the bow of the ship, but as the final headline noted, it was totally uncertain as to whether the explosion came from within the ship or from under it in the water. In other words, the specter of possible sabotage reared its head. This uncertainty, as well as the other, would also provide cannon fodder for both *The Journal* and *The World*.

In contrast to the acidic coverage coming out of Hearst's editorial rooms, *The World* correspondent Sylvester Scovel's reporting on the incident was downright mechanical. The only bravado in his account dealt with the courage of the survivors in the face of such adversity. Scovel noted that Sigsbee, who was, in his words, "badly injured in the face," was at the same time "very cool in giving orders to his officers and men." He added that "the officers also showed great coolness and valor in giving orders to men. . . . They were in their shirt sleeves having been hurled from their bunks at this moment."

Even the now-dismissed ambassador to Washington, Dupuy de Lome, was sought out for a statement, which appeared along with the other news of the disaster on page one. De Lome reportedly said, "This is dreadful, awful! I pray God this news is not true. Why, I have many dear friends on board the *Maine,* men that I knew intimately in Washington. I should feel their loss more than would most Americans." Continuing to firmly place his foot within his mouth, de Lome praised America and testified to his deep and continuing love for the country and its people. Then he supplied to the Yellow Press the justification they sought in advocating war. "Spain cannot afford to have a war with the United States," he boldly announced. It was music to the ears of the jingoists, who were increasing in number and influence by the day.

As Hearst was clamoring for the conflict to begin, Pulitzer was playing a far more cautious game. Unlike *The Journal, The World* questioned whether the *Maine* was even seaworthy. On the front page, following a somewhat flattering description of this fairly new product of the Brooklyn (New York) Navy Yard, *The World* revealed that the ship has suffered through a series of mishaps. Apparently, its design, which was a prototype for others of its class, was faulty. The ship drew three more feet of water in the forward areas than it did in the aft, causing the vessel to lean forward. Serious corrections had to be made before it became seaworthy. Then, while sailing through a severe storm off the coast of North Carolina, a large wave swept over the deck, and six sailors fell into the ocean. Three drowned. Furthermore, the ship's armor interfered with the water line and weakened the hull in that part of the ship. And to climax this sad tale of incompetence, it was discovered that the hull had the nasty habit of popping bolts, which in turn allowed water into the ship. The *Maine* spent a few weeks in dry dock having these ills rectified.

If there was one person who had plenty to lose if the hunger for war was not abated, it was President McKinley. Knowing that the situation in Cuba was becoming more dangerous by the day and aware of the fact that journalists such as Hearst and their allies were openly clamoring for American intervention, McKinley had steered a middle course, based on the belief that the dispute in Cuba could be resolved by reasonable people making reasonable demands. The effort did not go unnoticed, in particular by McKinley's detractors—among them, of course, William Randolph Hearst. He sent reporters into the field to interview the mothers of those sailors who had lost their lives in the explosion. He gleefully reported that the president, failing to act quickly against the Spanish following the disaster, had been hanged in effigy in Colorado and inspired street demonstrations in both Ohio and Virginia.

Nonetheless, the president stuck to his well-worn path of creative engagement. American pressure in the past had resulted in some limited reforms in the political life of the island. But now, the president was faced with a difficult set of choices. And like any good political professional would do, he set up a commission of inquiry to investigate the affair. On Friday, February 18, Pulitzer published the president's comments on the *Maine* affair on page one. McKinley's press release noted that

> based on information now in his possession the President believes that the Maine was blown up as the result of an accident and he hopes that the Court of Inquiry will develop that fact. If it is found that the disaster was not an accident, prompt and decisive steps will be taken in the premises. The finding of the Naval Court will develop the cause and until that is submitted nothing will be done.

The dedication to fact that had been one of Pulitzer's hallmarks began to erode. Scovel's dispatches from Havana became highly speculative. A headline on the top left-hand corner of the front page claimed that a torpedo had been identified as the cause of the disaster. One Scovel dispatch claimed that "it was not accidental either. Cubans or Spanish floated the torpedo under the waterline toward the Maine's forward magazine, or, while visiting the ship secreted in the afternoon a time bomb near the tons of piled powder" On the other side of page one, Arthur Houghton's description of the reaction of Spain's prime minister Sagasta stood in contrast. When contacted by *The World,* Sagasta remarked, "We were grieved and painfully surprised by the catastrophe to the Maine. We felt it doubly because the sad occurrence took place in our waters." However, *The World* also carried a short story on page four that indicated a Spanish officer had allegedly received a letter from a Spanish military officer in which the visit of the *Maine* to Havana was denounced. The letter declared that Cuban feelings against the United States were running high and further stated that something would happen that would astonish the world. Neither the writer nor the recipient of this letter were ever identified.

In spite of all the confusing and contradictory evidence that pointed in no special direction, William Randolph Hearst and Joseph Pulitzer were well aware they could benefit from the problems caused by the explosion. Hearst offered a $50,000 reward for anyone who could provide information leading to the arrest and conviction of those responsible. In retaliation, Pulitzer sent a crew of divers to Havana to inspect the wreck and draw conclusions. (The Spanish denied them access to the scene of the explosion.) Both newspapers published a cablegram allegedly sent by Captain Sigsbee to the secretary of the navy in which the commander stated that he knew the explosion was not an accident. Supposedly, the assistant secretary of the navy, Theodore Roosevelt, concurred with Sigsbee's conclusions. There was only one problem with the story: the communication was a fabrication.

The fake Sigsbee cable was only one of a number of falsehoods that appeared primarily in *The New York Journal* of William Randolph Hearst. As McKinley was formulating his response to the world, Hearst was piling lie upon lie to get America involved in the Cuban–Spanish conflict. On February 17, 1898, *The Journal* carried an article on page one in which it claimed to have proof that some kind of explosive device, possibly a torpedo or a mine anchored by the Spanish, was responsible for the damage to the *Maine*. A few days later, on February 20, the newspaper declared it now had conclusive proof that the explosive device was a mine, not a torpedo. And on February 25, *The Journal* carried a map supposedly showing all the Spanish mine installations in Havana harbor, something that was hotly disputed by the Spanish authorities. And if one good fib was not enough, *The Journal* claimed that divers hired by the newspaper had gone to Havana and had examined the sunken wreckage of the *Maine*. But as Pulitzer discovered, the Spanish were quite expert at preventing this kind of activity.

In the final analysis, there were no solid conclusions that could accurately point to the real cause of the *Maine* disaster. On March 21, 1898, the McKinley inquiry concluded that the explosion had been caused by a submarine mine. *The World* did not agree, stating that the commission of inquiry had pointed to a torpedo that struck the *Maine* on the port side just above the midship line. The newspaper also declared that this conclusion should have been no surprise because *The World* had been on top of the story and had revealed what was now obvious to one and all some weeks previously.

The Spanish, of course, did not agree with the American conclusions. Although they concurred with the claim that the ship's magazines had exploded, they disagreed on the how. The Spanish dismissed any explanation that included either a submarine mine or a torpedo. To them, the explosion had to be internal, and they suggested that the evidence clearly pointed to that fact. No one saw a tower of water jump from the sea at the time of the explosion, which would have been consistent with an external explosion. As well, the lack of dead fish was curious, for any explosion that took place outside the ship would have killed hundreds, if not thousands, of types of marine life. And finally, the Spanish asked what kind of magician would have been needed to get near the ship to plant a mine or launch a torpedo.

When war was finally declared, Hearst became delirious with joy. Rockets were purchased and set alight in the *Journal* building. The publisher offered a reward of $1,000 to any reader who could provide great ideas for conducting the war. But McKinley finally put a limit to the publisher's ambitions when Hearst offered to mobilize and equip his own unit to fight under the *Journal* banner.

Nonetheless, Hearst was determined to be part of the action. He chartered ten ships at a cost of $15,000 a day to collect information and to feed the nearly forty special editions of *The Journal* that were published at home. He cranked up the publicity to new heights when he announced that he would be publishing a version of *The Journal,* which he named the *Journal-Examiner,* for the benefit of the troops in the field. This odd expression of charity served him well back in New York and in his circulation war with Pulitzer. But alas, the war only lasted for four months. The United States suffered the loss of some five thousand military men in the conflict, but the country gained the Philippines, Guam, and Puerto Rico. And Cuba gained its independence. It would not be long before Hawaii, Samoa, and Wake Island would find themselves the "beneficiaries" of American expansionism.

In the final analysis, there is little doubt that it was the *Maine* incident that finally pushed the McKinley administration into a war with Spain. In spite of the popular myth that William Randolph Hearst provided a war for *The Journal* to exploit, it remains clear to most observers that one newspaper or newspaper editor could hardly have mustered up support for a war if the underpinnings of that support did not exist in the first place. As we have seen, there were other serious issues on the American agenda, such as currency reform, a rising and militant labor movement, and the need to counteract a series of economic setbacks. But in spite of its problems, the United States had visions of international influence and power. The Spanish-American War picked up where the Monroe Doctrine left off.

SEVEN

THE CORRESPONDENTS

The Spanish-American War marked the zenith in the influence of the Yellow Press on American journalism. The man who brought it to this high point was also the person who precipitated the crisis that led to its decline. On September 6, 1901, in Buffalo, New York, Leon Czolgosz pulled out a gun and took aim at William McKinley, fatally wounding the president. Violence against public officials was no rare occurrence in nineteenth-century America, but when a newspaper precipitated the action, well, that was a different story.

As a Republican, McKinley never fit the model of the successful political figure conjured up by Hearst and his like-minded colleagues. Furious with the president for his failure to immediately invoke war against Spain when *The New York Journal* called for it, Hearst embarked on a campaign to alienate *Journal* subscribers and readers from the Republican Party and its best-known figure. Cartoonist Frederick Opper devised a satirical series called "McKinley's Minstrels" in which the chief executive and the Ohio politico and businessman Marcus "Mark" Hanna were regularly ridiculed. When McKinley died some eight days following the shooting, attention turned to the Hearst papers, which were widely and roundly condemned for their wholesale attacks on McKinley. It did not help that the assassin had a copy of an extremely vindictive *Journal* article on McKinley in his pocket when he was apprehended.

Although Hearst was not a direct party to an incident that took place in February 1901 in San Francisco, the overwhelming condemnation of his editorial policies spilled over into the West Coast when the Democratic governor-elect of Kentucky, William Goebel, was fatally wounded. In an editorial credited to Ambrose Bierce, the crescendo building against the Hearst regime was reaching its peak. The normally pointed Bierce penned this little four-line rhyme in keeping with the Hearst policy on Republicans in general and McKinley specifically:

> The bullet that pierced Goebel's breast
> Can not be found in all the West;
> Good reason, it is speeding here
> To stretch McKinley on his bier.

When the poem appeared in the *San Francisco Examiner,* McKinley was very much alive. To Hearst's critics, the poem appeared to call for and justify the slaying of the president.

Hearst retaliated by accusing his detractors of taking advantage of the crisis to spill their venom on his newspapers. In the final analysis, of course, Hearst survived and lived to create a large newspaper and, later, electronic media empire that still exists today. But Yellow Journalism, which eventually gave way to different forms of activist journalism such as muckraking, never commanded the heights that it once did after the twentieth century dawned on Park Row.

It is no secret that Yellow Journalism could never have survived and prospered had it not had the right people in the right places at the right times—people who created and inspired the genre. It worked because it attracted a very special kind of person both in the editorial offices and on the street. Indeed, there was a Yellow Journalism personality. In the editorial rooms, this personality was obsessed with the scoop and being first with the grandest of first-person tales, to the point that there was often confusion in the merging of fact and fiction. It was no sin and Nellie Bly discovered it was no problem to have a hand in creating your own news. As Arthur Brisbane, one of the larger-than-life figures in Yellow Journalism, told *Cosmopolitan Magazine,* the agenda was "to get all the news into the office first, into the newspaper first, on the street and all over the country first . . . and to sift the kernel of fact from the mass of rumors, to exercise discretion and reasonable conservatism without falling behind in the fight for news priority and supremacy." As we shall soon discover, it was one of the Victorian age's miracles that Brisbane did not choke to death on his words. In the field, the attitude prevailed with a company of reporters who were, first and foremost, adventurers—individuals who, as was the case in the Spanish-American War, risked life and limb to get the news home.

It would be a demanding task to explore the mind-sets of everyone who followed orders from both Hearst and Pulitzer and the editors of the many copycat journals that appeared across the nation hoping to jump on a bandwagon where spirit and money supposedly flowed freely. However, the examination of a culture and a set of attitudes that produced this kind of journalism is a less challenging undertaking. In the final analysis, the names of a number of individuals consistently appear every time the concept of Yellow Journalism gets a hearing. The impact of these individuals will be examined and analyzed in the subsequent pages, as fitting representatives for both those who appear and those who do not appear in this text.

If there is one person who best epitomizes the culture of Yellow Journalism, it is Arthur Brisbane. The mercurial Brisbane came out of the journalistic training ground so generously supplied by one of New York's leading media citizens, Charles Dana. In 1887, Dana decided to take on some of the more established evening journals published in New York at that time, under the mastheads of the *Commercial Advertiser,* the *Mail and Express,* and the *Evening Post.* Dana was more cautious about opening a circulation war with the city's leading newspaper, the *New York Daily News.* In fact, Dana did not break the bank at Monte Carlo in funding his new adventure. His *Evening Sun* published only four pages and was priced at a cent a copy, a remnant of the halcyon days of the penny press. But the editor and owner did manage to attract some significant journalistic names to his staff, among them the twenty-five-year-old Arthur Brisbane.

Dana could hardly be called a Yellow journalist, but some of his ideas on how reporting should be conducted were later modified and exploited in the Yellow Press. It was at Dana's knee, so to speak, that the young Brisbane learned the value of telling the tales of human experience and composing them almost in the same vein as a shortened, narrative novel. And New York in the closing years of the nineteenth century was a working laboratory that a newly minted journalist could only ignore at his or her own risk. Its tenements teemed with people who spoke languages that only they understood. It was in New York, hidden behind walls owned by slum landlords, that women worked away sweating heavily over pieces of cloth as they tried to eke out a meager living for their families. And it was in New York that one of the grandest schemes of municipal corruption almost succeeded in remaining undetected until someone delivered a brown paper bag to the *New York Times* and the previously tranquil life of Tammany Hall's notorious Boss Tweed started to unravel.

In most respects, Brisbane was a walking set of contradictions. When he became an editorialist first with Joseph Pulitzer and later with William Randolph Hearst, his writing strongly advocated gender equality and especially the right to vote. Yet at home, he was a domineering, intransigent manager and commander. He constantly sermonized against gambling, but he was also one of New York's leading real estate speculators, a financial pastime that eventually made him a very rich man. He argued against Prohibition, but at the same time, he advised his readers that drinking even in moderation was a bad habit to get into. While Hearst was marching *Journal* readers off to war somewhere in the world, Brisbane's editorials were, for the most part, singularly pacifist. If nothing else, Brisbane shared the zeal for social reform that the two most important journalistic figures in his life, Hearst and Pulitzer, also promoted. Unlike his employers, Brisbane had been brought up in a devoted, socialist family, an influence that he often said shaped his world vision well into the later years of his life.

Brisbane's father, Albert, was a devotee of a branch of socialism known as Fourierism, named after the French intellectual Charles Fourier. Like all Victorian socialists, Fourier had little use for industrial capitalism, which, he argued, had been built on fraud, waste, and exploitation. However, unlike his fellow left-wing activists, Fourier believed the solution was to have everyone move into cooperative societies like the experimental Ruskin colonies that were beginning to emerge across the United States and parts of Europe.

The elder Brisbane's influence was minimal until 1853, when he and a group of fellow socialists founded the New York Free

Love League. The *New York Times* was not amused by this development and accused the league of holding large orgies at its Broadway Avenue headquarters. After constantly being hounded by the newspaper's editor, Henry Raymond, the city's finest began to regularly descend on the clubhouse, although they found little there to support Raymond's vision of a place filled with nonstop debauchery.

His father's approach to the world, a kind of a devil-may-care attitude, was not lost on the younger Brisbane. Journalism was a career that could accommodate young Arthur's life vision, and he knew that from his experiences with Charles Dana. So when William Randolph Hearst, using a few million dollars donated by his mother, began to raid the offices of competitive newspapers in New York, a golden opportunity arose for the ambitious Arthur.

Hearst had been laying checks on competitive journalists both to undermine the competition and to build his own stable of reliable employees. One such person was the editor of Pulitzer's *Sunday World*—Morrill Goddard, a man who made his own significant contributions to the emergence of the Yellow Press. Goddard convinced Hearst that he could not rise to the owner's expectations unless Hearst was prepared to hire the whole staff from *The World*. Hearst agreed, and Goddard, his editors and writers, and the office cat moved into Hearst's *New York Journal* offices. The defection was short-lived, for Pulitzer topped the Hearst offer. But Hearst retaliated, and Goddard and his fellow journalists became Hearst's property in 1896. Goddard's throne was turned over to Arthur Brisbane for what would prove to be a productive but tumultuous tenure under the very watchful surveillance of the owner.

Brisbane must have wondered how he would rebuild Pulitzer's weekend newspaper, which to that point had been successful.

Hearst had not killed the paper with his numerous staff raids, but he had certainly humbled it. Brisbane was initially forced to work with a staff that had also been assigned to both the evening and morning editions. What few in New York realized when his appointment was announced was that Brisbane was a Goddard in both experience and temperament. He had cut his teeth in Dana's London bureau, where he had the good fortune, for a journalist at least, of being present when Jack the Ripper was terrorizing Whitechapel. Brisbane devoted himself to the Ripper tale, often sending back reports so exaggerated and colorful that his New York editors found them to be stomach-turning. As Brisbane himself once noted, he knew that "murder, mayhem and mystery" sold newspapers. When Pulitzer, his second major employer, complained that his precious journal was turning into a late Victorian scandal sheet, Brisbane retaliated by trotting out the circulation figures and the increased advertising revenues. And when Nellie Bly confided in Brisbane that she wanted to return to work at *The World* to escape, in part, from a less than satisfying marriage, he rehired her. The building process was on its way.

It was well known in New York journalistic circles that Pulitzer trusted virtually no one. He had nicknames for his staff and even for some outsiders he felt could harm his enterprise. Employees were expected to spy on one another and report any dubious goings-on to the senior editor, who himself was being spied upon by another of the publisher's henchmen. Needless to say, the activity did not meet with favor among the employees. Cartoonist Walt McDougall noted that the spying caused "suspicion, jealousy and hatred." He related that two editors became alcoholics, one committed suicide, another left the field to go into banking, and one was committed to an insane asylum.

It was Pulitzer's penchant for micromanaging that finally

brought about the professional divorce between Brisbane and the publisher. The cleavage came in spite of the fact that Brisbane was earning the almost unheard-of sum of $15,000 per year. As noted earlier, Brisbane had strong views on most issues, both international and domestic. He wanted to write editorials, but Pulitzer resisted, strongly telling Brisbane that editorials were the exclusive right of the publisher: only the publisher could express opinions, since, as Pulitzer argued, all opinions that appeared in *The World* would be traced back to him in any case.

But Brisbane persisted. While the publisher was on one of his many junkets away from New York, Brisbane took the opportunity to publish a signed editorial in the *Evening World*. Of course, Pulitzer's spy operation proved to be quite useful, and the publisher soon learned that Brisbane had been insubordinate. Pulitzer was furious and suspended Brisbane for a week while telling him that if he wanted editorials in the various *World* editions other than the *Morning World,* he should reprint the commentary from the morning edition. Brisbane was about to fall into the hands of William Randolph Hearst.

Hearst had been disappointed in the performance of his evening edition of *The New York Journal,* and in 1896, he was seriously considering concentrating only on the morning edition. He was being battered by the Pulitzer papers. Pulitzer's *Evening World* was attracting no less than 325,000 readers per day, eight times more than the Hearst newspaper. When Hearst approached Brisbane about a job switch, the old socialist replied that the *Evening Journal* could be prosperous, and to prove it, he, Brisbane, would take a 50 percent cut in the salary he was earning with Pulitzer. But Hearst might have to pay at some point. Brisbane wanted a $1,000 bonus for every increase in circulation of ten thousand readers after he assumed the editor's post. Hearst agreed, and a legend was about to be born.

Brisbane's tenure with Hearst is a story from which mythological tales are made. The editor stayed with the publisher through thick and thin until he died in 1936. He was at Hearst's side when the publisher was clamoring for war against Spain. He defended Hearst when the publisher was accused of precipitating the assassination of McKinley, and he rode arm in arm with Hearst when he ventured into the treacherous field of politics. However, he was noticeably withdrawn when Hearst became infatuated with silent-screen star Marion Davies, with whom he had a torrid affair while still married. Even though it is doubtful that many contemporary figures within or beyond the field of journalism would remember the editor, a monument to Brisbane still stands at the entrance to Central Park at 102nd and Fifth.

To the end of his life, Brisbane was a staunch defender of Yellow Journalism. He was convinced that sensational stories caught the attention of readers and that it was through this attention that newspapers could precipitate real change social change. As he argued:

> The whole human race, according to the highest authority, has been exterminated once already because it wasn't going right and only the rainbow protects it from a repetition. They say the Hearst papers are Yellow. Remember that the sun is Yellow and we need a little sunshine. Think of the colors of the rainbow.

It is somewhat surprising that Morrill Goddard has not received as much scholarly attention as has Brisbane. When Goddard agreed to join the Hearst empire in the Hoffman House bar in January 1896, his *Sunday World* was the most successful newspaper in the United States, regularly topping the half-million mark in circulation each week. Goddard, as an editor, relied closely on the instincts that he had honed during his time on the street as a reporter. It did not take him long to learn that tales normally hidden behind closed doors, such as in the city morgue, had all the value to shock potential readers as the horror of any given situation involving violence. They also had the ability to prime the human curiosity gene to the point that subscribers could seldom resist reading about how nasty folks could be to one another.

In many ways, simplicity in delivering the news was a Goddard trademark. He was a great believer in the potential impact of pictures, arguing that they could communicate dozens of facts more quickly and effectively than the printed word. Pulitzer's *Sunday World* became home to dozens of talented artists, which made the weekend journal the largest publisher of illustrated news in the country. Of course, not one of the pictures escaped the editor's attention, and often, they were returned to the creator spiced with all sorts of suggestive material. Goddard also introduced the concept of comic strips, which, it was often said, were the only section of the *Sunday World* that Pulitzer could read without grimacing in pain.

Journalist and journalism critic Will Irwin has repeatedly stated that he believes Morrill Goddard was the originator of the concept of Yellow Journalism. Irwin points to the construction of the *Sunday World* under his leadership, which, of course, was on the newsstands before Hearst showed up on Park Row. It had large, blazing headlines accompanied by dozens of pictures and lots of misleading and sometimes dangerous information. Goddard actually carried a series of stories that argued that while dinosaurs were thought to be extinct, there were still parts of the world where they lived and thrived and that some of those locations were in the more remote locations of the United States itself.

Closer to home and far closer to the truth, Goddard made his mark by publishing some of the most sensational and investigative pieces of journalism that New York had seen in years. He was determined to get to the bottom of life in the slums, a subject that few would discuss openly for fear of recrimination by evil landlords. So, he hired a clergyman to live in Hell's Kitchen for a month and report back on his findings. He retained the determined Nellie Bly before her marriage to work as an investigative reporter in the wake of her series on abuse at the insane asylum for women on Blackwell's Island, which proved to be a *World* sensation. Bly exposed conditions in sweatshops and a women's jail, while debunking the myths surrounding a popular mesmerist; she also traveled across the country with Buffalo Bill's Wild West Show.

What made Morrill Goddard tick? In 1934, the editor himself provided some insights. In December of that year, Goddard, still editor of Hearst's *American Weekly,* gave a series of six lectures to a conference that was held in New York each year. The collected essays were privately published under the title *What Interests People and Why.* The lectures became one of the strongest defenses for Yellow Journalism and made Brisbane's pale in comparison. Goddard made no excuses for his approach to the profession, even to the point of invoking the Almighty himself:

> The American Weekly has been called sensational. It is sensational. The great events of history have been sensational. The great news events which sell newspapers have, for the most part, been sensational. The great events of the Old Testament which

stand out in our minds were sensational, and the miracles performed by the Savior were, every one of them sensational. Because a thing is sensational it is not necessarily objectionable or unfit to print. The more extraordinary, unexpected and sensational, the more likely to be interesting.

He drew a comparison between the Yellow Press and the then-modern phenomenon of themed magazines. He spoke to the fact that many magazines sold themselves on the basis of publishing some of the best fiction available in the country. But as he pointed out, no matter what activities the central characters became involved in—from illicit love affairs to financial skulduggery and even imaginary murders—the fact remained that the stories were just fiction and nothing else. Would it not be more gripping, he asked,

> if these novelists were able to make their stories narratives of the actual romances, intrigues, crimes or extraordinary exploits of genuine living human beings like the Vanderbilts, the Astors, the Belmonts, real Wall Street captains of finance and real lords who can be called by name and the truth substantiated by quoting court records and illustrated by using their portraits?

There was little reason to doubt Goddard's assertion that the truth was often stranger than fiction. The only problem that could arise from this position was the contentious factor that the editor called the truth. Goddard was in his prime, as were other newspaper barons, as the world around them underwent rapid change. With the centennial celebrations in Philadelphia still ingrained in the minds of many Americans, science and scientific development almost became a national obsession. Of course, this development did not escape Goddard's attention. But the editor was quick to point out that "blundering, half-baked pseudo-science will not do." Perhaps the dinosaurs would not agree.

Goddard felt that his *American Weekly* should do what it could to both exploit the national interest in matters scientific and bring the scientific community to its readers with a regular weekly insert. He told his New York audience on the first night that he spoke to the community that this was indeed a difficult task. Science and scientists were hardly cohesive. They lived and worked in their own special compartments, which separated them and their ideas from other scientists. Goddard treated this situation as a danger to the scientific community that the *American Weekly* had a duty to overcome. No, he did not want astronomers treating the common cold, but he felt that scientists could be sharing more information than they currently were doing. Consequently, the journal would continue its work to aid science by exposing "the fallacies, false teachings and scientific half-truths spread by public speakers or writers in which they were likely to mislead or endanger those not well informed."

In concert with both Hearst and Pulitzer, Goddard was at his finest when he took on the elites. He held the position that these folks were a different class of gangster than those who rose out of the slums to pursue a life of crime. In his mind and, of course, in the minds of the two editors for whom he toiled,

> the malefactors of wealth, position and influence who are the most dangerous and difficult to deal with [are the] oil magnates, debauching cabinet officers, dollar a year patriots sitting on the Treasury steps in Washington to grab and swindle on war contracts, the Power Trust with its paid propagandists, the Paper Trust poisoning the public with its inspired newspapers, steel companies with their secret agents to upset armament limitation

at Geneva, greedy captains of industry sending secret lobbyists to wheedle or bribe faithless servants of the people at Washington, eighty New York Lawyers brought before the bar in one batch for unethical practices, judges stepping down from the bench afraid to have the light of investigation turned on them, a New York police magistrate welcomed home with a testimonial dinner by criminals. A discouraging picture to contemplate.

It would appear that little had changed since that fateful day in the Hoffman House bar.

There were few more tragic figures who plied their trades in the cutthroat journalistic world of New York than Charles Chapin, who until very recently had also been largely ignored by media historians. Chapin was ideally suited for a career in journalism and in the Yellow Press at that. And he not only reported the news but also became the news. In 1918, while still working at *The World,* Chapin ran afoul of his creditors when some of his investments tanked on the New York Stock Exchange. He had been under serious stress for quite some time from both his workplace environment and the financial nightmare that was closing in on him. As a result, he decided that the only solution to his dilemma was to take his own life. He determined very quickly that he was not going to leave his wife behind to clean up the messes in which he was involved. As a consequence of this decision, he shot and killed her, with the idea that he would walk to a neighborhood park and do himself in. But he lacked the courage, especially to shoot himself in front of others. Throughout the night, he traveled to three different parks, and finally, when he saw a newspaper headline declaring that he was wanted for murder, he surrendered to the police. He spent the rest of his life in Sing Sing Prison, where he became renowned for bringing some beauty to the place by tending a number of rose gardens that he had designed and planted.

Chapin made a mark in his early career as the kind of reporter who would stop at nothing to get a story. While working in Chicago, he landed in the midst of a story about drug smuggling:

> I followed a daring opium smuggler over the Canadian border after he had escaped from treasury agents, and interviewed him in a hotel. He talked freely to me about his adventures, but in all the time I was with him he kept a revolver pointed at me. He apologized for his rudeness, said he didn't doubt that I was a newspaper man, but that he couldn't afford to run the risk of being captured. He had taken desperate chances the night before in attempting to visit his mother and had narrowly escaped with his life. For years he had been the most successful smuggler of opium operating along the Canadian border belonging to a ring that had its headquarters on Vancouver Island.

But even Chapin had his limits. When he covered the hangings of the Haymarket anarchists, he found the spectacle thoroughly disgusting and spiritually damaging.

Chapin came to Pulitzer largely through the back door. The publisher was totally unaware of Chapin's exploits in Chicago even after he arrived in New York in 1890. Pulitzer was in Paris in 1891 when he read an account of a massive railroad disaster in *The World*. He immediately cabled his editor, Ballard Smith, and inquired as to the identity of the reporter who wrote the story. When told it was Charles Chapin, Pulitzer told Ballard to give Chapin a large bonus and to make him city editor of the *Evening World*. The relationship would last nearly twenty years. And it would not be long before the name Chapin would send shivers down the spines of many an aspiring reporter and a few senior editors for extra good measure.

During Chapin's tenure, the *Evening World* became unbeatable. Rival editors would send junior reporters to local newsstands to pick up copies of the paper as it arrived. Immediately, the volume would be returned to the city desk, where staffers would determine whether both Chapin's paper and their own had the latest story. If it was an *Evening World* exclusive, rival editors often cribbed the Pulitzer story rather than face the wrath of the publisher's office upstairs.

Superman was not the first man of steel, Chapin was. He literally terrorized the people who worked for him. Even the smallest move that he considered as being out of order could lead to a dismissal. It was thought that he fired 108 reporters during his time with Pulitzer. And the fact that the publisher did not intervene only added to his fearsome reputation. Irving S. Cobb, a *World* reporter, noted that "in him was combined something of Caligula, something of Don Juan, a touch of the Barnum, a dash of Narcissus, a spicing of Machiavelli."

Perhaps the publisher was unaware or did not care about Chapin's worldview when he decided that the city editor could teach his young son, Joe, the ropes of the newspaper business. When Joe Jr. was brought to the dais upon which Chapin kept his desk and chair, he felt the chill that others before him had experienced: "The eyes that stared back at him were like disks of polished flint, deeply set in a gray, stern face. [Chapin's] expressionless mouth was more like a slash set beneath a close clipped, gray mustache. Grayness permeated all of Chapin's features." This was not going to be a relationship made in heaven. After young Pulitzer missed a few days of work, citing in one case as an excuse that the family butler had failed to awake him, Chapin fired him. The senior Pulitzer did not intervene.

There was little doubt that Chapin was a workaholic and expected others to behave in a similar fashion. When the Spanish-American War broke out, he rose at two in the morning and reported to his desk at four. He and his closest confidants never even stopped for lunch, and it would often be midnight before they would retire for the day. In his own words, he was never convinced that he was practicing Yellow Journalism. However, a glance at the *Evening World* might suggest otherwise, although Chapin never stooped to the depths that typified the Hearst newspaper's practice:

> I can't say that I was ever fully converted to such extreme sensationalism, though I don't think my worst enemy would accuse me of being an old fogy in presenting the news to the public. Flashy headlines were not the only innovation of that period. Editors used poster type in every edition, sometimes when the news wasn't important enough to justify extravagant display, so when a really big piece of news came along there was no way of attracting attention to it except by printing the headline in red ink.

Convinced or not, Chapin eventually became caught up in the delirium that a journalist could experience when faced with the prospect of covering a war: that just did not happen every day. But it had its victims as well. Managing Editor Ernest Chamberlain, anxious to get a jump on the story for the *Evening World,* issued an extra containing headlines stating that Congress had declared war on Spain before it did. Chamberlain's misdeed was soon discovered, and all but a few copies of the extra were retrieved. The overworked and exhausted Chamberlain was not so fortunate. His colleagues removed him from his desk and took him home, where he died a few days later. Ironically, within a month, war was declared, and it was up to Chapin to ensure that the *Evening World* was at the forefront of war reporting, just as he himself would be until events in 1918 shifted the course of his life forever.

Like every editor, Chapin had some days filled with good fortune and good luck. When Mayor William Gaynor of New York embarked on a sea journey to Europe, one of Chapin's reporters and his photographer were present for the send-off. Shortly after the mayor walked up the gangplank and set foot on the ship, a man appeared with a gun in his hand and aimed it at Gaynor. Noticing the potential assassin, the photographer raised his camera and took a picture at the precise moment that the gun went off and the mayor fell into the arms of the person closest to him. The wounds were superficial, and the mayor survived to govern another day. The photo of his brush with death was on the front page of Chapin's *World* within the hour.

Within New York's journalistic world, Chapin was both feared and revered. It was common knowledge that he had the most innovative approach to journalism of anyone working in the city at that time. Journalists suffered through his many moments of professional torture because he was able to promise them situations and incomes that few others could do until William Randolph Hearst came to the city in 1895. Many successful journalists tried to imitate his traits and manners. To their colleagues, they were said to possess Chapin stigmata.

Charles Chapin was not the only flamboyant personality who worked with Pulitzer and became a central figure in a shooting drama. That distinction was shared by John Cockerill, a longtime Pulitzer associate who had worked with the publisher back in his St. Louis days. He had a very simple definition of what constitutes news:

[a] hitherto unprinted occurrence which involves the violation of any one of the Ten Commandments and, if it involves a fracture of the Vth, VIth, VIIth or IX commandments and by those people whose names people have heard and in whose doings they are specifically interested by knowledge of their official and social position, then, it is great news.

Cockerill was two years older than his employer, but he joined the Pulitzer camp with a strong background in journalism. He had worked as a reporter, an editor, and a foreign correspondent for the *Cincinnati Enquirer.* When he agreed to go to work for Pulitzer, he was employed by the *Baltimore Gazette.* The move was a bit of a surprise to his friends and colleagues. The *St. Louis Post-Dispatch* was considered to be on the lower rungs of influential American newspapers, hardly the kind of journal that would attract the best and the brightest. Although he never stated his reasons for moving on from Baltimore, historians have speculated that it must have been due to the persuasive powers of Pulitzer himself. The Cockerill-Pulitzer tandem would prove to be one of the more successful partnerships in the age of Yellow Journalism.

Unlike Chapin, no matter what mood Cockerill was in, conciliatory or aggressive, he held the affection of most of those who worked for him. He was not afraid to pass along compliments, nor was he hesitant to rebuke sloppy work right on the city room floor. He was considered to be more energetic and involved in every aspect of the journal than the publisher himself. It wasn't until 1888, after his move to New York, that staffers noticed a decrease in the editor's interest in what was going on in the journal. Everyone had a theory, but Pulitzer believed that Cockerill was being distracted by his new wife, Leonara Barner, a stage actor who was young enough to be his daughter and then some.

Pulitzer and Cockerill had been reunited in New York in 1883, where the approach sometimes called New Journalism or Western Journalism was starting to make serious inroads in the existing journalistic culture. Cockerill was a major factor in the Blackwell's Island insane asylum investigation undertaken by Nellie Bly in 1893. Getting committed to an asylum was not Bly's first choice of a story to pursue. There were far less dangerous but equally inviting tales to be told. But when Bly kept pestering people at *The World* to look over her story ideas, Cockerill agreed to interview her, and he discussed the possibility of doing the asylum story with Pulitzer. In the end, Pulitzer approved the idea, and Bly agreed to undertake the investigation.

The relationship between Cockerill and Pulitzer was one of both admiration and tension. Each man was very strong-willed, and cracks began to show once the two were teamed in New York at the various editions of *The World*. Pulitzer, a confirmed Democrat, was disappointed when Cockerill decided to support Republican Benjamin Harrison in the race for the presidency in 1888, but citing freedom of the press, he decided not to challenge his editor. Another challenge would come later over a seemingly mundane issue of illustrations.

The power of pictures had been recognized ever since Frank Leslie's group of newspapers began to appear on New York streets prior to the Civil War. Until the emergence of halftoning, it was virtually impossible to print a clear, gray-scale photograph in the daily press. In fact, due to the expense of reproducing them, photos did not begin to appear regularly in the daily press until the second decade of the twentieth century. As a consequence, newspapers employed both artists and engravers who more often than not used this technology to copy the content of photos for publication in the daily journals. Slowly but surely, the notion that one could tell an important story through the use of illustration or, at the very least, anchor a major story by pulling in readers through pictures became an accepted part of the way newspapers sought readers.

During the mid-1880s, Pulitzer was becoming increasingly dismayed with the use of illustrations in his journals. He was primarily a word person. He was also not overly pleased with the mounting costs entailed in using both an artist and an engraver, even though this was a secondary consideration. Pulitzer ordered Cockerill to remove the illustrations from *The World* newspapers. With great reluctance and possibly after a stormy confrontation with the publisher, Cockerill complied. Almost immediately, circulation plummeted. Cockerill ordered that illustrations be returned to the newspapers, and, as he recalled, the newspapers "illustrated everything from advertisements, to death notices, and the circulation went up by leaps and bounds." Pulitzer was on the verge of losing control of his own creations.

At the dawn of the final decade of the nineteenth century, anyone who knew anything about newspapers could see that the Pulitzer empire was a great success in terms of both readership and income. The situation was not lost on two major players, business manager George Turner and editor in chief John Cockerill. Both men wanted a significant share of the spoils, and when Pulitzer refused to help line their respective pockets, the relationship between the employer and his employees grew increasingly tense and counterproductive. Pulitzer returned from a trip to Europe to confront the two dissidents, and when the smoke settled, Turner had been fired and Cockerill was about to be exiled to St. Louis, a journey he was unwilling to make. As a result, he resigned; two weeks later, he became the editor of the morning edition of the newly named *Commercial Advertiser.*

As the years passed, Pulitzer had time to reflect on the Cockerill case. When the journalist chose to leave *The World New York,* Pulitzer referred to him as "the Custer of Journalism, handsome and intellectual, a fighter if there was fighting to be done and infinitely proud to be a newspaperman." Pulitzer began to have second thoughts about his separation from his favorite editor. He repeatedly tried to lure him back to *The World,* but Cockerill was too busy being a newspaperman. He had left the *Commercial Advertiser* after a short sojourn and had taken up the post of foreign correspondent for the *New York Herald.* In 1896, he died in a barbershop in Egypt. The executor of his estate was none other than Joseph Pulitzer.

Compared with Goddard and Brisbane, Cockerill was closer in temperament on the sensationalism issue and its role in journalism to Charles Chapin. However, he often threw caution to the wind and printed material that may not have been substantiated. And like Chapin, he, too, became the centerpiece in a very disturbing tale of violence. He ended up pumping bullets into another human being, an act that clearly threatened not only his career but his life. The victim was a prominent St. Louis lawyer named Alonzo Slayback, who had also been a Civil War hero on behalf of the Confederacy. However, it was not Slayback who had provoked Cockerill but his law partner, Col. James O. Broadhead. The *St. Louis Post-Dispatch* had been on a nonstop and rather virulent campaign to prevent Broadhead from running for Congress. Cockerill's editorials had accused the colonel of being involved in corruption, paybacks, and numerous other forms of financial misbehavior. Slayback came to Broadhead's defense, accusing the *Post-Dispatch* of being a blackmailing rag and all those associated with it blackmailers themselves.

Eventually, Cockerill and Slayback came face to face with each other at an Elk's Club meeting. Slayback denied calling Cockerill

personally a blackmailer. But he did note that it was unlikely that
Pulitzer was behind the attacks on Broadhead, since the publisher
had been in New York for quite some time. However, the night
before the shooting, Slayback once again found a public forum in
which to lay a heavy hand on Cockerill and his newspaper. Cockerill was not the type of person to take this without a response. He
resurrected a strongly worded piece of invective from a young
lawyer named John Glover, who had also had a serious confrontation in a courtroom with Slayback. Cockerill published Glover's
card in the *Post-Dispatch,* much to Slayback's chagrin.

On October 13, 1882, Slayback entered the journal's offices
with vengeance on his mind. He confronted Cockerill, who was
meeting with his business manager, John McGuffin, and Victor
Cole, the composing room foreman. Apparently, Slayback attempted to slap Cockerill's face and demanded that the Glover
item be retracted. While the confrontation was going on, Slayback
noticed Cockerill's revolver lying on the desk. He then pulled out
his own pistol and pointed it at the editor. Then things got confusing. It seems the business manager jumped Slayback and succeeded in rendering his pistol inoperative. At the same time,
Cockerill grabbed his own gun and shot Slayback in the chest,
killing him instantly. Cockerill was never indicted for the shooting, and St. Louis buzzed with rumors that Pulitzer had called
upon his political friends to quash any further action. In terms of
both direct intervention in an affair and the style of reporting that
created the trouble to begin with, the St. Louis experience would
influence Cockerill when he took the reins of Pulitzer's New
York publications.

Thus far, it has been argued that the kind of editor that Yellow
Journalism attracted was a person who was not afraid to both report
and create the news. And when Yellow Journalism at last reached

the peak of its influence during the Spanish-American War, the major journalists who covered that conflict were also driven by the spirit of the scoop and a sense of rivalry with their counterparts from other journals. In some cases, in particular those of three major reporters, there did not seem to be a clear dividing line between fact and fiction or between reporting and participation.

Of the three journalists who will be highlighted in the remaining pages of this chapter, James Creelman best epitomized what it meant to be a reporter during the heyday of Yellow Journalism. It was Creelman who claimed he was present when the now-disputed wires between William Randolph Hearst and Frederic Remington were sent—those correspondences in which Remington advised Hearst that nothing was going in Cuba after the publisher sent him there to cover a local uprising and Hearst replied that if Remington could stick to supplying pictures, he himself would provide the war to go with them. Unfortunately, Creelman was in Europe at the time the correspondence allegedly took place, and no other witnesses to the events ever came forward. It was not the first time that Creelman had added a bit of color to spice up a news report.

Creelman came to prominence in New York after an illustrious and adventurous career as an expert interviewer on the international stage. He was not an American. He had been born in Montreal, Canada, but gravitated to the New York journalistic scene quite early in his career. From there, he developed contacts around the world that got him into the inner sanctuaries inhabited by some of the globe's more interesting personalities. He interviewed Count Leo Tolstoy on the nobleman's views on modern marriage. He lectured Pope Leo XIII on the strained relationships between Catholics and Protestants, in particular from the Catholic point of view. He traveled to the plains of the West to interview the aboriginal chief Sitting Bull.

All the signs that indicated Creelman could find professional comfort with the likes of Hearst and Pulitzer were there early in his career. In 1878, at the tender age of nineteen, he accepted an unusual challenge while working as a cub reporter on the *New York Herald*. During a particularly nasty day in the winter of that year while the young reporter was warming himself by the stove in the city room, an editor approached him with a story idea. It had come to the editor's attention that an inventor was claiming he had created an unsinkable suit that would keep people from drowning if they had the misfortune to be involved in a marine disaster. Creelman was urged to contact the inventor and try the suit out for himself. But his boss was a cautious man. He wanted the young reporter to drop by the obituary desk on his way out of the office just in case.

Creelman found the inventor and donned the suit, and with the inventor also equipped with his creation, the two men jumped into New York harbor not far from Fulton Street. The suits worked perfectly, but they lacked the motive power needed to get the hapless reporter and the terrified inventor back to the shore. The currents were moving toward the open ocean, and the two drifted out to sea until they had the good fortune to be spotted by a fishing boat and rescued. Then, at the tender age of twenty-one, Creelman was sent to cover a family feud in the Appalachian Mountains, where he spent more time dodging bullets than writing the tale of the Hatfields and the McCoys.

Creelman often dined at The Ship, a seafood restaurant near the New York docks. The eatery was owned by a flamboyant Irishman named Paul Boynton, who, along with dispensing seafood, was also an amateur deep-sea diver. On one of Creelman's visits, he and Boynton began discussing a British man-of-war that was visiting New York. It was moored at a pier close to The Ship. Boynton, citing his nationalistic, Irish sentiment, was not amused. As the night progressed, the restaurateur told Creelman that any diver worth his weight could get near enough to the ship to attach a bomb to the hull. Boynton offered to demonstrate his technique. The two set out in a borrowed boat to which was attached a weighted keg that looked like an explosive device. As the two daredevils approached the ship, they were caught in the floodlight that the crew used to scan the water for intruders. Boynton and Creelman were immediately apprehended by the British crewmen, who saw no humor in what they had done. After a lengthy interrogation, both were freed. It was this kind of reckless bravado that would characterize Creelman's reporting on the Spanish-American War.

Creelman learned early in his reporting career that sensationalism attracted readers, especially if that sensationalism had something to do with horrible atrocities. When he moved from the *New York Herald* to Pulitzer's *The World* in the early years of the 1890s, he was in a perfect situation to put his ideas to the test. Japan and China had gone to war over which country was going to end up running the Korean Peninsula. Creelman was on the scene when Japanese forces entered Port Arthur in Manchuria in 1894 and began, according to the reporter, to systematically eliminate the local population in the most savage way known to man at that point in history. He wrote:

> The Japanese troops entered Port Arthur on November 21 and massacred practically the entire population in cold blood. The defenseless and unarmed inhabitants were butchered in their

houses and their bodies were unspeakably mutilated. There was an unrestrained reign of murder which continued for three days. The whole town was plundered with appalling atrocities. The Japanese lapsed into barbarism. All pretence that circumstances justified the atrocities are false. The civilized world will be horrified by the details. The foreign correspondents, horrified by the spectacle, left the army in a body.

Creelman claimed that he had been offered a bribe by the Japanese invaders to look in another direction. He cabled Pulitzer that he had refused. He did not explain why the Japanese, who seemed to have little concern about massacring a whole town, would hesitate to have the reporter join the unfortunate citizens of Port Arthur below the ground.

However, as time marched on, Creelman faced challenges to his version of what took place at Port Arthur. The *New York Tribune* called the account "reckless sensationalism." The backlash to Creelman's distorted report among other journalists rose dramatically in the United States, to the point that the ambassador to Japan decided to make some serious inquiries. Edwin Dun left few stones unturned, tracking down and interviewing anyone he could find who had knowledge of what the Japanese did or did not do at Port Arthur. Dun concluded that Creelman's reporting was "sensational in the extreme and a gross exaggeration of what occurred." Yet that judgment would not deter Creelman's approach to journalism, as his reporting in the Spanish–American War would demonstrate.

By 1896, Creelman's reports on the Sino-Japanese War had entered into history. The correspondent had been sent to Cuba by Pulitzer to cover what would prove to be a rather bloody uprising against the Spanish colonial authorities. Spain was a declining

military and colonial power at that time, and the prospect of conducting a protracted guerrilla war, with all the problems inherent
in that method of warfare, was unappealing to Madrid. So, the
Spanish government decided to try to end the uprising as quickly
as possible. Officials sent one of their top generals, Valeriano
Weyler, to Cuba with explicit orders to do what he had to do to
stop the insurgency.

Shortly after his arrival in Havana, Creelman met the captain
general face to face:

> He was a short, broad shouldered man, dressed in a general's uni-
> form with a blood red sash wound around his waist. His head was
> too large for his body. The forehead was narrow, the nose and
> jaws prominent and bony; the chin heavy and projecting. The
> sharp lower teeth were thrust out beyond the upper rows, giving
> the mouth a singular expression of brutal determination. The
> eyes were gray and cold. The voice as harsh and guttural—a trace
> of his Austrian ancestry—and he jerked his words out in the curt
> manner of a man accustomed to absolute authority. It was a smile-
> less, cruel face, with just a suggestion of treachery in the crow's
> feet about the eyes, otherwise bold and masterful.

The good general, as Creelman would discover, was not a person
to be tampered with. But Creelman was determined.

Key to Weyler's strategy was the belief that if one separated the
population from the insurgents, the movement would die on the
vine. Weyler had created large camps called reconcentrados on the
outskirts of the island's towns and cities. They were guarded by
regular Spanish troops and were difficult to penetrate. Creelman
continued to hear tales in Havana that conditions in these settle-
ments were far from ideal. In fact, he had also heard there were
numerous deaths in the camps that were not being reported. As

well, rumors abounded that the Spanish army was systematically killing off the local and undefended population. This information was a godsend for a reporter such as Creelman. Once again, he dipped into his bag of tricks and dusted off the atrocity angle.

Creelman's first report hit the front pages of *The World* on May 1. It was, to say the least, a shocker. Pulitzer considered the report important enough to give it a full four columns. The reporter had been tipped off that Spanish soldiers were systematically killing civilians in the village of Campo Florida, near Havana. In typical Creelman fashion, he hired two Cuban guides, and the trio made their way to the village under the cover of darkness. There, they uncovered the bodies of thirty-three victims, all with their hands tied behind their backs. They were clearly not insurgents. Creelman published the names and death dates of all the victims and sent Weyler into a rage.

The reporter composed stories in Havana claiming that Spanish troops on the hunt for rebels had invaded hospitals and had lined up patients and shot them. The victims were primarily male, and their wives and children, according to the reporter, were forced to witness the savagery. Creelman also claimed that Cuba's roadsides were littered with corpses of victims of the famine and disease that were rampant in Weyler's concentration camps. When he was shown Creelman's articles, the general erupted. He ordered the correspondent to leave Cuba immediately or face the consequences. Exactly when Creelman left the island is still a mystery. Back in New York, *The World* reported that he was in hiding in Havana, writing more lurid accounts of Spanish cruelty. From August to November 1896, *The World* carried regular atrocity tales from its Cuban correspondent, wherever he may have been. Creelman, it appeared, had decided to become a propagandist for the Cuban rebels.

Cuba was now on the agenda back in the United States, where sympathy for the rebel cause was gaining support. The New York–based Cuban government in exile, known as the Junta, had approached the Republican Party to ask it to put a pro-Cuban plank in its 1896 convention program. The move was endorsed by the *New York Sun,* a step that clearly propelled both Hearst and Pulitzer into the Cuban support business. Creelman had lobbied key figures from both parties to ensure that American support for Cuban independence would not become a political football on the hustings that year.

It has often been argued that great actors actually become, spiritually at least, the characters that they bring to the stage and to the cinema. In many respects, the same can be said of determined reporters, but James Creelman almost took it one step too far. When war finally came to Cuba, the American fleet decided to dispatch a large contingent at Santiago de Cuba, where there was a navigable harbor that would greatly assist with the disembarking. As the American troops landed and proceeded inland, they came upon a fortified structure at a place called El Caney. Creelman, now working for Hearst, was with the soldiers, and he felt that he knew the best way to attack the fort with the fewest casualties. He continued to press his ideas on the officers on the scene, and finally, one told him to lead the charge. He concurred and ran about two hundred feet in front of the troops. When he arrived at the fortress, he discovered that only a few of the original defenders remained and that most of them had been severely wounded in the bombardment that preceded the capture. But Creelman, acting as a soldier this one time in his life, accepted the Spanish commander's surrender and turned his sword over to the American military.

Creelman's military adventures on that particular day were far from over. Following the surrender, he noticed that the Spanish flag had been knocked to the ground, and he set out to claim it. Suddenly, he felt a sharp pain in his back and realized that he had been shot by a wayward Spaniard who was unaware of the surrender of his mates. In great pain, the reporter was removed from the scene of the action, all the time wondering how he could finally write his dispatch and get it to the ship some ten miles away. Unexpectedly, he heard a familiar voice—the voice of his employer, William Randolph Hearst. Creelman explained his dilemma, and the publisher agreed to take Creelman's story and send it off.

In the final analysis, Creelman was a true practitioner of the art of Yellow Journalism. He sincerely believed that it was "that form of American journalistic energy which is not content merely to print a daily record of history, but seeks to take part in events as an active and sometimes decisive agent." In many respects, Yellow Journalism was the precursor of today's public journalism. For Creelman, the culture of Yellow Journalism was something to be revered. He turned on his critics:

> How little they know of "Yellow Journalism" who denounce it! How swift they are to condemn its shrieking headlines, its exaggerated pictures, its coarse buffoonery, its intrusion upon private life and its occasional inaccuracies! But how slow they are to see the steadfast guardianship of public interests which it maintains! How blind to its unfearing warfare against rascality, its detection of prosecution of crime, its costly searchings for knowledge throughout the earth, its exposures of humbug, its endless funds for the quick relief of distress.

Like Creelman, Sylvester "Harry" Scovel had the blood of an adventurer running through his veins. And like Creelman, he sensed a good story in the rebellion against Spain that was taking place in Cuba. Both Creelman and Scovel wanted Pulitzer to send them to the island to report firsthand on what was taking place there. Pulitzer finally relented, deciding that Creelman would be better equipped to scour the city of Havana for news about the ruling Spanish authority and Scovel had the experience and talents to seek out the rebels and report on what they were up to. That decision came close to backfiring.

Scovel was an unlikely candidate for a job as a top-flight reporter. Everything in his life indicated that he was, first and foremost, out for a good time. Stability was hardly a word he understood or used. He had been born into a religious Presbyterian family on July 29, 1869, in Pennsylvania's Allegheny County. He had been sent to college at the age of nineteen in order to prepare himself to fulfill his parents' desire that he enter the clergy. The young Sylvester had other plans, though, and he left his postsecondary education without completing his degree. He would later return to Wooster College to pursue a career as an engineer, but in his youth, it was the lure of adventure that eventually drew Sylvester Scovel to journalism.

In introducing its newest personality after he joined the newspaper, *The World* noted that "from his earliest boyhood [Scovel] showed a daring spirit and a fondness for sports." Sports was not his only pursuit. He spent a year on a cattle ranch on the western plains, where he took up roughriding with a vengeance, developing a serious expertise in the sport. His adventures also took him to ranches in Colorado, Wyoming, and Utah. However, being a ranch hand was not the kind of endeavor that brought a decent living. He retreated from the West and took up residence in Cleveland, where he entered the hardware business. But selling nails, nuts, and bolts hardly brought out the kid in Scovel, and he finally gave it up. His next "career move" took him to the Cleveland

Athletic Club, where he became general manager. His spare time was spent with the First Cleveland Troop, a well-trained and effective state militia unit. His membership in this group only whetted his appetite for becoming involved in more things militarily. Sylvester Scovel had all the grit it would take to become a success in the world of Yellow Journalism, although his entry into the genre was never planned.

In 1895, the lure of the fight in Cuba could no longer be denied. Scovel was off to report on a war. He had contacted a number of newspapers and promised to furnish them with firsthand reports from the rebel side of the fence. He left his residence in Havana to journey into the interior, where the majority of rebel activity was taking place. He spent about six months with the guerrilla army of Gen. Maximo Gomez before returning to the capital; there, the ruling Spanish authorities ordered him to leave the island. Apparently, Scovel then went into hiding for a while. In the meantime, his work had come to the attention of Pulitzer, who ordered his Cuban bureau chief to make an offer to Scovel to join *The World* and return to Gomez and his fighters. Later, Scovel left Cuba and returned to New York to work on several assignments in the country before once again convincing Pulitzer to send him back to the island.

Scovel had acquired the confidence of the guerrilla leader on a number of counts. First and foremost, he could communicate with the general in Spanish, although Scovel could hardly claim full fluency. Since his conversations were in the native tongue of the chief rebel, there was no suspicion that he was hiding something from his hosts. To do so would be quite dangerous anyway. He traveled on horseback regularly, carrying his worn-out typewriter with him. He chose to remain unarmed. As his reporting began to get under the skin of the Spanish government in Havana, it only strengthened his credibility with Gomez and his ragged band of fighters.

After meeting some of his competitors from newspapers such as *The New York Journal* and *New York Herald*, Scovel quickly learned the value of beating his opponents with a well-timed scoop. For him, doing so was simply an extension of the sense of adventure that had driven him most of his life. However, his zeal left something to be desired. In its haste to get its stories into print in the continental United States, *The World* either only lightly edited Scovel's copy or, in some cases, ignored even glaring errors in his transmissions. In this respect, Scovel shared a journalistic culture with the likes of James Creelman.

If one felt that Creelman's graphic accounts of atrocities in Cuba could make one's skin crawl, there would be no relief in the passages composed by Scovel. He told his readers that the Spanish were attempting to destroy the Cuban economy by burning sugarcane fields. To accomplish this feat, he claimed that soldiers doused snakes in inflammables, set them on fire, and freed them to wriggle their way through the cane fields, where they ignited the stalks of the plants before finally expiring due to their injuries. Scovel admitted to Creelman that the tale was largely fictional but believed he was forced to write this kind of tale because Pulitzer was having second thoughts about reporting that told lurid tales of Spanish atrocities against humans. The publisher drew the line when a dispatch told of an intoxicated Spanish officer who had murdered fifty old men, cut up their bodies, and fed their remains to a pack of dogs. By this standard, the tale of smoldering snakes seemed positively passive.

On a later junket to Cuba, Scovel spent some time in the

province of Pinar del Rio. It was there that he explored the relationship between the Spanish occupiers and the local population. He told of one Spanish soldier's dealings with a female captive from whom he was trying to extract information. The woman, at least in the mind of the soldier, was not being cooperative, so he tore off her dress. The captive began to cry uncontrollably, but that did not bother the inquisitor. After removing her dress, he still did not hear what he wanted, so he pulled out his sword and began to slash the unfortunate victim until she passed out and ultimately died in a pool of her own blood. According to Scovel, she was not the only one to suffer terribly that day. Others lost their heads, which were hung on the door of the local grocer. Only when the sun went down did the locals had enough courage to retrieve the bodies and bury the victims. As with most Scovel tales of atrocity, no corroboration was provided.

On his second sojourn in Cuba, Scovel got himself into serious trouble. He had been arrested by a small band of Spanish soldiers because they mistook him for a mercenary called El Inglesito. The soldiers actively debated whether or not to shoot Scovel on the spot. Fortunately for the reporter, they chose to hand him over to the Spanish authorities, who at once declared him to be an American spy and a colonel in the rebel army. Scovel denied both charges, but the Spanish were not convinced. He was sentenced to death by firing squad.

Specifically, Scovel faced four very serious charges. He was accused of communicating with the enemy, which in itself was a capital offense; passing Spanish lines without permission, which he did when trying to find a place to file his reports; traveling without a military pass, which, of course, was not required by the rebel army with whom he spent most of his time; and obtaining a false police pass under a false name. It was not until the day of his scheduled execution that he finally convinced Spanish authorities of his real identity.

There was a very good possibility that Scovel would have faced an array of loaded guns at a prison in Cuba had not Pulitzer decided to turn up the journalistic heat on the Spanish. As noted earlier, Scovel's case was aided and abetted by the unfortunate passing of Ricardo Ruiz in the custody of the Spanish. As related in the earlier chapter, Ruiz, although born and brought up in Cuba, had emigrated to the United States in order to practice dentistry. He had taken out American citizenship as well. Eventually disillusioned with life in the country, he returned to Cuba, where he set up a busy practice. However, in the heat of the rebellion, Ruiz was accused of being a rebel soldier and was promptly arrested. Under very suspicious circumstances, he died in prison. In order to free Scovel, Pulitzer felt that the Spanish had to be portrayed in the worst possible light. Hearst and *The New York Journal* also took up the battle cry in Scovel's defense.

The Hearst paper printed a wildly distorted tale of misdeeds under the headline "AMERICAN SLAIN IN SPANISH JAIL," in which the story of the unfortunate Ruiz was related in all its gory details, many of which were figments of Hearst's fertile imagination. Pulitzer, who had been pressuring American politicians in the Scovel case and organizing massive defense meetings, jumped on the bandwagon with Hearst in order to save his wayward reporter. The campaign worked. While the authorities were debating Scovel's fate, he was given a cell with a carpeted floor and a rocking chair, gifts from the wife of the U.S. consul in Havana. He was not denied creature comfort.

Although he was facing a death sentence, Scovel was not to be left out of the biggest story of his career. He wrote a daily account of his life at the hands of the jailers. The wife of the American consul visited Scovel on a daily basis and was his contact for smuggling out his reports. In one of his communiqués, he denied a charge by the Spanish ambassador that he was nothing more than a rebel himself. He also related that he was given numerous opportunities to escape but feared being shot if he attempted to do so. He was soon released.

There is little doubt that Scovel was a fellow traveler with Gomez's troops. His first report upon being released by the Spanish described a skirmish in which fifteen hundred Cubans had been harassing some three thousand regular Spanish troops. He claimed that during the battle, he had been shot in the leg. However, he was reluctant to provide any substantial proof of the incident.

Scovel's journalistic career became much easier when, in 1898, the Spanish government recalled Captain General Weyler, who had proven to be a scourge to all American journalists when he lowered the tight cap of censorship shortly after arriving to conduct the war against Gomez and his followers. He was replaced by the more amenable Gen. Roman Blanco. In spite of a relaxation in the relationship between the population and the Spanish and the American reporters, life was still extremely difficult in Cuba. Scovel reported that homelessness was a national tragedy. He quoted the U.S. vice-consul when he remarked that he thought that about one-third of Havana's population of fifty thousand went without food and shelter on a daily basis. Even President McKinley was moved by Scovel's story. He donated $5,000 of his own money for a Red Cross relief drive.

It has often been claimed that good journalism can be a creature of luck, of being in the right place at the right time when something of great significance happens. Scovel was the recipient of such luck on the evening of February 15, 1898, while dining in a Havana restaurant with his wife. A loud sound coming from the harbor shook the restaurant with a vibration that Scovel felt in his seat. The American battleship the *Maine* had been destroyed and now lay on the bottom of Havana harbor. Although its captain, Charles Sigsbee, and one other officer had survived, the blast took the lives of 269 American sailors. Needless to say, Scovel left his dinner and hurried to the waterfront. His first report to New York basically said that the ship had been destroyed, but he refused to speculate on a possible cause. His caution did not last long. In his report the next day, he included several rumors about the incident, especially one that claimed a doctor had overheard discussion of a plot to blow up the ship. He quoted a so-called dynamite expert who declared that the explosion was no accident. And he reported that Captain Sigsbee's report, which blamed the Spanish, had been suppressed. Scovel was proving beyond a shadow of a doubt that he clearly belonged in the world of Yellow Journalism. His pedigree was never in question.

The Spanish argument that Scovel was an American spy was not without merit. He had been carefully examining Spanish installations wherever he went and dutifully reported his findings back to the American military. He also carried messages from the American high command to General Gomez in the interior. In every respect, he was the Victorian version of Mata Hari, and if justice had prevailed, there was a fairly good chance that he would have suffered the same kind of fate, which, of course, he had duly earned. At any rate, by 1899, calm was settling over the Cuban countryside, and Pulitzer decided that Scovel was no longer needed in Havana. He offered to send his star reporter to Europe to be his chief correspondent. But journalism was losing its luster for Scovel. He told Pulitzer that he wanted to return to his first profession, engineering, and he did.

At least initially, Richard Harding Davis had little in common with people such as Arthur Brisbane, Morrill Goddard, Charles Chapin, James Creelman, and Sylvester Scovel. He plainly did not fit into the mold of a Yellow Press reporter, yet in his early career in New York, he was attracted to the genre until William Randolph Hearst did a rewrite of one of his stories, which, as noted earlier, left Davis with considerable anger and with no post at *The New York Journal*.

Davis broke into the frantic world of New York journalism following a series of newspaper jobs in Philadelphia, the first of which he owed to a face-to-face meeting with the editor of the *Philadelphia Record* and his father. James S. Chambers Jr. was not overly excited about the prospect of having a young trainee in his newsroom, since Davis's appointment had been confirmed without his knowledge or approval. And then, there was the matter of Davis's sartorial demeanor, which would be a point of great discussion throughout his newspaper career and indeed his entire life.

He usually reported to work dressed in a fine, English-cut suit and carrying a cane that was large enough that Chambers dubbed it the Davis railroad tie. His devotion to wearing kid gloves was a particular annoyance to Chambers, who "was ready to suspect his applicant of owning a dress suit, a college education and a willingness to drink afternoon tea—anything but entrance requirements for the Fourth Estate."

Life with Chambers would prove to be a test of wills, not as bad as one might encounter with the likes of Charles Chapin but no Sunday picnic either. Chambers took out his resentment over Davis's hiring by assigning him to the boring and mundane stories that had to be covered. He was often given desk duty writing obituaries, a common starting point for many a cub reporter. When he was allowed into the field, it was generally to cover those things no one else wanted to cover, such as flower shows, agricultural exhibits, and museum openings. Davis immediately began to take liberties with the copy. He had always pictured himself as a kind of literary figure in the making, and the type of story he covered on the *Record* led him to believe he could flirt with the various kinds of style to which he was exposed. Chambers did not agree, and three months after being imposed on the editor, Davis was invited to set up shop on the street.

In spite of being fired by the temperamental Chambers, Davis had started to acquire a reputation for flair within the Philadelphia press corps. After leaving the *Record,* he was hired by Albert H. Hoeckley, city editor of the *Philadelphia Press.* This time, Davis was determined to please his employer, and for the first time in his life, but not the last, he donned the clothes of a reporter. The English-cut suit, the cane, and the kid gloves were all put in the closet for the time being.

The *Press* was the kind of newspaper that gave satisfaction to the young reporter. It was a lively, aggressive member of Pennsylvania's journalistic community. Hoeckley gave Davis room to grow, and he became enthralled when one of his stories made the front page. He was quickly building a reputation as a first-rate writer. But despite what he contributed in terms of a literary approach to journalism, he fell down on collecting and verifying facts. Perhaps the task was just too mundane for a man of his talents. Over time, as he became more secure in his post at the *Press,* the fancy clothes returned from the closet. His habits did not always endear him to his colleagues, who often found him somewhat distant and aristocratic.

Davis finally demonstrated the kind of mettle that was necessary to work in the Yellow Press when he agitated for a dangerous assignment that could have brought him bodily harm. The city had been plagued by a series of well-planned burglaries that the police department seemed unable to curtail. Davis argued that if someone unknown to the gang committing these crimes was able to gain the confidence of its members, the crooks could be exposed and arrested, giving the *Press* an exclusive like no other at the time. An undercover cop was out of the question, since one could not take the chance that a gang member could identify a plainclothes officer. But a reporter, usually unseen by readers, could provide the proper disguise.

So, Davis parked his well-designed clothes back in the closet, exchanging them for the kind of things thought to be worn by gang members. He acquired a shabby suit, complemented by a flannel shirt and a cap that he wore tipped to one side of his head. He worked his way around the more forbidden parts of town until someone invited him to visit the lair occupied by the bandits. He carefully observed the behavioral patterns of the gangsters, determined to avoid contact with the suspects until he was able to imitate their speech patterns and body language. The gang soon realized that Davis was the kind of fellow who could help them plan a big heist. But when the gang showed up to execute the robbery, the police were waiting. They got their men, and the *Press* got its exclusive. In 1889, Davis was convinced that he was ready for New York.

Richard Harding Davis may have thought that his excellent work in Philadelphia would provide him with an open door in New York. It did not. His reputation had preceded him, and the hard-bitten journalists on Park Row gave him the insulting nickname "Beau Brummell of the Press." He should have been a natural. He was college educated, at a time when more and more reporters came with such qualifications. He had a depth of knowledge on literature and world affairs. He was athletic and while at college had played halfback on a football team. An average musician, he could hold his own as a singer or guitar player.

While pondering whether he should invade the sacred golden dome of *The World New York,* Davis decided to visit Charles Dana's *New York Sun* to make a pitch to the editor of its evening edition, Arthur Brisbane. Davis mentioned that he was going to see Pulitzer, and Brisbane intervened by inviting him to a discussion in his office at the *Sun.* Davis never made it to Pulitzer's office, at least not then. He left Brisbane with a position and a salary of $30 per week. He would stay with the *Sun* until he accepted an offer to become managing editor at *Harper's Weekly* in 1891.

In his early years with Brisbane, Davis covered the police beat, among others, assigned to produce some graphic tales of human misdeeds. He gained the confidence of the police department, which was always ready to feed him good information for a juicy tale or two. But like all beats, this one had a life expectancy. Davis moved to *Harper's Weekly* not just for the chance to head a journal but also to give himself time for other pursuits. His desire to create more literary pieces, both in fact and fiction, had returned. He combined his work at the magazine with traveling around the world and composing a series of short stories and books. His growing reputation did not escape the always wandering eye of William Randolph Hearst. In 1895, Hearst hired him to cover a Yale-Princeton football game. In the following year, Hearst sent him to Russia to interview Czar Nicholas II. In 1896, he was in Cuba with artist Frederic Remington to cover the steadily growing uprising. It was at that time that the now-disputed claim by Remington that he could find no conflict inspired a response by Hearst that if Remington could supply pictures, he could provide a war to go with them. In 1897, Davis covered the Greco-Turkey War for the *Times* (London).

As Hearst would discover, Davis's allegiance to the fundamental principles, if you could call them that, of Yellow Journalism had its limits. Like most other reporters sent to the scene in the mid-1890s to cover the Cuban uprising, he found that evidence was hard to come by: the rebels were waging a hit-and-run war outside the cities, which made reporting on the conflict difficult. This proved to be no obstacle for *The New York Journal*. A little problem with facts never deterred the determined Hearst, who published numerous accounts of bloody battles between insurgents and Spanish troops that were created in the minds of the approximately thirty reporters, including Davis, who wrote the stories on the terrace of the Hotel Inglaterra in Havana. Even the most persistent analyst would have difficulty separating fact from fiction in these transmissions.

By January 15, 1897, Davis's field companion, Frederic Remington, had abandoned Cuba and returned home. February would prove to be an extremely active month for Davis. The events of that month would include the incident that drove a wedge between the publisher and the reporter. In the meantime, Davis had plenty of news upon which he could report accurately. There was no more graphic tale than Davis's report on the execution of a young rebel by a Spanish firing squad. The story hit a nerve with Americans back home.

Adolfo Rodriguez was indeed a rebel. He had joined the insurgency near the town of Santa Clara, where his family kept a farm. In December 1896, he was captured by the Spanish and taken before a military court. That month, he was tried, convicted, and sentenced to death, as were a number of other insurgents from the same area. He was to meet his fate on the morning of January 19, the first of a group of rebels who would be executed on successive mornings. Davis described the scene as Rodriguez was prepared for his fate:

> The Cuban's arms were bound, as are those of the statue, and he stood firmly, with his weight resting on his heels like a soldier on parade, and with his face held up fearlessly, as is that of the statue. But there was this difference, that Rodriguez, while probably as willing to give six lives for his country as was the American rebel, being only a peasant, did not think to say so, and he will not, in consequence, live in bronze during the lives of many men, but will be remembered only as one of thirty Cubans, one of whom was shot at Santa Clara on each succeeding day at sunrise.

There is little doubt that Davis harbored a deep sentiment for the Cuban people in their battle against Spain. While reporting on the unfortunate Rodriguez, he noted that members of the firing squad had been lined up in such a manner that if they were to shoot, they would hit several of their own men. Just as the order to shoot Rodriguez was about to be given, someone noticed the problem, and the execution was halted. Davis described the incident as "one of the most cruelly refined, though unintentional acts of torture that one can very well imagine." Eventually, the Spanish carried out the order, and Adolfo Rodriguez fought no more.

Just a few days following the Rodriguez incident, the *Olivette,* a ship bound for the United States, was boarded by several Americans in Havana. As noted earlier, among the passengers was Clemencia Arango, a Cuban citizen whose brother was a prominent member of the insurgent army. Arango was allegedly one of a number of young women who were searched by the Spanish authorities before leaving the port, an incident that drew the attention of Richard Harding Davis. By the time the story of the incident appeared in *The Journal,* the women had been strip-searched by leering Spanish male detectives. The story also carried a drawing by Remington in which the women were clearly devoid of any clothing. *The Journal* treated the incident as an insult to both the United States and womanhood and carried highly exaggerated accounts of it in all its details for three days running. The only problem was that the incident had never occurred.

Back in New York, Joseph Pulitzer smelled a rat. He ordered Sylvester Scovel to dig up the truth of the matter. Scovel interviewed Arango, who denied that she or any of the others had been strip-searched by male officers. She told *The World* that the examination was conducted by female agents in a private room in the vessel. Pulitzer seized the moment to blast *The Journal* in *The World* with an inflammatory headline that read, "THE UNCLOTHED WOMEN SEARCHED BY MEN WAS AN INVENTION OF A NEW YORK NEWSPAPER." Hearst ignored *The World*'s challenge.

Ultimately, it was not Arango and the other women who became victims in this case. Richard Harding Davis was the biggest loser. He was so furious with Hearst that he immediately divorced himself from the publisher and vowed he would never submit another word to Hearst or any of his journals again. Veteran reporter William Abbot noted that "it was characteristic of the Hearst methods that no one suffered for what in most papers would been an unforgivable offense, and I never heard the owner of the paper, in public or in private express the slightest regret for the scandalous fake." Fortunately, all was forgotten, and Richard Harding Davis survived professionally to report on another day.

Davis was present when the American fleet dropped its cargo of fighting men at Santiago de Cuba after the Spanish-American War finally got under way. Sailing toward Cuba, he felt a sense of enthusiasm among the troops, which he believed would be good for overall morale, not to mention a quick victory. However, he was a bit taken aback when one of the men on the ship who was writing to his wife advised her not to believe any of the battle stories that might appear in both *The World* and *The New York Journal.* Death was a real possibility, and he was not interested in anything but the truth should he fall in battle.

When it came time to release the troops and begin the assault, Davis complained that journalists were being forced to occupy the last boats to leave for the encounter. The reporter was ready to meet his obligations, dressed as he was in full khaki battle fatigues. But the invasion's commander, Gen. William Shafter, had no sympathy for the journalist or any other journalist for that matter. When Davis claimed that he should be allowed to go on one of the first boats, he told the general that he was a "descriptive writer." Shafter replied, "I don't give a damn what you are, I'll treat all of you alike." He did. The rift between Davis and Shafter continued for a lifetime.

If Davis had been a modern man, it could be claimed that he had a flair for the media. He became an international celebrity for a number of reasons. His artist friend Charles Dana Gibson painted him as the male counterpart to the Gibson Girl, one of the artist's own creations. He had written an extensively popular novel called *Gallegher,* which detailed the adventures of a newsboy who became a detective. The book, much the equivalent of the modern-day *All the President's Men,* portrayed journalism as a career full of excitement and glamour. A typical day for Richard Harding Davis could be described as "shrapnel, chivalry and sauce Mousseline, and so to work the next morning on an article."

Although the three editors and three journalists discussed in the preceding pages represent the culture and genre of Yellow Journalism in 1890s' New York, they were far from an exclusive group. There were literally hundreds of editors and reporters across the United States who wanted to turn their journals into miniversions of the Hearst and Pulitzer publications. Within New York itself, there were whole newspaper communities that reported on many of the same events that attracted the editors and journalists at *The World* and *The New York Journal*. However, many of these young men and women were not the dedicated journalists that Creelman and Scovel were. They thought more like Richard Harding Davis, who regarded journalism as the first step in honing one's skills to become a prominent literary figure. To them, as one journalist described it, a job on a major newspaper was a tuition-free professional school education. One such person was the talented and frail Stephen Crane.

Crane had arrived in New York in 1892, preceding Hearst by three years. At the time, publishers and editors were concentrating their recruitment efforts on potential reporters who had a flair for the dramatic. In other words, the kid who could tell the best story regularly got the nod when seeking employment. Crane needed nourishment, of course, which he obtained by his work in journalism. But his heart was in the novel, and in 1893, he finished his book *Maggie, a Girl of the Streets: A Story of New York*. He set out to find a publisher, and when all efforts failed, he issued the book himself. Two years later, he found a publisher for *The Red Badge of Courage,* which became an instant hit. In 1896, the Maggie story, based on his observations as a reporter, was reissued, and Crane was on his way to becoming a well-known figure in New York literary circles.

It was almost predictable that Crane's name would show up on a list of desirable writers compiled by William Randolph Hearst. Crane was soon to join one of the best reporting staffs in American journalism, one that also included Mark Twain, Julian

Hawthorne, Richard Harding Davis, and Murat Halstead. Hearst was determined to conquer New York and all of the continental United States with his blustery and exaggerated approach to journalism, and the world was to be open to his vision as well. While Crane was working on a number of sketches about life on the other side of the tracks—in this case, New York's notorious Tenderloin district—Hearst had him lined up to cover a war between Greece and Turkey. The journalist-cum-novelist had to set aside his stories to travel to the scene of the action halfway around the world.

When the tensions between the United States and Cuba kept inching closer to open warfare, Crane decided to join the navy, but he failed the physical and was forced to return to journalism. Upon receiving an invitation to work for Pulitzer, he gladly accepted and was assigned to join Sylvester Scovel in Havana. To that point, he had never seen a real war, but his *Red Badge Of Courage* was so graphic that few believed him when he declared his innocence in this regard. However, he found the literary techniques he employed in the novel quite useful when covering the war for *The World*. His dispatches, although not as bombastic as those of Scovel and Creelman, could not disguise the fact that the novelist and the reporter in him had some difficulty sorting out the role that each should play in the conflict.

Crane found himself defending his personal and professional honor after Hearst publicly accused him of disloyalty after he had reported that the behavior of the New York Seventy-first Regiment was less than exemplary on the raid on San Juan Hill. Crane had stated that the troops seemed demoralized, which eventually resulted in an uncharacteristic retreat from the scene of battle. One of Hearst's typical headlines read, "SLURS ON THE BRAVERY OF THE BOYS OF THE 71ST REGIMENT / THE *WORLD* DELIBERATELY

ACCUSES THEM OF RANK COWARDICE AT SAN JUAN." The Hearst report neglected to mention the fact that the regiment had come under heavy fire from the Spanish defenders and that one in every eight soldiers was hit in the fusillade. The remainder of the article defending the Seventy-first was nothing but pure fiction in a typical Hearst style.

Stephen Crane did not live long enough to register an extensive set of bibliographical references in American literature. On June 5, 1900, he, like many others during the period, succumbed to tuberculosis. He believed that he had contracted the disease when the boat in which he was returning to Cuba in 1896 was wrecked, leaving the author and a number of others shipwrecked in the Caribbean Sea. He relived that nightmare in the 1898 work *The Open Boat and Other Tales.*

In every respect, reporter Jimmy Hare was an innovator and creator. He was one of a kind—a photojournalist who covered world events in pictures until his retirement in 1931. He had been born on October 3, 1856, in London, England, the son of an expert cabinetmaker who then moved on to manufacturing cameras. It was this instrument that attracted the young Hare, who recognized its potential as a storytelling vehicle. He kept pressing his father to design a much smaller and more mobile camera for use on the streets of London. The older Hare refused to recognize the validity of his son's ideas, and the two parted company. In the 1880s, the younger Hare moved from manufacturing cameras to using them for journalistic purposes.

By 1895, Hare had turned his love for photography into a career. He became the full-time photographer for the *Illustrated American Magazine.* His mandate included taking pictures of yacht club regattas and parades, and later on, he photographed the inauguration of William McKinley. After a fire destroyed the offices of the magazine, Hare contacted *Collier's Weekly,* offering to go to Cuba and take pictures both of the wreckage of the battleship *Maine* and of life during that tense period on the island. Robert Collier, the magazine's publisher, did not hesitate to accept Hare's offer.

Hare crossed paths with Sylvester Scovel at about the time that the Spanish–American War broke out. Scovel convinced the photographer to take pictures of Spanish defense installations, which he, Scovel, would pass on to the American military. Hare then experienced the bravado of his new companion when he agreed to board a small boat and journey to Cuba to inform General Gomez that America was coming to his rescue. Scovel also convinced the correspondent for the *Chicago Tribune,* Henry James Whigham, to join the expedition. It was an adventure Hare would never forget, later writing of "five mortal hours under the lock of this half ton sailing boat in a hole barely large enough for one with the sun beating down on us while we made our way over the shallows." The return trip was no less adventurous. He and Whigham got separated from Scovel, so they decided to steal a boat and make their way back to Key West over ninety miles of water. They were spotted by the U.S. torpedo boat *Winslow* and picked up. Unfortunately, the boat soon encountered a Spanish battleship, and the fight was on, to be photographed by Hare. The only American officer to die in the Spanish–American War, Ensign Worth Bagley, fell in this encounter.

Hare's Spanish–American experiences ended when the United States invaded the island at Santiago de Cuba. But the war bug had bitten him. In 1904, he covered the war between Russia and Japan. In 1911, he was in Mexico to photograph the Mexican revolution. *Collier's Weekly* hired him once again to cover the conflict in the Balkans in 1912. When Hare discovered that *Collier's* had no interest in having him photograph World War I, he offered his services to *Leslie's Weekly* and was sent to England.

Hare's photography during the Spanish-American War brought a sense of realism to the conflict that no illustration, no matter how good, could accomplish. Much of his work from his many travels has been saved, and much of it can be seen in the Gould volume cited in this chapter. For those interested in viewing motion pictures of the Spanish-American War, many exist on the Thomas Edison web site at http://memory.loc.gov/ammem /edhtml/edmvhm.html.

The story of the role of editors and reporters in the heyday of Yellow Journalism could cover many more pages, but much of it has already been told by Joyce Milton. Readers interested in the place in history given to George Bronson Rea, Frank Norris, Murat Halstead, and Frederic Remington, among others, can find references in Milton's book on Yellow Journalism and reporters. The mission of this chapter was to explore the culture that produced Yellow Journalism, with an eye to explaining how the various activist participants shaped the genre and where it fits into the larger world of journalistic practice. It is hoped that the discussion of the lives of Arthur Brisbane, Charles Chapin, Morrill Goddard, Sylvester Scovel, James Creelman, and Richard Harding Davis accomplished that purpose.

EIGHT

THE ILLUSTRATORS

Anyone present when President Ulysses S. Grant and Emperor Don Pedro of Brazil fired up the mighty and massive double Corliss engine in Philadelphia in 1876 could have no doubt that the world would soon belong to America. The engine stood on a platform that was no less than fifty-six feet across. It operated two cylinders that rotated a thirty-foot flywheel that produced 1,400 horsepower of energy, enough to drive all the machinery in Mechanical Hall. The machine was a modern miracle, a product of a new technological age that would soon propel American might and know-how well beyond the nation's borders. The new age created the perfect environment for both economic and political imperialism. And America would not hesitate to take its place on the global stage until it ran headlong into Woodrow Wilson's scheme for world government, the League of Nations, long after the age of the Yellow Press had reached a peak of influence that it could no longer sustain.

America needed a new raison d'être, and industry and technological advances were to be the backbone of a new society. In the centennial year, Americans, conscious of their heritage, realized that their country had been born in blood and had been again bathed in blood in the previous decade. In spite of economic crises such as the one that hit in the 1870s and another in the early 1890s, Gilded Age America had much about which to be optimistic. And needless to say, the Yellow Press had no hesitation in advancing American causes anywhere it chose to do so. If America had a premier cheerleader, it was the fast and fancy press of the late 1890s and the early years of the twentieth century.

Late Victorian America was a colorful mosaic that had been assembled in many of the large coastal cities on both the Atlantic and the Pacific. Believing as did Chinese immigrants that America was indeed the Golden Mountain, people arrived in the thousands, some to face the prospect of collecting fantastic riches, others to die prematurely in the environmental horror of the new industrial state. It was to these potential new readers that both William Randolph Hearst and Joseph Pulitzer directed much of their attention. The Yellow Press shared their triumphs and their tragedies. The Yellow Press supported their causes and fought their enemies. As we have seen, the news was lively, the editorial page was pointed and direct, and the journals published copious quantities of illustrations of the daily news, the weekend comics, and political cartoons. The role of the illustrator in making the Yellow Press what it was cannot be underestimated during this period of its influence and glory.

Good artists were worth their weight in gold to an editor in late Victorian America. With the stroke of a pen or a brush, they could communicate messages to even the partially literate, messages that would be missed in the columns of wordy dialogue that shared the pages of the Yellow journal. Although he was not the first cartoonist with attitude to grace the pages of America's journals,

Thomas Nast would be the first really effective political analyst who used drawings instead of words.

For a three-year period following the Civil War, Nast devoted much of his work in *Harper's Weekly* to a series of savage attacks on William "Boss" Tweed, head of the Irish social club Tammany Hall. To Nast, the club was more than just a place where the sons of Eire could get a cold drink on a hot night; it was the very epitome of political corruption. A year after Nast began publishing his thoughts on Tweed and his henchmen, the *New York Times* began to publish a series based on Nast's accusations, which, along with the cartoons, finally brought an end to Tweed's reign. The Boss did not take the intrusions into his affairs lightly. The Harper brothers, who published the majority of texts used in New York public schools, were threatened with the cancellation of their license. Nast received so many death threats that he finally had to move to an unknown location to protect his wife and children.

There is no evidence to suggest that William Randolph Hearst and Joseph Pulitzer were fully aware of the impact of the Nast cartoons in *Harper's Weekly,* but they would have had to be blind and deaf not to know what was going on. Hearst had assumed control of his father's *San Francisco Examiner* on March 4, 1887, determined to bring circulation up to almost unbelievable heights. He reached back into his own experience to recruit people he knew from his past ventures, including E. L. "Phinney" Taylor, who had created the still-revered *Casey at the Bat*; Ambrose Bierce, who was assigned to work as a columnist; and Samuel Chamberlain, who had New York experience with both *The World* and *The Herald*. Among the hires was a little-known artist from Silverton, Oregon, named Homer Davenport. He would become one of Hearst's most important players when the publisher moved to New York City.

Illustrations became an essential part of late Victorian journalism if for no other reason than that it was far cheaper to hire a good artist to sketch the daily news than it was to try to reproduce photographs. Since the invention of halftone technologies, it was feasible in terms of hardware to include photographs as a journalistic expression. Photographs appeared on a regular basis in much of the illustrated press and various other types of magazines, but they did not make a breakthrough in the daily press until well into the early decades of the twentieth century. Nonetheless, members of an editorial community that included Nast and, later on, *Puck* founder Joseph Keppler and Hearst's political cartoonist Homer Davenport were key players in the development of the illustration as a central element in journalism.

Of all the New York publishers in the age of the Yellow Press, it is quite likely that Hearst was the first to realize the communicative power of drawings. However, he was not the first publisher to include an ongoing series of political cartoons. That honor must be bestowed on Pulitzer, who began a regular series on August 10, 1884. By the time they were at each other's throats in the press wars of the late 1890s, both men knew that illustration could bridge the gap between the fairly well-educated person, on one side, and the newly arrived immigrant whose ability in English was questionable, on the other. For both communities, the picture, whether an illustration or a photograph, represented reality. It would be quite some time before the validity of this observation would be challenged. Hearst's interest in his news-oriented drawings got the publisher involved in reviewing the artwork, to the point that he spent more time with his illustrators than he did with his reporters and senior editors. He had a reputation as a cartoon aficionado.

It did not take Hearst and Pulitzer long to realize that the illustrations that communicated the news on their front pages could easily be adapted as vehicles for commentary. The single message contained in most cartoons that espoused political causes could touch the heart and soul of an interested reader in a way the full-length editorial could not. In Pulitzer's world, as opposed to that of his rival, the front-page illustration or political cartoon was just a vehicle to incite the reader to go to page four and read the editorials. In Hearst's analysis, "Cartoons could capture the sense of reform and social conflict by directing their [the owners' and editorial managers'] frustration at those robber baron monopolists who absconded with public money, appropriated the public trust and profited off the backs of the poor." And of course, when the Spanish-American War broke out, Hearst and in particular Homer Davenport relayed the tales of American bravado largely through full-page illustrations and political cartoons.

Anyone who wishes to review the illustrated content of the Yellow Press at the turn of the century will find a number of artist credits near the bottom of each of the drawings. Only a few of these artists created a legacy that extended into the twentieth century, and only a handful are remembered by journalism historians today. The names of Ray Brown, Horace Taylor, Frank Bowers, and others have drifted in virtual obscurity, leaving us to remember the aforementioned Homer Davenport, Frederick Opper, Jimmy Swinnerton, and Walt McDougall. This list is by no means comprehensive.

McDougall came to prominence as the cartoonist who side-tracked James Blaine's quest for the presidency in 1884. He and fellow cartoonist Valerian Gribayedoff started drawing commentary on the Blaine-Cleveland run for the presidency as early as August 1884. The cartoons were particularly mean-spirited and pointed. With large captions such as "The Flesh Pots of Plunder—

The Republican Party's Last Chance," "The Feast of Aldermanic Vultures," and "How the City Is Plucked by the City Hall Birds of Prey," these cartoons started showing up in *The World* in September.

The errant Blaine let down his normally rigid guard on the evening of October 29, 1884, at a banquet at Delmonico's Hotel attended by the city's movers and shakers, all of whom were raising money for his anticipated campaign. McDougall knew that this political orgy was about to take place and drew an acidic cartoon that he offered to Joseph Keppler at *Puck*. Keppler did not practice censorship as a rule, but he was conscious of offending the man likely to be the next president. He rejected McDougall's cartoon.

Not discouraged by the turn of events, the artist journeyed over to Pulitzer's *World* and offered the cartoon there. Since Blaine was a member of the Republican Party that Pulitzer hated, any work that made the candidate uncomfortable would find its way into Pulitzer's newspaper. On October 30, 1884, McDougall's cartoon entitled "The Royal Feast of Belshazzar Blaine and the Monkey Kings" was spread over seven columns in *The World*.

The cartoon was particularly vicious. It showed Blaine dining with the cream of the New York robber baron set, people such as railroad tycoon Jay Gould, steel magnate Andrew Carnegie, John Jacob Astor, William H. Vanderbilt, and Chauncey DePew. They were pictured dining on Gould Pie, Lobby Pudding, and Monopoly Soup. Particularly damaging was the caricature of a starving couple and a ragged child whose pleas for food were turned down by the elites.

The cartoon was based on the biblical tale of Belshazzar, an Old Testament prophet and Babylonian ruler who sat near a wall containing writing that brought about the destruction of the city. To

Blaine's further chagrin, the cartoon was distributed by Pulitzer to other New York State publications. In the final analysis, Blaine lost the state, a defeat that cost him the election.

With the publication of the cartoon, Pulitzer came to the conclusion that McDougall would soon be a wanted property around New York. He offered him the grand sum of $50 a week to join *The World* permanently. McDougall accepted. When James Gordon Bennett Jr. offered him $75 a week to join the *Herald,* Pulitzer upped the ante to $110. Unlike many other editors, reporters, and artists who jumped ship on a regular basis, McDougall remained with Pulitzer for sixteen years. During that period, Pulitzer never questioned McDougall's work and never discussed his ideas for political cartoons.

McDougall was not a cartoonist who limited himself to drawing at the office. He often asked reporters if he could accompany them on major stories in order to get a feeling for the kind of drawings that could emerge from certain situations. One such situation was Nellie Bly's release from the notorious women's asylum on Blackwell's Island:

> *The World's* cartoonist Walt McDougall accompanied Hendricks [Pulitzer's attorney]. Left alone in the inner court yard for a few minutes, McDougall recalled years later almost having his clothes ripped off by a raging crowd of female maniacs, idiots and plain bugs. "The way the mob rushed me, one would have thought I was the first train out after a subway hold-up."

The granddaddy of all political cartoonists would prove to be Homer Davenport. He had been a brakeman on the Northern Pacific Railroad, and when that did not satisfy his career appetite, he took a job as an animal caretaker in a traveling circus. Eventually, he became an artist on Portland, Oregon's *Oregonian*. It was not a happy relationship. Recalling the day he left his hometown of Silverton, Oregon, to become Hearst's cartoonist in San Francisco, he remembered:

> It was a bashful trip for me, as I had left a few months before to be the artist on the *Oregonian* at Portland and the whole town went into a half holiday and the streets were decorated. I even bid them goodbye for ever; but I was fired and came back before some of the flower decorations had wilted.

His next trip home would be more triumphant.

In his memoirs, Davenport recalled that his father had always protected him from hard labor because his mother wanted her son to grow up to be a cartoonist, a profession that did not suit a man with scarred hands. So, in spite of his disaster in Portland, he never gave up the dream of being one. It was his father who took him to Woodburn, a small community on the Southern Pacific Railroad where one could board a train to San Francisco. This time, he would not return with his tail between his legs.

The young Davenport soon joined the team of artists and cartoonists at the *San Francisco Examiner* under the leadership of William Randolph Hearst and his art chief, Charles Tebbs. Soon, the overpowering Collis P. Huntington, the chief executive officer of the Southern Pacific Railroad, came in contact with Davenport and his fellow cartoonist Jimmy Swinnerton. Huntington did not have a clean record with the authorities, having been charged with violation of the Interstate Commerce Act of 1887. However, he and his enterprise survived the calamity and lived to see another day, including one notable day in 1894.

The summer of 1894 would be an economic nightmare in the United States. The downturn in the economy involved just about every American, including rich ones such as Collis P. Huntington.

As income from his railroad began to plummet, the robber baron asked the federal government, through the U.S. Senate, to pass what he described as a funding bill but others would call a subsidy. So, while the nation starved, Huntington tried to tap the public purse. It was an issue made for Davenport and Swinnerton, and both responded in kind. But kind they weren't.

When Hearst decided to take on New York, he chose to take many of the *San Francisco Examiner* staff with him, including Homer Davenport. Hearst would find New York quite amenable to his concept of journalism. Early in his days in the city, he initiated a reader contest in which the big prizes would be the bicycles that were very popular in New York at the time. He also adopted a strong, pro–Democratic Party policy line that he expected to have followed in his editorial policy, much of which was expressed in the political cartoons of Davenport and Swinnerton.

Hearst banished all news regarding Republican presidential hopeful William McKinley and his campaign manager, Ohio senator Mark Hanna, to the back pages of *The Journal*. But he made one exception: the cartoons of Davenport and Swinnerton could still appear on page one, and the more vicious they were, the more prominence they would receive. Hanna was regularly depicted as a fat, bloated individual with a suit tailored from dollar bills, holding a puppet on a string that could not be mistaken for anyone other than McKinley. And as cartoon historian Paul Somers noted, "By the end of the century, Charles Nelan, Homer Davenport and James Montgomery Flagg would crystallize a vigorous, jingoistic Uncle Sam to stand guard over the palm and pine of the growing American empire."

This discussion of illustrators must necessarily include some references to Richard Felton Outcault, whose drawings were at the center of one of the most costly personnel raids in American journalism history. Although he is better known for his little balding kid in a yellow nightshirt—the cartoon character known as the Yellow Kid, who supposedly gave Yellow Journalism its name—Outcault did contribute some editorial cartoons to the New York press at the height of the battles between Hearst and Pulitzer. His first major position was with the Edison Laboratories, where he took a post as an artist for the company's manuals. He moved on from there, and by 1892, he was in demand in New York's art world.

Like Jacob Riis and Stephen Crane, Outcault was fascinated by life on the seamier side of New York City. In 1892, he began to sketch urban waifs, one of whom became the model for the Yellow Kid. His first major sketch appeared on March 4, 1893, in a magazine called *Truth* that needed all the help it could get. The editor knew Outcault was good, and he was cheap. For the next two years, the artist contributed a weekly series featuring urchin children to the magazine. It was also there that he worked with George Luks, who one day would also draw the Yellow Kid.

Across town on the more prosperous Park Row, Joseph Pulitzer was about to launch his first colored comic supplement in his Sunday newspaper. Although many of the local glossies carried color drawings, Pulitzer's entry into the field was a first for newspapers. Richard Outcault joined *The World* with a publication on September 16, 1894. His contribution was a six-panel, captioned narrative in black and white. His first colored cartoon was published as a series in late 1894, although the *Yellow Kid* strip as we know it today was still under construction.

The character first appeared on February 17, 1895, accompanying a reprinting of the Fourth Ward Brownies, a set of cartoon urchins that was originally published in *Truth* on February 9. But the character of the Yellow Kid had yet to show the consistency that would be apparent in later drawings. That consistency would be established on January 5, 1896, when Outcault drew the Kid in a cartoon entitled "Golf—The Great Society Sport as Played in Hogan's Alley." When the Kid evolved in 1896, he caught the attention of William Randolph Hearst, who immediately offered Outcault an outrageous sum to draw for *The New York Journal*. The cartoonist accepted. When Outcault left Pulitzer to sketch for Hearst, *The World* publisher retaliated by hiring Luks to draw the Yellow Kid for his own Sunday supplement. Although he did so for a year and a half, Luks never captured the spirit that its originator had brought to the strip.

The *Yellow Kid* comic strip was never political in a direct way, but it addressed some serious social concerns that should have been on the discussion table in fashionable New York. Much of the inspiration for the comic came from Jacob Riis's photographic study of the slums of New York, entitled "How the Other Half Lives." Stephen Crane had also attempted to bring a similar dialogue to the city when he prowled the Tenderloin in search of both stories and salvation. In that respect, the *Yellow Kid* was very political, although none of Outcault's work can be compared to or seen in the same light as that of Homer Davenport, Jimmy Swinnerton, and Walt McDougall, all of whom were directly political.

It is in the drawings that appeared in the press between 1854 and 1898 that we get a sense of the growing importance of the United States in world politics. The memory of conflicts past was gradually fading, and America was stepping out. It was a bit too late to emulate the success of European powers such as Britain, France, Germany, Spain, and Portugal, with their significant land-holdings around the globe that, taken together, almost constituted a European monopoly. America had to export its influence in different ways, although land grabs were not out of the question. The remaining pages of this study will return to the second half of the nineteenth century to explore how America's illustrators and cartoonists treated the new state.

In February 1854, the New York–based magazine *Yankee Notions* addressed the issue of an expanding America in a cartoon. The drawing focused on the conversation of a so-called Young American who was presenting an option to the king of the Sandwich Islands, which had been named by the British explorer James Cook in 1778. The islands, now known as America's fiftieth state, Hawaii, were in danger of being expropriated by the American government. In a slang typical of the day and age, the American diplomat told the king, "We want to buy you out, lock, stock and barril [*sic*]." In a response not unlike that uttered by Marlon Brando in *The Godfather,* the American envoy offered his majesty a deal he could not refuse, telling the king, "Yer know yer can't hold 'em long—must give up." The Hawaiians consistently refused such offers until William McKinley annexed the territory in 1898 during the imperial fever that resulted in the Spanish-American War. The drawing provides us with a very early glimpse of American ambitions on the world stage, ambitions that were, of course, interrupted by the Civil War.

In the period leading up to the North-South conflict, a number of magazines that published politically oriented cartoons took up the case for American expansion. In March 1857, *Yankee Notions* once again addressed the question. In a drawing in that issue, Uncle Sam (then known as Brother Jonathan) sat on the North Pole examining lands and places that he felt would fit nicely into the American family. With a satiric point of view, the artist noted that Jonathan was hardly limiting himself to places on earth, although he did desire all the territory east of the Jordan River. In this case, that desire had been set aside so that Jonathan could take what he really desired, the planet Venus.

The May 19, 1860, *Vanity Fair* published a cartoon that poked fun at the declining importance of Britain as an imperial power. The message was a bit premature but reflected the difficulties that the United States had had with Great Britain since 1776, in a relationship that had the potential to deteriorate into war at any given moment. In the cartoon, there was a clear suggestion that Admiral Matthew Perry's forced opening of Japan to Western markets and thus Western ideas did not sit well with the British. In fact, a very strong, young, and virile Jonathan was shown with a Japanese doll in his possession, and he was on the verge of removing John Bull's belt, which would naturally loosen anything attached to this rather large body. The drawing marked the end of subjects dealing with imperial ambitions, while the United States embarked on a path to solve its own internal problems.

Although Cuba was not yet part of American expansionist ambitions, *Vanity Fair* did draw attention to the first uprising that was taking place there in the early 1860s, which would ultimately result in the American invasion of the island some three decades later. The island had long been a part of Imperial and Catholic Spain, an empire that came uncomfortably close to the borders of the English-speaking and predominately Protestant United States and extended southward to touch the shores of Antarctica. The relationship between Old World Spain and New World America was polite but uneasy in the middle years of the nineteenth century. When Spain faced an uprising in its Cuban colony, Americans turned their attention southward in sympathy for the rebels there. But there was more at stake, as a cartoon from June 2, 1860, demonstrated. In that piece, a hunter took aim at a whale named

Cuba. The caption below the drawing noted that if young America did not react to events in Cuba, there was likely to be an intervention by its old enemy, Great Britain; of course, that would never do.

A drawing that appeared in *Frank Leslie's Budget of Fun* took a different look at American expansionist dreams. As noted earlier, at the midpoint of the century, Great Britain was considered to be the largest obstacle to any imperial ambitions on the part the American nation. In this cartoon, an Irish general named O'Killian was apparently returning from a successful battle with the British in Canada. Canada was considered to be a thorn in the American body politic for no other reason than that many Americans felt leaving the British with four colonies to the north and a couple of large virgin territories represented a failure by the United States to take command of its own future. The traditional enemy still shared an extensive border with America.

O'Killian and his band of merry men were Fenians, members of a society devoted to achieving Irish independence by any means possible. In some ways, they were the forerunners of the Irish Republican Army founded by Michael Collins. The Fenians, from camps inside the United States, carried out a number of raids on British territory in Canada armed with the belief that this would destabilize the British military, which could not effectively fight a war in both Canada and Ireland. However, by the early 1870s, the Fenians were no longer, and British complaints about American complicity had faded from the international scene. America learned that allying itself with international battles in which it really had no interest was both foolish and quite damaging to its future goals.

The subject discussed in another Frank Leslie cartoon, this one published in June 1866, dealt with the growing obsession with Europeans practicing politics in North America. In this drawing, the United States confronted the emperor of Mexico, himself not a local, to complain about the way that the country was being governed—represented, in this case, by a very ill young woman with a very large crown on her head. The American reminded Louis Napoleon that North America was a sphere of influence in which the United States had to dominate and that the U.S. government had drawn up a policy known as the Monroe Doctrine to enforce its position. In case the Mexicans and Louis Napoleon did not get the intent of the message, the American stated pointedly that the emperor had to be prepared to surrender jurisdiction over Mexico to the United States.

There was little doubt about the editorial position of the Frank Leslie journals when a cartoon entitled "Uncle Sam's Bird" appeared in the February 1866 edition of *Frank Leslie's Budget of Fun*. The cartoon was simple and yet effective. In it, a large bird was climbing into the sky with a document in its talons that appeared to be a map. The caption confirmed it was a map of North America that the bird had been invited to take home and remodel, and the artist did not mean the paper map.

As the dust settled from the War between the States, America had dabbled in imperial expansion in Hawaii, Mexico, and Canada. It would now turn its attention to the growing political problems in Cuba, problems that had been set aside during the Civil War. *Punchinello*'s first cartoon on the subject, published on April 2, 1870, treated the growing military and humanitarian crisis on the island with a sense of whim. In it, one man was standing and one was sitting. Both were indulging in rather large cigars, which became the focal point of the discussion. In this cartoon, the desire to annex Cuba was suggested only by the fact that America had to have a steady supply of quality cigars.

Another drawing that appeared two issues later took the Cuban situation far more seriously. It showed two leading American politicians, Secretary of State Hamilton Fish and Senator Charles Sumner, looking out of a room with a half door at a woman in apparent distress leaning on the stoop below the door. She was pleading for help. But when the two discovered that she was Cuba, they retreated, not wishing to get involved. Cuba was Spain's problem, and there was a significant body of thought in the United States that imperialism and military adventure should not go hand in hand.

The subject of imperialism was addressed directly in a cartoon that appeared in *Frank Leslie's Budget of Fun* at the end of 1870. In the sketch, President Ulysses S. Grant was drawn as a large bird of prey—undoubtedly an eagle, but the head was covered with a large hat that made the bird species unidentifiable. To his left, there was a cracked egg marked "Imperialism" from which another young bird of prey was beginning to emerge. Speaking to his offspring, the president remarked, "Now I recognize you as one of my own."

In 1889, America stepped forward and challenged one of the world's most effective imperial and military powers. The difference of opinion arose over the fate of a group of islands in the South Pacific known as Samoa. The islands, populated by a fierce and warlike people, had never willingly submitted to any form of foreign conquest. Yet their critical location on the Pacific trading routes brought them visitors from most European powers as well as the United States, all of whom used the islands as refueling depots. When Germany began to show an interest in the islands, the United States immediately laid claim to the territories, a move that was the subject of a cartoon that appeared in *Judge* in 1889.

There was no mistaking who held the hot hand. While a native was pictured standing next to a palm tree on the beach, the German chancellor Otto von Bismarck towered over a small American equipped with only a slingshot and a bag of uncooked Boston beans. The central message of the cartoon was to send American diplomat Ben Butler to represent the United States because there was a feeling that he would not be intimidated by the gruff and tough Bismarck.

Much of the cartoon work in the 1890s focused on either political corruption or American ambitions in Cuba and Spanish holdings in Puerto Rico and the Philippines. American cartooning, especially that with a pointed, no-holds-barred message, became prevalent when the Yellow Press encouraged—no, insisted—that President McKinley invade Cuba, take possession of the island, and end Spanish influence in North America. The United States was defining a new imperial age in which it was determined to be the leader. The Yellow Press egged it ever onward.

One of Hearst's cartoonists, who did not sign his work, took advantage of the tragic circumstances of the *Maine* explosion to criticize both those who allegedly destroyed the battleship and the vultures on Wall Street who hoped to profit from the incident by keeping the United States out of what they regarded as an internal matter. In the Wednesday, March 2, 1898, issue of *The New York Journal,* Uncle Sam was pictured at the site of the wreckage in what appeared to be an attempt to retrieve the remains of the vessel from Havana harbor. Circling about were hundreds of large, mean-looking birds with captions on their feathers that read, among others, "Wall Street broker" or just plain "broker." The Spanish were mercifully spared in this drawing, but their supposed involvement in the *Maine* disaster would be brought up in subsequent cartoons in the newspaper.

It was Walt McDougall who attempted to make humor out of

a situation that emerged over the sinking of the *Maine*. President McKinley had tried to sidetrack accusations that the Spanish garrison in Havana had somehow been responsible for the attack. To calm the increasing tensions over the issue, the president created a board of inquiry that had considerable range to investigate the tragedy. Part of that investigation would deal with the possible actions of the Spanish and their captain general, Valeriano Weyler.

Weyler was not amused by the situation and called on the United States to apologize for even thinking that Spain could participate in such a horrible event. He argued that until the United States offered an apology, no Spanish soldier could wear a military uniform with honor. McDougall's cartoon showed a gathering of Spanish military types at a wall upon which Weyler's proclamation was posted. The soldiers had obeyed orders in a certain respect in the drawing, shedding their uniforms for various other types of nonmilitary garb, including barrels.

Early in the Spanish-American conflict, Homer Davenport continually reminded *Journal* readers that Spain was not the nation's only enemy. On Friday, March 4, 1898, he drew a cartoon of one of his favorite subjects, Mark Hanna, under the caption "The Administration's First Birthday." Behind Hanna, Uncle Sam was shown dancing with a Spanish military figure holding a model of the *Maine*. Sitting on the ground behind both was a small, withered person with Cuba written on his chest. Surrounding Hanna were a series of documents pointing to his numerous deficiencies and his questionable friends, such as John D. Rockefeller. Hanna was also accused of being involved in the massacre of nineteen strikers at the Lattimer Mine in Hazelton, Pennsylvania, in 1897.

On Thursday, March 17, 1898, Davenport managed to cram a number of themes into a cartoon captioned "Now, Darn You, Fight." The drawing was part of Hearst's continuing campaign to draw the United States into a war with Spain over Cuba. At the center of the cartoon was the perennial Republican bogeyman Mark Hanna, dressed in his suit of dollar bills. Standing in front of the political operative was a large eagle wiping his talons on a stars-and-stripes flag. However, the bird could not take off and represent America because Hanna had him chained around his wings, which were now immobile; a large ball with a chain, marked "Wall Street" in reference to the financial community's opposition to the war, prevented the bird from moving at all.

Richard Outcault's contribution to the war effort in the pages of *The Journal* came in a series called *The Huckleberry Volunteers*. The drawings, like those of *The Yellow Kid,* were ensemble efforts focusing on the young. On Friday, April 8, 1898, one of Outcault's panels appeared under the caption "They Are Fired by Patriotism and Start Off to Exterminate Spain or Anything Else." The long title was not the only wordy contribution from the young marchers who were banging drums and carrying the Stars and Stripes along with a number of "weapons of war," including garden rakes. According to one of the signs, the Huckleberry Volunteers were all colonels. And of course, Wall Street was pointed out as one of the villains preventing the good America from rescuing imprisoned Cubans from Spanish tyrants.

Bob Carter, another of Hearst's political cartoonists, brought the battle with Spain into perspective on Monday, May 16, 1898. His illustration showed an obviously pleased Uncle Sam, with a cigar clenched between his teeth, discussing the American campaign with the symbol of the state—the bald eagle. The eagle had three badges attached to his feathers, which revealed clearly the plans that the United States had for dealing with the Spanish. An observer would quickly note that the campaign would be extended beyond Cuba, which had only one badge, marked with the city of Matanzas. The other two badges were designated as the Philippines capital of Manila and the island of Porto Rico [*sic*].

Walt McDougall put the polishing touches to an American age of imperialism with a cartoon in *The Journal* on Tuesday, June 30, 1898. He depicted a terrified Spanish official who had just awakened from what he thought was a bad dream only to discover the reality of the situation. Under the caption "A Terrible Nightmare," the unfortunate Spaniard realized his nightmare was real: there was little or nothing that could be done to stop the United States from capturing the best jewels in the Spanish colonial crown. The age of imperialism had arrived in America as the first days of the twentieth century dawned across the world.

NINE

CONCLUSION

It has been a century and then some since the Yellow Press ruled the journalism community in New York City and in smaller centers where publishers and editors looked on in envy as Hearst and Pulitzer reported readerships that often had the word *million* somewhere in the circulation claim. It is not difficult, but sometimes confusing, to assess the impact that the heyday of this genre has had on modern news-delivery systems. Although Hearst and Pulitzer were probably oblivious to the slow decline that characterized Yellow Journalism following the turn of the century, the printed word within itself continued to be the major player in both information delivery and storytelling until someone in the 1920s got the bright idea that radio could also perform many of the same tasks. So, what is needed in this section of the study is not a review of a technical legacy but rather a look at the intrusions into modern journalistic culture.

American newspapers had always depended on some sort of external funding to guarantee their survival. The funds often came from a mix of sources, such as political friends, newsstand sales, government printing contracts, and classified advertising. The circulation wars that broke out between Hearst and Pulitzer, battles that would eventually engulf the entire journalistic community in the United States, brought the concept of marketing to the press. Journalism became a commodity, something to be bought and sold. The very idea of a value-driven media in the money culture of New York City was hardly foreign. After all, huge fortunes were being made by New York society insiders such as J. Pierpont Morgan, Jay Gould, Andrew Carnegie, and John Jacob Astor and outsiders such as P. T. Barnum. Why should Hearst and Pulitzer, it could be argued, be any different?

One of the first things of note in the transition from the early days of the *New York Sun* to its later reincarnation under the leadership of Charles Dana was an increasing dependence on advertising revenues. It was then that the relationship between the press and the department store—John Wanamaker's in New York City, to be precise—began. It would be one of the most lasting alliances between the media and the merchant class, a relationship that would exist through almost the entire twentieth century. It was also at this time that other media creations, such as advertising agencies and the measurement of newspaper readership, developed, all for the benefit of advertisers.

Anyone who has studied the history of American media will not be surprised at these claims. But it is important to recognize that, first and foremost, it was the late Gilded Age press that extended a welcome to those who ran businesses, those who had money to spend and a message to communicate. This attitude, helped in a significant way by newspapers, later became the standard approach when radio arrived in American households. Many radio licenses were held by newspaper owners, who had little or no idea of what to do with the new medium but recognized that being on the ground floor, no matter how expensive, was better than finding oneself knocking at the door of opportunity and being refused entry. (We saw an unfortunate manifestation of this mind-set years later with the dot.com crisis of the mid-1990s.) When New York radio station WEAF sold its first advertisement in the 1920s, the move was hardly courageous. The station's owners had Hearst and Pulitzer to thank for turning the new medium over to commercial interests. The broadcasters were just following a pattern set years earlier.

With the concept of commerce comes competition, and just as we see today, advertising rates and readership were intertwined in the late Gilded Age. It was not enough to report the facts of the day's events; those facts had to be interpreted and placed in a setting where readership could be attracted and retained. There was always the fear that pushing the boundaries would take journalism beyond its sacred duty to inform to a plain where entertainment superseded fact. And as we have seen, that certainly took place in the reporting of the Spanish-American War.

But in the final analysis, what was going on in Cuba was but a temporary impasse in the lives of most Americans. It was nice to get up in the morning, wave Old Glory, and exhort the government to deal with the dastardly (it was claimed) Spanish regime on the island and declare once and for all that American righteousness would prevail in the end. But America could not continue to fight wars for the satisfaction of the daily press, if indeed it had ever done so. So, to keep the momentum going, the press turned to crime and corruption, both themes that remain with us today in newspapers, on radio, and in television reporting. It is a sphere where all too often, as Jayson Blair and Steven Glass have proven recently, fact and fiction can become confused.

Crime reporting can be a specifically touchy subject. Within this realm, the press is seldom asked to authenticate what appears in print or on the air. Yet at the same time, the press is regularly accused of being biased, misreporting significant events, and, in some cases, practicing the kind of sensationalism that Hearst and Pulitzer brought to the media scene in the closing decade of the nineteenth century. Crime reporting is real, it is true—at least, that is what we often hear. The television picture of the bleeding suspect, the injured victim, or the damaged domicile is taken as fact in a way that impacts negatively on the more vulnerable members of our society. It is a phenomenon, created by the electronic press in particular, that fosters the belief that violent crime is close to being an epidemic even when statistics show that it is on the decline.

In essence, what we have is the contemporary version of the Yellow Press or, at the very least, a distorted sense of the value of sensationalism. Here, we can clearly find fault with the editorial decision making that leads to this kind of visual and very disturbing reporting, with routine parts edited out to include quick clips of the more exciting elements of a real-life tale. And when this sort of thing starts to dominate the way reporting and editorial decision making are undertaken, seniors across the land don't stop watching these newscasts. They go to the hardware outlet and buy bigger and more secure locks for their homes.

It is more difficult to argue about the ongoing emphasis on corruption as a front-page entity. Certainly, events in the country's financial markets going back in time have been less than savory. Although it cannot be denied that corruption from the inside has created the types of tragedies that broke out during the 1990s, the overemphasis on sensationalism in this regard moves these stories beyond the purview of the daily press that originated the tales of uncontrollable greed and criminal manipulation and on to other media to become salable and marketable products. The film *Wall*

Street and the Enron story *The Smartest Guys in the Room* present situations when crime can actually pay, although not necessarily for the perpetrator.

The major problem with this kind of journalism, as it was in the Victorian age of the Yellow Press, is the tendency to undermine those institutions, both private and public, charged with running the country. Modern media, learning from Hearst and Pulitzer, know that crime and corruption sell. Of course, this fact of life then excludes or at least diminishes extensive reporting on things that are undertaken to benefit American society. If there is a choice between extensive coverage of complicated social security reforms or a juicy murder or two, it doesn't take much imagination to see which topic will get to the front page or top the evening television news.

The Yellow Press of Hearst and Pulitzer was very much a personal pursuit for both publishers and all those who copied their successes and avoided their failures. In every respect, the newspapers that they published were their own windows on the world, although Pulitzer was not nearly as forceful as his rival in putting his viewpoint on page one: Orson Welles's *Citizen Kane* was not made about the Hungarian immigrant. In the twenty-first century, there is a major difference in media ownership and practice due to a significant degree of evolution in news technologies and concentrated corporate ownership.

It was Karl Marx who first noted that capitalism, which is based on the principle of competition, does anything it can to *avoid* competition. In most modern societies, this reality has resulted in the creation of the megacorporation that seeks to eliminate competitors by gobbling them up when the time is right. In the media world, it has also led to a blending of product. One can find, for example, one city's big media clearly duplicated in another. In an age of multichannel availability, in which I include both the electronic and the printed press, the need to diversify and appeal to local communities is more critical than ever. As de Tocqueville noted, newspapers make associations and associations make newspapers. Can we apply the same criteria to the modern news media?

The Yellow Press in the age of Hearst and Pulitzer shaped the generation that followed with fresh concepts of marketing, reporting, layout, design, and storytelling, but the modern media have relegated the concept of community to the backstage of human existence. In the success that both publishers enjoyed, the sense of understanding a constituency or a community, one not locked into focus groups, was incredibly strong. One can certainly question of the validity of their respective editorial approaches, but one cannot question their understanding of the world in which they lived and worked. It is the one lesson from the two Victorians, now long dead, that should be revisited.

NOTES

CHAPTER ONE

2 *Representations of crime influence:* Joy Wiltenburg, "True Crime: The Origins of Modern Sensationalism," *American Historical Review* 109, no. 5 (December 2004): 1.

3 *Capturing the carnage:* Michael Carlebach, *The Origins of Photojournalism in America* (Washington, D.C., and London: Smithsonian Institute Press, 1992), p. 7.

Marvels of the century: Harold Innis, *The Bias of Communication* (Toronto, London, and Buffalo, N.Y.: University of Toronto Press, 1951), p. 27.

4 *Age of great excess:* Frederick Siebert, Theodore Peterson, and Wilbur Schramm, *Four Theories of the Press* (Urbana and Champaign: University of Illinois Press, 1956), pp. 44, 74.

5 *Ideological straitjacket:* John C. Nerone, *Last Rights: Revisiting Four Theories of the Press* (Urbana and Champaign: University of Illinois Press, 1995), pp. 42–43.

Theological impurities: Andrew M. Osler, *News: The Evolution of Journalism in Canada* (Toronto, Ontario: Copp, Clark Pittman, 1993), p. 55.

6 *Where the press is free:* Edward Dumbald, *Jefferson: His Political Writings* (New York: Bobbs-Merrill, 1955), p. 93.

Liberty of the press: John Stuart Mill, *On Liberty* (Glasgow, UK: William Collins and Sons, 1962), p. 141.

A necessary connection: Alexis de Tocqueville, *Democracy in America,* vol. 2 (New York: Vintage Books, 1945), p. 120.

7   *Information to constituencies:* David Paul Nord, *Communities of Journalism* (Urbana and Champaign: University of Illinois Press, 2001), p. 5.
A model of information: Ibid., p. 6.
The marketplace of ideas: Nerone, p. 43.
Approach to journalism: David Mindich, *Just the Facts: How Objectivity Came to Define American Journalism* (New York: New York University Press, 1998), p. 130.

8   *Daily press in America:* Nord, p. 6.
Function or misfunction: James W. Carey, *Communication as Culture: Essays on Media and Society* (Boston: Unwin, Hyman Publishers, 1989), p. 20.

9   *Ritual view of communication:* Ibid.
Need to conquer the spaces: Ibid., p. 21.

10   *Five short years:* Harold Innis, *Empire and Communications* (Toronto, London, and Buffalo, N.Y.: University of Toronto Press, 1972), pp. 160–61.

11   *Passages from Confucius:* Ramsay Cook, *The Regenerators* (Toronto, London, and Buffalo, N.Y.: University of Toronto Press, 1991), p. 87.

12   *Havana cigars:* Available at http://www.kirjasto.sci.fi/bhecht.htm.

13   *Drinking and working:* Fred Fedler, *Lessons from the Past* (Prospect Heights, Ill.: Waveland Press, 2000), pp. 176–77.

14   *Pulitzer was an outcast:* Denis Brian, *A Life: Pulitzer* (New York: John Wiley and Sons, 2001), pp. 163–64.
Establishment of a journalism school: Ibid., pp. 277–78.

15   *Mandate to improve:* Ibid., pp. 283–85.
Degree program in journalism: Mindich, pp. 115–17.
Attacked religion: L. J. Budd, "Color Him Curious about Yellow Journalism," *Journal of Popular Culture* 15, no. 2 (Fall 1981): 26.

16   *Depended more on fact:* Mindich, pp. 64–68.
Scare heads: Ted Curtis Smythe, *The Gilded Age Press, 1865–1900* (Westport, Conn., and London: Praeger Publishers, 2003), p. 210.

16   *The same could apply:* Michael Schudson, *Discovering the News: A Social History of American Newspapers* (New York: Basic Books, 1978), pp. 5–6.

17   *To economic survival:* Ibid., p. 3.

18   *Less crime around:* Marshall McLuhan, *Understanding Media* (Cambridge: Massachusetts Institute of Technology Press, 1994), p. 205.

   The construction of realities: Hanno Hardt and Bonnie Brennen, eds., *News Workers: Toward a History of the Rank and File* (Minneapolis: University of Minnesota Press, 1995), p. 2.

CHAPTER TWO

21   *Morris won the seat:* Frank Luther Mott, *American Journalism* (New York: Macmillan, 1962), pp. 32–33.

   Truth was a defense: Ibid., p. 37.

22   *The charges were true:* Jean Folkerts and Dwight L. Teeter Jr., *Voices of a Nation,* 3rd ed. (Boston and London: Allyn and Bacon, 1998), p. 43.

   Birth of the penny press: George H. Douglas, *The Golden Age of the Newspaper* (Westport, Conn.: Greenwood Publishing, 1999), p. 4.

   Population growth was hardly explosive: Ibid., pp. 11–12.

   Events in the local communities: James Melvin Lee, *History of American Journalism* (Garden City, N.Y.: Garden City Publishing, 1923), p. 145.

23   *The journalistic vocabulary:* Kevin Barnhurst and John Nerone, *The Form of News: A History* (New York and London: Guilford Press, 2001), p. 15.

   The printer's newspaper: Ibid., pp. 17–18.

24   *Boston's largest minority:* Mott, p. 217.

   Viability of the marketplace: Lee, pp. 187–188.

   Emergence of popular newspapers: Douglas, p. 3.

25   *Printed in their sheets:* Lee, p. 203.

25 *Culture of their respective communities:* Barnhurst and Nerone, p. 1.
Learning to read and write: Sidney Kobre, *Development of American Journalism* (Dubuque, Iowa: William C. Brown Publishers, 1969), p. 198.
This first issue: Douglas, p. 5.

26 *Previously anonymous people:* Ibid., p. 6.
Craft of reporting: Ibid., pp. 6–7.
Completely anonymous news hound: Barnhurst and Nerone, p. 17.

27 *Manly observer of events:* Ibid.
Final humiliation: Mott, p. 225.

28 *Urchins called newsboys:* Lee, p. 206. Also see Jon Bekken, "Newsboys," in Hanno Hardt and Bonnie Brennen, eds., *News Workers: Toward a History of the Rank and File* (Minneapolis: University of Minnesota Press, 1995), pp. 190–225.
These communities: Kobre, *Development of American Journalism,* p. 221.
Illicit sex relations: Mott, p. 228.

29 *Obsessed with facts:* Douglas, pp. 24–27.
Competitive spirit: Ibid., pp. 19–20.

30 *On lower Wall Street:* Ibid., p. 29.

31 *As freshly as ever:* Isaac C. Pray, *Memoirs of James Gordon Bennett and His Times* (New York: Arno Press, 1970), pp. 205–6.
Truth, morals and virtue: Ibid., p. 214.

32 *Surprised by the results:* Mindich, pp. 15–16.
A New York prostitute: For present purposes, she will be named Ellen, although many other accounts refer to her as Helen. An 1836 pamphlet referred to her as Ellen as well.
She landed in New York: David Anthony, "The Helen Jewett Panic: Tabloids, Men, and the Sensational Public Spheres in Antebellum New York," *American Literature* 69, no. 3 (September 1997): 488.
The Reverend Mr. Tappan: Pray, p. 210.

33 *Intimate details:* Douglas, p. 33.
Erotics and aesthetic beauty: Anthony, p. 488.
Proceeded to dissect: Ibid.

34 *Dismissed the story:* Pray, p. 210.
       Marie Roget: Kobre, *Development of American Journalism,* p. 225.
       Cases passed into history: Mott, p. 297.
       Took their own lives: Lee, p. 223.

35 *The great triumvirate:* Douglas, p. 70.
       Elizabeth Cochrane: Ibid., p. 73.
       Famous humor magazines: Ibid., pp. 77–78.

37 *No expense is spared:* Mott, pp. 375–76.
       Manage the newspaper: Smythe, p. 6.

38 *The source of the Nile:* Lee, pp. 356–57.

39 *A kidnapper and his victim:* Ibid., pp. 356–60.
       So it did: A. P. Herbert, *The Best Cartoons from "Punch"* (New York:
       Simon and Schuster, 1952), back page.

40 *Convince the skeptics:* Joshua Brown, *Beyond the Lines* (Berkeley, Los
       Angeles, and London: University of California Press, 2002),
       pp. 7–8.
       Special Tweed supplement: Lee, p. 329.

41 *Fat and bloated:* Paul Somers, *Editorial Cartooning and Caricature*
       (Westport, Conn., and London: Greenwood Press, 1998), p. 7.
       A vulture: See more on Tweed and Nast in David R. Spencer,
       "Bringing Down Giants: Thomas Nast, John Wilson Bengough
       and the Maturing of Political Cartooning," *American Journalism*
       15, no. 3 (Summer 1998): 61-88.
       Blanket the marketplace: Brown, pp. 62–63.

42 *Well into the 1880s:* Ibid., p. 67.
       Political cartoons: Lee, p. 362.

43 *Edwin Stanton:* Mindich, pp. 65–70.
       Owners struggled on: Rodger Streitmatter, *Voices of Revolution: The Dis-
       sident Press in America* (New York: Columbia University Press,
       2001), pp. 54–55.

44 *Prostitution should be legalized:* Edwin G. Burrows and Mike Wallace,
       Gotham: A History of New York City to 1898 (New York: Oxford
       University Press, 1999), pp. 983–84.

45 *More flamboyant approach:* Ibid.
Went on a rampage: Streitmatter, *Voices of Revolution,* p. 75, available at "Comstock, Anthony," Infoplease, http://www.infoplease .com/ce6/people/A0813136.html.

46 *Made a substantial income:* Burrows and Wallace, p. 984.

47 *Wholesome moral sentiment: Woodhull and Claflin's Weekly,* July 2, 1870.
In June 1876: Streitmatter, *Voices of Revolution,* p. 75.

48 *When the woman asked:* Ibid., pp. 74–75.

49 *Taken away from you:* Available at "Angela Fiducia Tilton Heywood," http://www.zetetics.com/mac/19thcent/aheywood.html.
Dead within the year: Streitmatter, *Voices of Revolution,* p. 76.
An abrasive ideologue: Ibid., p. 67.

50 *A perfect sanity: Lucifer the Light Bearer,* January 26, 1901.
Three years later: Streitmatter, *Voices of Revolution,* pp. 76–77.

CHAPTER THREE

54 *Brave new world:* Marion Tuttle Marzolf, *Civilizing Voices: American Press Criticism, 1880–1950* (New York and London: Longman Publishing, 1991), p. 7.
Demands from the working class: C. G. Pernicone, "The Bloody Ould Sixth: A Social Analysis of a New York City Working-Class Community in the Mid Nineteenth Century" (Ph.D. diss., University of Rochester, 1973), p. 181.

55 *Such proposals:* Edward Winslow Martin, *The Secrets of the Great City* (Philadelphia: Jones Brothers, 1868), p. 84.
A better place to be: Ibid., p. 398.

56 *Economic climate:* Burrows and Wallace, pp. 1041–42.
Persistent failures: Ibid., p. 1042.
Subscription-supported journals: Ibid., pp. 1048–49.

57 *Upping the ante:* Ibid., p. 1074.
Old Knickerbockers: Ibid.

59 *Dying in custody:* Bruce Shapiro, ed., *Shaking the Foundations* (New York: Thunder's Mouth Press, 2003), pp. 26–27.

   Theodore Roosevelt: Linda H. Davis, *Badge of Courage: The Life of Stephen Crane* (New York: Houghton Mifflin, 1998), p. 160.

   John Swinton: Shapiro, p. 40.

60 *Filthy cellars:* Davis, p. 52.

   American city today: Pernicone, pp. 35–36.

61 *Numerous small colonies:* Tyler Anbinder, *Five Points* (New York and London: Free Press, 2001), p. 345.

   The Five Points area: Pernicone, p. 32.

   Ill-gotten gains: Martin, p. 78.

   Saint Peter himself: Ibid., p. 189.

62 *Life in his hand:* Davis, p. 52.

   The cobbled streets: Burrows and Wallace, p. 1090.

63 *Manhattan's residents:* Ibid., p. 1162.

64 *Dives and opium dens:* Brooks McNamara, *The New York Concert Saloon* (Cambridge: Cambridge University Press, 2002), pp. 97–99.

   Defiled the Sabbath: Ibid., p. 1.

   Fanciful costumes: Ibid., p. 104.

65 *Fronts for prostitution:* Martin, p. 417.

66 *Bowery residents:* Burrows and Wallace, p. 1142.

   Inventor Thomas Alva Edison: Ibid.

   Tendency to poverty: Ibid., pp. 1158–59.

   Children's Aid Society: Ibid., p. 1161.

67 *In drinking establishments:* Martin, p. 284.

   Turnover in talent: Ibid., p. 303.

68 *Visitors to the city:* Ibid., pp. 358, 356.

   Few stones unturned: Burrows and Wallace, pp. 1163–64.

69 *Host of speakers:* Herbert H. Gutman, ed., *Who Built America?* vol. 1 (New York: Pantheon Books, 1989), p. 321.

   Property and prosperity: Ibid., pp. 326–27.

70 *General Trades Union:* Ibid., p. 332.

   National Labor Union: Ibid., pp. 537–38.

71   *Fall from grace:* Shapiro, p. 57.

72   *Charges were dismissed:* Davis, pp. 158–60.
         Stories spoke for themselves: Michael Robertson, *Stephen Crane: Journalism and the Making of Modern American Literature* (New York: Columbia University Press, 1997), pp. 76–77, 101.

73   *This number increased:* Innis, *The Bias of Communication,* pp. 160, 173.
         A daily circulation: Marzolf, p. 8.
         Standard and Poor's: Burrows and Wallace, pp. 1044–46.

74   *Manhattan and its bordering cities:* Ibid., pp. 1053–58.
         Electricity became the norm: Ibid., pp. 1058–68.

CHAPTER FOUR

77   *The mass media:* New York did not go unchallenged in this century. Chicago was also making large economic and political waves, which was reflected in that city's press as well; Hearst later became a major player there when he founded a newspaper in the Windy City.
         The modern newspaper was born: Meredith and David Berg comment on style in W. Joseph Campbell, *Yellow Journalism: Puncturing the Myths, Defining the Legacies* (Westport, Conn., and London: Praeger Publishers, 2001), p. 151.

78   *Battleground for press supremacy:* Smythe, p. 208.
         Pictures by the thousands: Michael Carlebach, *American Photojournalism Comes of Age* (Washington, D.C., and London: Smithsonian Institute Press, 1997), p. 12.

79   *Improved typesetting techniques:* Barnhurst and Nerone, pp. 81–82.

80   *Remained competitive:* Ibid., p. 82.
         Virtually moribund "World": Anthony Smith, *The Newspaper: An International History* (London: Thames and Hudson, 1979), pp. 159–60.

82   *Press technology:* Barnhurst and Nerone, p. 113.

87   *Gribayedoff's drawings:* Kobre, *Development of American Journalism,*
p. 380.

CHAPTER FIVE

96   *Gilman did not bend:* Denise D. Knight, "Charlotte Perkins Gilman,
William Randolph Hearst and the Practice of Ethical Journalism,"
American Journalism 11, no. 4 (Fall 1994): 337.
This is the secret: Ibid., pp. 337–38.

97   *She responded:* Ibid., p. 339n22.
Place of comfort: Fedler, p. 155.
Revisionist histories: Stephen Vaughan and Bruce Evensen, "Democracy's Guardians: Hollywood's Portrayal of Reporters, 1930–
1945," *Journalism Quarterly* 68, no. 4 (Winter 1991): 829.

98   *Grabbing suspects:* Fedler, pp. 155–60.
No room left: John. P. Ferré, "The Dubious Heritage of Media Ethics:
Cause and Effect Criticism in the 1890's," *American Journalism* 5,
no. 4 (1988): 191.

99   *Left the premises:* Ibid., p. 195.
Needed a diversion: Ibid., p. 195–96.

100   *Benjamin Day:* Mott, pp. 310–11.
Pure-minded and clean: Ferré, pp. 196–97.

101   *List of crimes:* Ibid., pp. 197–98.
No takers: Ibid., p. 200.

102   *Midnight candle:* Burrows and Wallace, p. 1214.

103   *Hearts and souls:* Mott, pp. 436–38.
Heart of the Victorian newspaper: Ibid., p. 438; also see John D. Stevens,
Sensationalism and the New York Press (New York: Columbia Uni-
versity Press, 1991), p. 68.

104   *Sing Sing Prison:* James McGrath Morris, *The Roseman of Sing Sing*
(New York: Fordham University Press, 2003), p. 3.

105 *Hurly-burly world:* Ibid., pp. 44–48.

   Steffens noted: Lincoln Steffens, *The Autobiography of Lincoln Steffens* (New York: Harcourt, Brace and World, 1931), pp. 314–15.

   Get this tragedy: Ibid., p. 317.

107 *Death of an inmate:* Brooke Kroeger, *Nellie Bly* (New York: Times Books (Random House), 1994), pp. 85–87.

   Story of horror: Burrows and Wallace, pp. 1152–53.

108 *On her way:* Kroeger, p. 92.

109 *Just as sane:* Nellie Bly, *Ten Days in a Mad House* (New York: Ian L. Munro, n.d.), chap. 1, available at "Ten Days in a Madhouse," A Celebration of Women Writers, http://digital .library.upenn .edu/women/bly/madhouse/madhouse.html.

110 *My flesh felt creepy:* Bly, chap. 12.

   Populist approach: Brian, p. 125.

   Marketing mentality: Upton Sinclair, *The Brass Check* (Urbana and Chicago: University of Illinois Press, 2003), p. xix.

111 *Passing out bread:* Burrows and Wallace, p. 1214.

   Fascinated with police work: Ben Procter, *William Randolph Hearst: The Early Years* (New York: Oxford University Press, 1998), pp. 98–99.

114 *More of this lurid crime:* Ibid., p. 99.

   Nack and the unfortunate Thorn: Evening Journal and Advertiser; see the coverage from Sunday, June 27, 1897, to August 1, 1897, for a more detailed look at *The Journal's* coverage of this event.

115 *Auburn Prison:* Procter, p. 114.

   His employers: New York Times, August 2, 1898.

116 *Scar on one finger: World New York,* June 30, 1897.

117 *Day's fictional series:* Burrows and Wallace, pp. 643–44.

119 *I came here to die: New York Journal and Advertiser,* August 8, 1897.

   This generous lover: Ibid.

CHAPTER SIX

124 *Bankers on Wall Street:* Burrows and Wallace, p. 1215.

Manifest Destiny: Hiley H. Ward, *Mainstreams of American Media History* (Boston: Allyn and Bacon, 1997), p. 282. As well, see Burrows and Wallace, p. 1215.

125 *Clash of paradigms:* W. Joseph Campbell, "1897: American Journalism's Exceptional Year," *Journalism History* 29, no. 4 (Winter 2004): 190.

A national disgrace: Rodger Streitmatter, *Mightier Than the Sword* (New York: Westview Press, 1997), p. 69.

126 *Confidence of our readers:* Benedict Karl Zobrist, "How Victor Lawson's Newspapers Covered the Cuban War of 1898," *Journalism Quarterly* 38, no. 3 (1961): 325.

Reporting on this topic: Ibid., p. 328.

Treatment of Manifest Destiny: Ward, p. 282.

127 *Holy war in the name of freedom:* J. Stanley Lemons, "The Cuban Crisis of 1895–1898: Newspapers and Nativism," *Missouri Historical Review* 60, no. 1 (1965): 74.

128 *Lost the support:* Daniel Simundson, "The Yellow Press on the Prairie: South Dakota Daily Newspaper Editorials Prior to the Spanish American War," *South Dakota History* 2, no. 3 (Summer 1972): 212.

Valeriano Weyler: Ibid., pp. 218–19.

Eastern wire services: Ibid.

129 *No story too improbable:* Mark. M. Welter, "The 1895–98 Cuban Crisis in Minnesota Newspapers: Testing the Yellow Journalism Theory," *Journalism Quarterly* 47, no. 4 (1976): 722.

130 *Cuban crisis:* Joseph A. Fry, "Silver and Sentiment: The Nevada Press and the Coming of the Spanish American War," *Nevada Historical Society Quarterly* 20, no. 4 (1977): 225, 233.

131 *Martial virtues of Napoleon:* William E. Leuchtenburg, "The Needless War with Spain," *American Heritage* 8, no. 2 (1957): 33.

131 *True statesmen:* Ibid.

132 *Sugar tariff:* Folkerts and Teeter, p. 267.

133 *A formidable power:* Proctor, pp. 101–2.
Tight censorship: Sidney Kobre, *The Yellow Press* (Tallahasee: Florida State University Press, 1964), p. 283.
Admitted the error: Ibid., p. 282.

134 *New York journalistic scene:* Proctor, p. 78.
Searched in private: Campbell, "1897: American Journalism's Exceptional Year," p. 195.
Incidents of this nature: Kobre, *Development of American Journalism,* p. 495.

135 *Conducted in private:* Joyce Milton, *Foreign Correspondents in the Heyday of Yellow Journalism* (New York: Harper and Row Publishers, 1989), pp. 141–42.
Esteemed freak contemporaries: Mindich, p. 130.
Front-page headline: Kobre, *The Yellow Press,* p. 285.

136 *Stretch of the imagination:* Marcus M. Wilkerson, *Public Opinion and the Spanish American War* (New York: Russell and Russell, 1932), p. 84.
Committing an outrage: Kobre, *The Yellow Press,* p. 286.

137 *State Department: World New York,* February 22, 1897.
Referred to Ruiz: Wilkerson, p. 84.

138 *Isle of Pines:* Bill Blackbeard, *R. F. Outcault's "The Yellow Kid"* (Northampton, Mass.: Kitchen Sink Press, 1995), p. 111.
Faced the firing squad: Wilbur Cross, "The Perils of Evangelina," *American Heritage* 19, no. 2 (1968): 36.

139 *Jungles of Camaguey: New York Journal,* August 17, 1897.

140 *The Inquisition:* Ibid.
Life behind bars: Ward, p. 273.
Clara Barton: Ibid.

141 *Speaking tour:* Blackbeard, p. 113.

141 *Pinkerton agents:* Wilkerson, p. 12.
A slush fund: Ibid., p. 28.

141 *Infuriated American public opinion:* Ibid., p. 44.
  Intended only for the eyes: Smythe, p. 188.

142 *Cranked up the campaign:* Procter, p. 116.
  A low politician: Quoted in Wilkerson, p. 92.

143 *Baying sounds of victory:* Wilkerson, pp. 93–95.

144 *Remember the* Maine: Procter, p. 116.

145 *Possible sabotage: World New York,* February 16, 1898.
  Hurled from their bunks: Ibid.

146 *Music to the ears:* Ibid.
  In dry dock: Ibid.

147 *Hanged in effigy:* Streitmatter, *Mightier Than the Sword,* p. 81.
  Naval Court: World New York, February 18, 1898.
  Time bomb: Ibid.

148 *Sad occurrence:* Ibid.
  A fabrication: Proctor, p. 116.

149 *This kind of activity:* Ibid., p. 117.
  McKinley inquiry: David F. Trask, *The War with Spain in 1898* (Lincoln and London: University of Nebraska Press, 1981), p. 35.
  Obvious to one and all: World New York, March 21, 1898.

150 *What kind of magician:* Trask, p. 35.
  Mobilize and equip: Stevens, p. 97.
  Gained the Philippines: Streitmatter, *Mightier Than the Sword,* pp. 82–83.
  "Beneficiaries" of American expansionism: Folkerts and Teeter, pp. 268–69.

CHAPTER SEVEN

154 *Assassin had a copy:* Procter, p. 167.
  McKinley on his bier: Ibid.

155 *Fight for news priority:* Charles H. Brown, *The Correspondents' War* (New York: Charles Scribner's Sons, 1967), p. 132.

156 *Arthur Brisbane:* Kobre, *The Yellow Press,* pp. 31–34.
Brisbane's editorials: Ray Vanderburg, "The Paradox That Was Arthur Brisbane," *Journalism Quarterly* 47, no. 2(1970): 281.

158 *Henry Raymond:* Burrows and Wallace, pp. 768, 812.
Hearst retaliated: Brian, p. 198.

159 *Murder, mayhem and mystery:* Ibid., p. 199.
Became alcoholics: Ibid., pp. 161–62.

160 *Pulitzer was furious:* Ibid., pp. 223–24.

161 *Hearst agreed:* Ibid., p. 224.
Colors of the rainbow: Quoted in John Tebbel, *The Life and Good Times of William Randolph Hearst* (New York: Dutton Publishers, 1952), p. 297.

162 *Half-million mark:* Hy B. Turner, *When Giants Ruled* (New York: Fordham University Press, 1999), p. 123.
The city morgue: Ibid., p. 116.
Concept of comic strips: Ibid., p. 117.

163 *Debunking the myths:* Joyce Milton, *The Yellow Kids* (New York: Harper and Row Publishers, 1989), p. 173.
Some insights: Smythe, p. 183.

164 *Extraordinary, unexpected and sensational:* Morrill Goddard, *What Interests People and Why* (New York: Published privately, 1935), p. 7.
Genuine living human beings: Ibid., p. 4.

165 *Pseudo-science will not do:* Ibid., p. 18.
Common cold: Ibid.
Fallacies, false teachings: Ibid., p. 39.

166 *A discouraging picture:* Ibid., p. 41.
Wanted for murder: Charles E. Chapin, *Charles E. Chapin's Story* (New York: Beekman Publishers, 1974), pp. 313–18.

167 *Smuggler of opium:* Ibid., pp. 102–3.
Large bonus: Ibid., p. 160.

168 *Rival editors:* Morris, p. 3.
Irving S. Cobb: Ibid., p. 12.
Made in heaven: Ibid., p. 171.

169 *Printing the headline:* Chapin, pp. 180–82. The extreme sensationalism to which he referred is *The Journal's* coverage of the Spanish-American War.

170 *Forefront of war reporting:* Ibid., pp. 173–74.
Chapin's "World": Ibid., p. 364.
Chapin stigmata: Morris, p. 5.

171 *Ten Commandments:* Brian, pp. 1–2.
Persuasive powers: Smythe, p. 86.
Leonara Barner: Brian, p. 133.

172 *Her story ideas:* Kroeger, p. 85.
Benjamin Harrison: Brian, p. 137.

173 *Pulling in readers:* Brown, pp. 36–38.
Losing control: Smythe, p. 115.
The morning edition: Brian, p. 159.

174 *Executor of his estate:* Ibid., p. 206.
Financial misbehavior: Ibid., p. 59.

175 *St. Louis buzzed:* The story is contained in most volumes dealing with journalism history. The two used here are Smythe, pp. 88–89, and Brian, p. 59.

176 *Provide the war:* James Creelman, *On the Great Highway* (Boston: Lothrop, Lee and Shepard, 1901), pp. 177–78.
Creelman was in Europe: Campbell, *Yellow Journalism,* p. 72.

177 *Sitting Bull:* Milton, *Foreign Correspondents,* p. 93.
Appalachian Mountains: John McNamara, *Extra! U.S. War Correspondents in Action* (Plainview, N.Y.: Books for Libraries Press, 1945), pp. 55–56.

178 *Both were freed:* Milton, *Foreign Correspondents,* p. 233.

179 *The foreign correspondents:* Brian, pp. 180–81.
Creelman's reporting: Campbell, *Yellow Journalism,* pp. 72–75.

180 *Suggestion of treachery:* Creelman, pp. 158–59.
Large camps: Kobre, *The Yellow Press,* p. 284.

181 *Names and death dates:* Brown, p. 37; Brian, pp. 204–5.
Famine and disease: Wilkerson, pp. 32–33.

182 *Cuban independence:* Joseph E. Wisan, *The Cuban Crisis as Reflected in the New York Press* (New York: Octagon Books, 1965), pp. 169–70.
Commander's surrender: Smythe, pp. 189–90.

183 *Explained his dilemma:* Procter, pp. 61–62.
Journalistic energy: Creelman, p. 174.
Unfearing warfare: Ibid., p. 177.

184 *City of Havana:* Brian, p. 203.
Lure of adventure: Brown, p. 45.
Showed a daring spirit: Ibid.

185 *Whetted his appetite:* Ibid.
Gomez and his fighters: Ibid., pp. 45–47.

186 *Strengthened his credibility:* Darien Elizabeth Andreu, "Sylvester H. Scovel, Journalist, and the Spanish American War" (Ph.D. diss., Florida State University), pp. 3–5.
Glaring errors: Ibid., p. 27.
Smoldering snakes: Brian, p. 204.

187 *Tales of atrocity:* Wilkerson, p. 34.
El Inglesito: Brian, p. 203.
Death by firing squad: Ibid., p. 216.

188 *False police pass:* Wisan, p. 222.

189 *Substantial proof:* Brian, p. 203.
Red Cross: Ibid., p. 228.

190 *Captain Sigsbee's report:* Ibid., p. 229.
Version of Mata Hari: Ibid., p. 234.

191 *Annoyance to Chambers:* Fairfax Downey, *Richard Harding Davis: His Day* (New York and London: Charles Scribner's Sons, 1933), p. 32.

192 *Set up shop:* Ibid., pp. 33–36.
Distant and aristocratic: Ibid., pp. 36–38.

193 *Got their men:* Ibid., pp. 42–43.
Beau Brummell of the Press: J. McNamara, p. 69.

194 *An average musician:* Ibid.

194 *Managing editor:* Ibid., pp. 69–70; Downey, pp. 52–54.

195 *The Greco-Turkey War:* J. McNamara, pp. 70–72.
Fact from fiction: Campbell, *Yellow Journalism,* p. 11.

196 *Santa Clara:* Richard Harding Davis, *Cuba in War Time* (New York: R. H. Russell, 1899), p. 67. The statue to which Davis referred is that of Nathan Hale in New York City.
Acts of torture: Ibid., p. 67.

197 *The incident:* Campbell, *Yellow Journalism,* p. 114; Procter, pp. 104–5.
Hearst ignored: Brian, p. 214.
William Abbot: Procter, pp. 104–5.

198 *Anything but the truth:* Trask, p. 196.
Davis and Shafter: Walter Millis, *The Martial Spirit* (Boston and New York: Houghton Mifflin, 1931), p. 264. The story is also related in Trask, p. 318.
A typical day: Milton, *Foreign Correspondents,* p. 110.

199 *Stephen Crane:* Robertson, p. 75.
The Maggie story: Ibid., pp. 76–77.
Best reporting staffs: Procter, p. 81.

200 *Scene of the action:* Robertson, p. 109; Procter, p. 100.
His dispatches: Brian, p. 234.

201 *Pure fiction:* Procter, p. 131.
Younger Hare: Lewis L. Gould and Richard Greffe, *Photojournalist: The Career of Jimmy Hare* (Austin and London: University of Texas Press, 1977), pp. 10–11.

202 *Robert Collier:* Gould and Greffe, pp. 10–11.
For five mortal hours: Ibid.

CHAPTER EIGHT

207 *Tweed's reign:* Streitmatter, *Mightier Than the Sword,* p. 51.
His own experience: Turner, p. 120.

208 *Bestowed on Pulitzer:* Lee, p. 362.

208 *Cartoon aficionado:* Stevens, p. 88.

209 *The sense of reform* : Chris Lamb, *Drawn to Extremes* (New York: Columbia University Press, 2004), p. 70.
Large captions: Kobre, *The Yellow Press,* pp. 53–54.

210 *Starving couple:* Brian, p. 93.

211 *Jumped ship:* Ibid., p. 162.
First train out: Kroeger, p. 93.

212 *Bid them goodbye:* Homer Davenport, *The Country Boy* (Chicago and New York: M. A. Donohue, 1910), p. 178.
Tail between his legs: Ibid., 180.

213 *Kind they weren't:* Procter, p. 74.
Dollar bills: Ibid., pp. 82, 92, 125.
Vigorous, jingoistic Uncle Sam: Somers, p. 3.

215 *Never captured the spirit:* Blackbeard, pp. 1–55.

216 *A deal he could not refuse: Yankee Notions* 2, no. 2 (February 1854).

217 *Imperial ambitions: Vanity Fair,* May 19, 1860.

218 *Young America: Vanity Fair,* June 2, 1860.
American body politic: Frank Leslie's Budget of Fun, July 1866.

219 *Mexicans and Louis Napoleon: Frank Leslie's Budget of Fun,* June 1866.
Map of North America: Frank Leslie's Budget of Fun, February 1866.

220 *Imperialism and miltary adventure: Punchinello* 1, nos. 2–3 (April 1870).
Speaking to his offspring: Frank Leslie's Budget of Fun, December 1870.

221 *Gruff and tough Bismarck: Judge* 15, no. 388 (1889).
Uncle Sam: New York Journal, March 2, 1898.

222 *Shedding their uniforms: New York Journal,* March 3, 1898.
Series of documents: New York Journal, March 4, 1898.

223 *Financial community's opposition: New York Journal,* March 17, 1898.
Rescuing imprisoned Cubans: New York Journal, April 8, 1898.

224 *Other two badges: New York Journal,* May 16, 1869.
Age of imperialism: New York Journal, June 28, 1898.

BIBLIOGRAPHY

BOOKS AND THESES

Allen, Douglas. *Frederic Remington and the Spanish American War.* New York: Crown Publishers, 1971.

Anbinder, Tyler. *Five Points.* New York and London: Free Press, 2001.

Andreu, Darien Elizabeth. "Sylvester H. Scovel, Journalist, and the Spanish-American War." Ph.D. diss., Florida State University, 2003.

Barnhurst, Kevin, and John Nerone. *The Form of News: A History.* New York and London: Guilford Press, 2001.

Bekken, Jon. "Newsboys." In Hanno Hardt and Bonnie Brennen, eds., *News Workers: Toward a History of the Rank and File.* Minneapolis: University of Minnesota Press, 1995.

Blackbeard, Bill. *R. F. Outcault's "The Yellow Kid."* Northhampton, Mass.: Kitchen Sink Press, 1995.

Bly, Nellie. *Ten Days in a Mad House.* New York: Ian L. Munro, n.d. Available at A Celebration of Women Writers, http://digital .library.upenn.edu/women/bly/madhouse/madhouse.html.

Brian, Denis. *A Life: Pulitzer.* New York: John Wiley and Sons, 2001.

Brown, Charles H. *The Correspondents' War.* New York: Charles Scribner's Sons, 1967.

Brown, Joshua. *Beyond the Lines.* Berkeley, Los Angeles, and London: University of California Press, 2002.

Burrows, Edwin G., and Mike Wallace. *Gotham: A History of New York City to 1898.* New York: Oxford University Press, 1999.

Campbell, W. Joseph. *Yellow Journalism: Puncturing the Myths, Defining the Legacies.* Westport, Conn., and London: Praeger Publishers, 2001.

Carey, James W. *Communication as Culture: Essays on Media and Society.* Boston: Unwin, Hyman Publishers, 1989.

Carlebach, Michael. *The Origins of Photojournalism in America*. Washington, D.C., and London: Smithsonian Institute Press, 1992.

———. *American Photojournalism Comes of Age*. Washington, D.C., and London: Smithsonian Institute Press, 1997.

Chapin, Charles E. *Charles E. Chapin's Story*. New York: Beekman Publishers, 1974.

Cook, Ramsay. *The Regenerators*. Toronto, London, and Buffalo, N.Y.: University of Toronto Press, 1991.

Creelman, James. *On the Great Highway*. Boston: Lothrop, Lee and Shepard, 1901.

Davenport, Homer. *The Country Boy*. Chicago and New York: M. A. Donohue, 1910.

Davis, Linda H. *Badge Of Courage: The Life of Stephen Crane*. New York: Houghton Mifflin, 1998.

Davis, Richard Harding. *Cuba in War Time*. New York: R. H. Russell, 1899.

de Tocqueville, Alexis. *Democracy in America*. Vol. 2. New York: Vintage Books, 1945.

Douglas, George H. *The Golden Age of the Newspaper*. Westport, Conn.: Greenwood Publishing, 1999.

Downey, Fairfax. *Richard Harding Davis: His Day*. New York and London: Charles Scribner's Sons, 1933.

Dumbald, Edward. *Jefferson: His Political Writings*. New York: Bobbs-Merrill, 1955.

Emery, Michael, Edwin Emery, and Nancy L. Roberts. *The Press and America*. 9th ed. Boston: Allyn and Bacon, 2000.

Fedler, Fred. *Lessons from the Past*. Prospect Heights, Ill.: Waveland Press, 2000.

Folkerts, Jean, and Dwight L. Teeter Jr. *Voices of a Nation*. 3rd ed. Boston and London: Allyn and Bacon, 1998.

Goddard, Morrill. *What Interests People and Why*. New York: Published privately, 1935.

Gould, Lewis L., and Richard Greffe. *Photojournalist: The Career of Jimmy Hare*. Austin and London: University of Texas Press, 1977.

Gutman, Herbert H., ed. *Who Built America?* Vol. 1. New York: Pantheon Books, 1989.

Hardt, Hanno, and Bonnie Brennen, eds. *News Workers: Toward a History of the Rank and File.* Minneapolis: University of Minnesota Press, 1995.

Herbert, A. P. *The Best Cartoons from "Punch."* New York: Simon and Schuster, 1952.

Innis, Harold. *The Bias of Communication.* Toronto, London, and Buffalo, N.Y.: University of Toronto Press, 1951.

———. *Empire and Communications.* Toronto, London, and Buffalo, N.Y.: University of Toronto Press, 1972.

Kobre, Sidney. *The Yellow Press.* Tallahasee: Florida State University Press, 1964.

———. *Development of American Journalism.* Dubuque, Iowa: William C. Brown Publishers, 1969.

Kroeger, Brooke. *Nellie Bly.* New York: Times Books (Random House), 1994.

Lamb, Chris. *Drawn to Extremes.* New York: Columbia University Press, 2004.

Lee, James Melvin. *History of American Journalism.* Garden City, N.Y.: Garden City Publishing, 1923.

Martin, Edward Winslow. *The Secrets of the Great City.* Philadelphia: Jones Brothers, 1868.

Marzolf, Marion Tuttle. *Civilizing Voices: American Press Criticism, 1880–1950.* New York and London: Longman Publishing, 1991.

McLuhan, Marshall. *Understanding Media.* Cambridge: Massachusetts Institute of Technology Press, 1994.

McNamara, Brooks. *The New York Concert Saloon.* Cambridge: Cambridge University Press, 2002.

McNamara, John. *Extra! U.S. War Correspondents in Action.* Plainview, N.Y.: Books for Libraries Press, 1945.

Mill, John Stuart. *On Liberty.* Glasgow, UK: William Collins and Sons, 1962.

Millis, Walter. *The Martial Spirit.* Boston and New York: Houghton Mifflin, 1931.

Milton, Joyce. *Foreign Correspondents in the Heyday of Yellow Journalism.* New York: Harper and Row Publishers, 1989.

———. *The Yellow Kids.* New York: Harper and Row, 1989.

Mindich, David. *Just the Facts: How Objectivity Came to Define American Journalism*. New York: New York University Press, 1998.

Morris, James McGrath. *The Roseman of Sing Sing*. New York: Fordham University Press, 2003.

Mott, Frank Luther. *American Journalism*.New York: Macmillan, 1962.

Nerone, John C. *Last Rights: Revisiting Four Theories of the Press*. Urbana and Champaign: University of Illinois Press, 1995.

Nord, David Paul. *Communities of Journalism*. Urbana and Champaign: University of Illinois Press, 2001.

Osler, Andrew M. *News: The Evolution of Journalism in Canada*. Toronto, Ontario: Copp, Clark Pittman, 1993.

Pernicone, C. G. "The Bloody Ould Sixth: A Social Analysis of a New York City Working-Class Community in the Mid Nineteenth Century." Ph.D. diss., University of Rochester, 1973.

Pitz, Henry C. *Frederic Remington: 173 Drawings and Illustrations*. New York: Dover Publications, 1972.

Pray, Isaac C. *Memoirs of James Gordon Bennett and His Times*. New York: Arno Press, 1970.

Procter, Ben. *William Randolph Hearst: The Early Years, 1863–1910*. New York: Oxford University Press, 1998.

Robertson, Michael. *Stephen Crane: Journalism and the Making of Modern American Literature*. New York: Columbia University Press, 1997.

Schudson, Michael. *Discovering the News: A Social History of American Newspapers*. New York: Basic Books, 1978.

Shapiro, Bruce, ed. *Shaking the Foundations*. New York: Thunder's Mouth Press, 2003.

Siebert, Frederick, Theodore Peterson, and Wilbur Schramm. *Four Theories of the Press*. Urbana and Champaign: University of Illinois Press, 1956.

Sinclair, Upton. *The Brass Check*. Urbana and Chicago: University of Illinois Press, 2003.

Smith, Anthony. *The Newspaper: An International History*. London: Thames and Hudson, 1979.

Smythe, Ted Curtis. *The Gilded Age Press, 1865–1900.* Westport, Conn., and London: Praeger Publishers, 2003.

Somers, Paul. *Editorial Cartooning and Caricature.* Westport, Conn., and London: Greenwood Press, 1998.

Steffens, Lincoln. *The Autobiography of Lincoln Steffens.* New York: Harcourt, Brace and World, 1931.

Stevens, John D. *Sensationalism and the New York Press.* New York: Columbia University Press, 1991.

Streitmatter, Rodger. *Mightier Than the Sword.* New York: Westview Press, 1997.

————. *Voices of Revolution: The Dissident Press in America.* New York: Columbia University Press, 2001.

Tebbel, John. *The Life and Good Times of William Randolph Hearst.* New York: Dutton Publishers, 1952.

Trask, David F. *The War with Spain in 1898.* Lincoln and London: University of Nebraska Press, 1981.

Turner, Hy B. *When Giants Ruled.* New York: Fordham University Press, 1999.

Ward, Hiley H. *Mainstreams of American Media History.* Boston: Allyn and Bacon, 1997.

Wilkerson, Marcus. *Public Opinion and the Spanish American War.* New York: Russell and Russell, 1932.

Wisan, Joseph E. *The Cuban Crisis as Reflected in the New York Press.* New York: Octagon Books, 1965.

ARTICLES

Anthony, David. "The Helen Jewett Panic: Tabloids, Men, and the Sensational Public Spheres in Antebellum New York." *American Literature* 69, no. 3 (September 1997): 487–514.

Budd, L. J. "Color Him Curious about Yellow Journalism." *Journal of Popular Culture* 15, no. 2 (Fall 1981): 25–33.

Campbell, W. Joseph. "1897: American Journalism's Exceptional Year." *Journalism History* 29, no. 4 (Winter 2004): 190–200.

Cross, Wilbur. "The Perils of Evangelina." *American Heritage* 19, no. 2 (1968): 36–107.

Ferré, John. P. "The Dubious Heritage of Media Ethics: Cause and Effect Criticism in the 1890's." *American Journalism* 5, no. 4 (1988): 191–203.

Fry, Joseph A. "Silver and Sentiment: The Nevada Press and the Coming of the Spanish American War." *Nevada Historical Society Quarterly* 20, no. 4 (1997): 222–239.

Knight, Denise D. "Charlotte Perkins Gilman, William Randolph Hearst and the Practice of Ethical Journalism." *American Journalism* 11, no. 4 (Fall 1994): 336–347.

Lemons, J. Stanley. "The Cuban Crisis of 1895–1898: Newspapers and Nativism." *Missouri Historical Review* 60, no. 1 (1965): 63–74.

Leuchtenburg, William E. "The Needless War with Spain." *American Heritage* 8, no. 2 (1957): 33–95.

Pomerantz, Sidney I. "The Press of a Greater New York." *New York History* 39, no. 1 (1958): 50–66.

Schuneman, R. Smith. "Art or Photography: A Question for Newspaper Editors of the 1890s. " *Journalism Quarterly* 42, no. 1 (1965): 43–52.

Simundson, Daniel. "The Yellow Press on the Prairie: South Dakota Daily Newspaper Editorials Prior to the Spanish American War." *South Dakota History* 2, no. 3 (Summer 1972): 211–260.

Spencer, David R. "Bringing Down Giants: Thomas Nast, John Wilson Bengough and the Maturing of Political Cartooning." *American Journalism* 15, no. 3 (Summer 1998): 61–88.

Vanderburg, Ray. "The Paradox That Was Arthur Brisbane." *Journalism Quarterly* 47, no. 2 (1970): 281–287.

Vaughan, Stephen, and Bruce Evensen. "Democracy's Guardians: Hollywood's Portrayal of Reporters, 1930–1945." *Journalism Quarterly* 68, no. 4 (Winter 1991): 829–838.

Welter, Mark. M. "The 1895–98 Cuban Crisis in Minnesota Newspapers: Testing the Yellow Journalism Theory." *Journalism Quarterly* 47, no. 4 (1976): 719–724.

Wiltenburg, Joy. "True Crime: The Origins of Modern Sensationalism."
   American Historical Review 109, no. 5 (December 2004): 1377–1403.
Zobrist, Benedict Karl. "How Victor Lawson's Newspapers Covered the
   Cuban War of 1898."*Journalism Quarterly* 38, no. 3 (1961):
   323–331.

WEB SITES

http://www.infoplease.com/ce6/people/A08336.html
http://www.loc.gov/rr/hispanic/1898/weyler.html
http://memory.loc.gov/ammem/edhtml/edmvhm.html
http://www.kirjasto.sci.fi/bhecht.htm
http://digital.library.upenn.edu/women/bly/madhouse/madhouse.html
http://zetetics.com/mac/19thcent/aheywood.html

NEWSPAPERS AND MAGAZINES

Evening Journal and Advertiser [*New York Journal*], New York (1897–1898)
Frank Leslie's Budget of Fun, New York (July 1866)
Judge, vol. 15, no. 388, New York (1889)
Lucifer the Light Bearer, Chicago (1901)
New York Times (1898)
New York World [*The World New York*], (1897–1898)
Punchinello, vol. 1, nos. 2, 3, New York (April 1870)
Vanity Fair, New York (1860)
Woodhull and Claflin's Weekly, Brooklyn, N.Y. (1870)
Yankee Notions, New York (1854)

David R. Spencer is a professor in the Faculty of Information and Media Studies at the University of Western Ontario in London, Canada. During his tenure at the university, he has held the Rogers Chair in Journalism and New Information Technology. He is a past chair of the History Division for the Association for Education in Journalism and Mass Communications, as well as a past president of the American Journalism Historians Association. His research interests focus on the nineteenth-century press in both Canada and the United States.

Geneva Overholser holds the Curtis B. Hurley Chair in Public Affairs Reporting in the Washington bureau of the Missouri School of Journalism. The former *Washington Post* ombudsman, she was a member of the *New York Times* editorial board and editor of the *Des Moines Register.*